"*The Divine Right of Capital* is brilliant. So simple. So direct. And so beautifully written. It is the start of some very basic rethinking. This could be a very important book. I think we have found our Thomas Paine for the new millennium."

—DAVID KORTEN, author, *When Corporations Rule the World*

"This book is a marvelous piece of work—clear, concise, and beautifully written. It raises all the right questions with insight and provocative observations."

—DEE HOCK, founder and CEO emeritus, Visa International

"I am impressed by this book's deconstruction of the corporation. It is clear, paradigm-shifting, and convincing. The parallel between the blindness in our own society and the aristocratic privileges of the Old Regime is devastatingly effective."

—BERNARD LIETAER, author, *The Future of Money: Creating New Wealth, Work, and a Wiser World*, formerly with the Belgian central bank

"I enjoyed this work immensely. Kelly's image of being an antiques collector but rummaging through antique thoughts rather than artifacts has a great charm. If we are to move to a more fair and sustainable world, it is imperative that we understand the concepts she presents."

—JIM TARBELL, co-host, Corporations and Democracy radio program, Caspar, California

"I am quite astonished at the clarity and sophistication of this work. It is a fresh voice in the corporate responsibility movement, a movement that too often results in well-meaning and high-minded talk without really grappling with the issues the way Kelly does."

—DAVID ELLERMAN, economist, The World Bank

"I found this book startlingly thought-provoking and enjoyable."

—BOB EDDY, management consultant and adjunct faculty member, Rosemont College

"Reading this work left me breathless. It addresses the life topics I have wrestled with for twenty-five years, and someone articulate and passionate is finally giving voice to these thoughts. I think this could be one of the most important books I will ever see on the shelves. I have read Marjorie Kelly's writing for years, and I love the spirit and intelligence and passion she takes on with her writing. I love her voice. Her voice is the perfect voice."

—TERRY SOUTH, area general manager, Showtime Networks Inc.

"The book brims—actually spills over—with unsanctioned ideas and imaginative new directions. The style is like a loose and friendly conversation, an invitation to think and talk about what is possible, what might work. I believe this book is an important step toward generating a new politics."

—WILLIAM GREIDER, author, *One World, Ready or Not*,
from the Foreword

"This volume challenges conventional wisdom about the corporation with facts, wit, and verve. We have long needed a real iconoclast like Marjorie Kelly."

—JOHN LOGUE, director, Ohio Employee Ownership Center,
Kent State University

"This book offers an elegant and powerful argument for workplace democracy and for a new way of thinking about corporations."

—DONNA WOOD, professor of management,
University of Pittsburgh

"Your work has made a deep impression on me. I find it morally inspiring and insightful."

—ALBERT SPEKMAN, senior consultant of an
S&P 500 financial institution, Bronx, New York

"I have read this work with great admiration. Having read countless books on business ethics, I can say this is a breakthrough work. It could even range on the same level as Francis Fukuyama's work. The approach is revolutionary."

—JACQUES CORY, International Business Programs, Israel

"I loved reading this. Marjorie Kelly has systematically deconstructed a sacred cow—that corporations exist to maximize shareholder wealth—and reconstructed a social vision for a truly democratic system that rewards all who are responsible for profits, particularly employees. I hope everyone who reads this can identify a way to contribute to reaching the goal of true democracy."

—LESLIE CHRISTIAN, president, Progressive Investment Management

"I found this work just excellent. I have been showing it and loaning it to friends."

—PHILIPP MUESSIG, pollution prevention specialist,
Minnesota Office of Environmental Assistance

"I have read this work with great pleasure—yes, even joy. It's sharp and right on the dot. It has a wonderful style and great passion."

—ROLF OSTERBERG, former chairman, Swedish Newspapers Association,
and author, *Corporate Renaissance: Business as
an Adventure in Human Development*

The Divine Right of Capital

Dethroning the Corporate Aristocracy

Marjorie Kelly

BERRETT-KOEHLER PUBLISHERS, INC.
San Francisco

Berrett-Koehler Publishers, Inc.
235 Montgomery Street, Suite 650
San Francisco, CA 94104-2916
Tel: (415) 288-0260   Fax: (415) 362-2512   www.bkconnection.com

ORDERING INFORMATION

Quantity sales. Special discounts are available on quantity purchases by corporations, associations, and others. For details, contact the "Special Sales Department" at the Berrett-Koehler address above.

Individual sales. Berrett-Koehler publications are available through most bookstores. They can also be ordered direct from Berrett-Koehler: Tel: (800) 929-2929; Fax: (802) 864-7626; www.bkconnection.com

Orders for college textbook/course adoption use. Please contact Berrett-Koehler: Tel: (800) 929-2929; Fax: (802) 864-7626.

Orders by U.S. trade bookstores and wholesalers. Please contact Publishers Group West, 1700 Fourth Street, Berkeley, CA 94710. Tel: (510) 528-1444; Fax (510) 528-3444.

Printed in the United States of America

Printed on acid-free and recycled paper that is composed of 50% recovered fiber, including 10% postconsumer waste.

Library of Congress Cataloging-in-Publication Data
Kelly, Marjorie, 1953–
   The divine right of capital: dethroning the corporate aristocracy/by Marjorie Kelly;
foreword by William Greider.
      p. cm.
   Includes bibliographical references.
   ISBN 1-57675-125-2
   1. Capitalism—Moral and ethical aspects. 2. Social responsibility of business.
   3. Business ethics. 4. Big business. 5. Power (Social sciences). 6. Business and politics.
   7. Democracy. 8. International business enterprises. 9. International economic relations.
   I. Title.
HB501 .K427 2001   2001035700

Copyediting by Sandra Beris. Proofreading by Carolyn Uno.
Book design and composition by Beverly Butterfield, Girl of the West Productions.

FIRST EDITION

06 05 04 03 02 01   10 9 8 7 6 5 4 3 2 1

Contents

To
Miriam Kniaz

Can it be believed that the democracy which has overthrown the feudal system and vanquished kings will retreat before tradesmen and capitalists?

❧

ALEXIS DE TOCQUEVILLE
Democracy in America

Foreword

THE UNASKED QUESTION that hovers over American politics and smothers public life is this: Do corporations have too much power in our society? As a younger reporter covering political campaigns, I occasionally asked this of candidates, mainly to watch them squirm and duck for cover. But during the 2000 Presidential campaign, I had an opportunity to ask the question of Senator John McCain, a conservative Republican in most respects but a man blessed with an incautious nature. Do corporations have too much power in America? "Without a doubt, without a doubt," he answered without hesitation. "I see it every day in Washington."

So I think it is possible now that many more Americans of all stations are ready to listen to Marjorie Kelly and her insistent, probing questions and arguments. Her book is intended as a free-spirited provocation—a gloriously incautious and intelligent plea to think anew and to act. It reads not like another gloomy recital of familiar economic complaints but more like an enthusiastic tour of a far horizon—a time when Americans find the will and the way to correct the systemic failures of economic institutions.

What Kelly offers in the first half of her book is a diagnosis of why corporations spin off so many social ills. In her view, problems such as wealth inequality, corporate welfare, and industrial pollution are like the fevers and chills of the economy. The underlying illness is shareholder primacy, the corporate drive to make profits for shareholders, no matter who pays the cost. Corporations do indeed hold too much power in the world today, but Kelly says the more invisible problem is that the wealthy hold too much power over corporations. In the interest of making the rich richer, corporations are in effect levying absurd private taxes on the rest of us (to paraphrase Adam Smith, as Kelly does). Financial powers have become an economic aristocracy.

The solution is economic democracy, and in the second half of the work, Kelly draws on ancient radical thinkers like Thomas Paine, as well as more contemporary theorists, to assemble a menu of fundamental reform propositions. She also deliberately leaves room for doubt, disagreement, and playful speculation. "I only presume to offer hints, not plans," Thomas Paine wrote. Kelly likewise generously explains that what she offers is a rough draft, and if it encourages others to make better drafts, it has served its purpose.

The book brims—actually spills over—with unsanctioned ideas and imaginative new directions, all utterly unacceptable to those in the orthodox circles of economics, business, government. But the style is like a loose and friendly conversation, an invitation to think and talk about what is possible, what might work.

As a small business owner and business journalist, Kelly is grounded in the real world of enterprise. She has earned her conviction that nothing less than systemic structural change is needed. For fourteen years, she has edited and published *Business Ethics*, a publication that chronicles the many efforts to establish social responsibility in business and investing. Her publication is both hopeful cheerleader and tough critic. She remains idealistic herself but says that in recent years she has become increasingly discouraged at how little enduring change has been accomplished. Legislation, social investing, business ethics, and other progressive initiatives have in some measure made business more humane, she believes, but the overall result seems to her the opposite: corporations are focused more ruthlessly than ever on shareholder gain, to the exclusion of all competing values—from employees to the environment to social equity. It was this discouragement that led her to search for deeper answers.

Can we imagine an economy in which firms are typically owned in large part by the people who work there? In which corporate boards of directors are required to exercise broad fiduciary obligations to all of the stakeholders in the company—employees and community as well as absentee owners? Can we imagine a broader, more inclusive understanding of property rights? Kelly believes all these are possible. And she shows how in beginning ways they are already becoming reality, with nearly twelve hundred employee-owned firms thriving today, thirty-two states already having stakeholder laws redefining fiduciary duties, and courts beginning to recognize community property rights.

Kelly puts big questions on the table. But she also offers smaller steps that can move us forward, explaining all with a sense of history that helps us understand how we got to the present circumstances. Along the way she introduces new language with which to discuss the structure of modern corporations. Perhaps most provocatively, she introduces the phrase *wealth discrimination*, showing its kinship to sex and race discrimination. The principle of equality, in her view, has no meaning unless it is also established in economic terms: "Under market principles, wealth does not legitimately belong only to stockholders. Corporate wealth belongs to those who create it, and community wealth belongs to all."

Those are fighting words, of course, and the people who presently hold the high ground of economic power in society will not be amused. But the strength of Kelly's case is that it restores democratic principles in the economic context—demonstrating that structural changes in business, far from being radical, are grounded in the founding ideals of America and are required to sustain the democratic idea. Kelly wants to provoke a fighting spirit in America and other democratic nations. She aims to stimulate active curiosity and doubt about the current nature of the system and how far democracy has drifted from its first principles. Her flood of ideas are so numerous and profound, no one should expect to agree with all of them—and certainly I didn't. But I believe this book is an important step toward generating a new politics, and I share Marjorie Kelly's optimism that this is possible. What she essentially is after is a lively time of argument and inquiry in which the oldest, deepest questions—what it really means to live in a democracy—are back in play again, and people are once again in motion toward achieving their democratic ideals.

WILLIAM GREIDER
author, *Who Will Tell the People: The Betrayal of American Democracy* and *One World, Ready or Not: The Manic Logic of Global Capitalism*

Preface

FROM A WORLD once dominated by monarchy and aristocracy, civilization in the twentieth century crossed a great divide into a new world of democracy. But we have democratized only government—not economics. This book examines how our corporate worldview remains rooted in the predemocratic age, and how we can transform it.

It is a book about wealth privilege, which is the hallmark of aristocracy. Wealth privilege means serving the wealthy few and disregarding the many. It is a bias built into the design of the corporation, particularly its central mandate to maximize returns to shareholders. This is a mandate out of step with both democratic and market ideals.

We are often told stock ownership is being democratized today. But the truth is, of all financial wealth held by households, the wealthiest 10 percent hold 90 percent. And wealth is not being spread democratically today. It is concentrating in fewer and fewer hands. In the last two decades, the wealthiest 1 percent have doubled their share of national household wealth, from 20 percent to close to 40 percent.[1]

This massive concentration gives the wealthy virtual sovereignty over both our economic and our political systems. We may have done away with the divine right of kings, but we find ourselves in the grip of a new divine right of capital.

The democratic ideals of America's founding fathers show the way out. That way leads to economic democracy, to a new economic order that respects the workings of the market while reclaiming its gifts for the many rather than for the few. Calls for economic democracy may be painted as anti-business, but that's a bit like painting George Washington as anti-government. In truth, an economic democratizing process means extracting aristocratic bias from business institutions while leaving the institutions themselves substantially intact, and healthier.

I myself am a small business owner, as were my father and grandfather before me.[2] As a business publisher and journalist, I have seen that a democratic evolution in business has been trying to happen for some time—with growing attention to environmental stewardship, employee profit sharing, family-friendly policies, and good corporate citizenship. Fourteen years ago, I cofounded the publication *Business Ethics* to support this rise in corporate social responsibility, believing that voluntary change by progressive businesspeople would transform capitalism. I no longer believe that.

The turning point in my thinking came at a seminar years ago, when business theorist and author David Korten and I found ourselves arguing in the halls, off and on, for three days—with me insisting that many businesses were becoming more humane and David insisting that change at the company level wasn't enough, that we needed systemic change.

David's premise is one I've come to accept, for in the years since that seminar, over and over again I've seen the failure of voluntary change by individual companies. I have seen corporations announce family-friendly policies, only to turn around and lay off tens of thousands. I have seen companies pursue environmental stewardship, but only to the extent that it enhances the bottom line. I have seen companies create profit-sharing incentives, but at the same time hold down wages and cut benefits. I have seen corporations become generous citizens, but only as they demand far more in tax concessions.

After more than a decade of advocating corporate social responsibility and seeing its promise often thwarted, I've come to ask myself, *What is blocking change?* The answer is now obvious to me. It's the mandate to maximize returns for shareholders, which means serving the interests of wealth before all other interests. It is a systemwide mandate that cannot be overcome by individual companies. It is a legal mandate with which voluntary change can't compete.

This mandate, quite simply, is a form of discrimination: wealth discrimination. It is rooted in an ancient, aristocratic worldview that says those who own property or wealth are superior. It is a form of entitlement out of place in a market economy.

We can move to a true market economy, where all economic rights are equally protected, and where all persons are equally empowered to pursue self-interest. We can design new economic structures—new ways to hire CEOs, new financial statements, new concepts of fiduciary duty, and new forms of citizenship in corporate governance—that embody both democratic and market ideals.

If changing economic structures in this way now seems impossible, an opening for change can come. It may already be coming, if the end of the bull market dampens the stock market hysteria that has gripped us for so long. Financial powers may seem omnipotent today, but we should remember that the power of kings was once as great.

The institution of kingship dominated the globe for millennia as a nearly universal form of government stretching back to the dawn of civilization. The very idea of monarchy once seemed eternal and divine, until a tiny band of revolutionaries in America dared to stand up and speak of equality. They created an unlikely and visionary new form of government, which today has spread around the world. And the power of kings can now be measured in a thimble.

August 2001   MARJORIE KELLY
Minneapolis, Minnesota

Acknowledgments

THIS BOOK is the product of many minds. Karl Mannheim, one of the founders of the sociology of knowledge, perhaps said it best in his 1936 work *Ideology and Utopia:* "Strictly speaking it is incorrect to say that the single individual thinks. Rather it is more correct to insist that he participates in thinking further what other men have thought before him." If writers like John Locke, Voltaire, Thomas Jefferson, and Thomas Paine had the original thoughts of democracy, others today are carrying this stream of thought into economics. For opening the channels in which my own thought has flowed, I would particularly like to acknowledge a handful of contemporary writers who have deeply influenced me—David Korten, Ralph Estes, Richard Grossman, David Ellerman, and Margaret Blair. Korten and Grossman both offered key ideas foundational to this work as well as valuable feedback on the manuscript. Estes provided the seminal insight that stockholders today are not funding corporations. Ellerman clarified my thinking on employees' right to a voice in corporate governance. And Blair's writing opened up to me the world of progressive corporate governance scholarship.

Other writers and thinkers mentioned in this book, whose names are too numerous to repeat here, have also had a great and apparent influence on my thinking. I feel particularly indebted to Richard Ashcraft, Peter Barnes, Robert Benson, Robert Beyster, John Boatright, Edward Carberry, Robert Dahl, John Kenneth Galbraith, Jeff Gates, Hazel Henderson,

Andy Law, Thomas Linzey, Jane Mansbridge, Carl Mayer, Teresa Michals, Lawrence Mitchell, Marleen O'Connor, Eric Orts, Lynn Stout, Gordon S. Wood, William Wynn, and Alan F. Zundel.

My publisher, Steve Piersanti of Berrett-Koehler, had the original idea of building this work around a half-dozen core principles, and thus played a vital role in giving the book its shape. He and Alis Valencia generously gave me the early opportunity to publish the four opening chapters of the book in a pamphlet entitled "Is Maximizing Returns to Shareholders a Legitimate Mandate?" as part of the Beyond the Bottom Line series. They helped me to begin getting these ideas out into the world in 1999 via that pamphlet, which led to fruitful feedback that influenced the rest of the book. For opportunities to present the work publicly in its early stages, I am grateful to Donna Wood (and the wolf pack), George Brenkert, Jim Tarbell, Teresa Yancey Crane, and Michael Lerner. I want particularly to acknowledge feedback from Heidi Von Weltzien-Hoivon at a Society for Business Ethics meeting; she persuaded me that the book would be incomplete without addressing the issue of money in politics. Some research and ideas from the book first appeared in different form in *Business Ethics*, and I wish to thank the many people who contributed in various ways to those early articles (many of which can be found on the Web site www.DivineRightofCapital.com).

I wish to offer very warm and deep thanks to Karen McNichol of the *Business Ethics* staff, who contributed to this book in so many ways—creating the Web site, finding out-of-print books and articles, researching facts, tracking down individuals, arranging travel, doing publicity, and in general keeping *Business Ethics* running with smoothness during my long absences while working on the book. She is one of those once-in-a-lifetime colleagues who has created the underlying structure of order that makes all of my work possible. I also wish to thank my brother Bradley Kelly for research assistance and much-needed emotional support. And I'm grateful to editorial intern Tom Klusmann, whose excellent work at *Business Ethics* bought me precious time for work on the book.

A number of individuals generously took the time to read an early draft of the entire manuscript and offer many constructive comments, including Leslie Christian, Allan Paulson, Peter Rachleff, Maggie Stuckey, and Donna Wood. For assistance with certain portions of the manuscript in various stages I am grateful to Kent Greenfield, John Logue, Deborah Groban Olson, and Terry South. Some of these individuals helped read the work for accuracy in historical, legal, and other areas, but any errors remaining in the work are of course my own. I also wish to thank the many individuals who generously provided endorsements for the work, and in the process offered me welcome reassurance.

A book that simply sits on the shelf is only half complete. Energetic work in getting this book out to the public was provided by publicist Pat Rose, marketing director Kristen Frantz, and by all the members of the Berrett-Koehler staff, who in a tangible sense are partners in this book. Special thanks to Jeevan Sivasubramaniam for his words of encouragement and enthusiasm. For the design of the cover, I'd like to thank Pat Thompson of Triangle Park Creative in Minneapolis, who for many years has been both a colleague and a friend. As one of those rare designers gifted with words as well as images, she crafted the final subtitle of this work—which took her only a moment, after countless others had wrestled with it for weeks. The tasteful interior design of the book was done by Beverly Butterfield.

For the final flow of the manuscript I am indebted to copyeditor Sandra Beris, with whom it has been a rare pleasure to work. She elegantly slashed out redundancy and overkill, and like a sculptor brought forth the natural shape of the manuscript. William Greider graciously provided a foreword for this work, as well as ideas used in the writing of it.

Finally, I would like to acknowledge the skillful wordsmithing of Miriam Kniaz, my partner and the cofounder of *Business Ethics*. She participated at every stage of this book, contributing both key ideas and moral support. She wrestled with me paragraph by paragraph through difficult chapters and insisted on clarifications that—despite my initial obstinacy—proved enormously beneficial. She was with me in the antiques store when I found *Whitaker's Peerage, Baronetage, Knightage, and Companionage* and encouraged me to splurge on this seemingly ridiculous purchase. I am grateful for her support, which in countless ways made this book possible, and vastly more fun.

M.K.

Introduction

IN AN ERA when stock market wealth has seemed to grow on trees—and trillions have vanished as quickly as falling leaves—it's an apt time to ask ourselves, Where does wealth come from? More precisely, where does the wealth of public corporations come from? Who creates it?

To judge by the current arrangement in corporate America, one might suppose capital creates wealth—which is strange, because a pile of capital sitting there creates nothing. Yet capital providers—stockholders—lay claim to most wealth that public corporations generate. Corporations are believed to exist to maximize returns to shareholders. This is the law of the land, much as the divine right of kings was once the law of the land. In the dominant paradigm of business, it is not in the least controversial. Though it should be.

What do shareholders contribute, to justify the extraordinary allegiance they receive? They take risk, we're told. They put their money on the line, so corporations might grow and prosper. Let's test the truth of this with a little quiz:

Stockholders fund major public corporations—true or false?

False. Or, actually, a tiny bit true—but for the most part, massively false. In fact, most "investment" dollars don't go to corporations but to other speculators. Equity investments reach a public corporation only when new common stock is sold—which for major corporations is a rare event. Among the Dow Jones industrials, only a handful have sold any new common stock in thirty years. Many have sold none in fifty years.

The stock market works like a used car market, as former accounting professor Ralph Estes observes in *Tyranny of the Bottom Line*. When you buy a 1997 Ford Escort, the money goes not to Ford but to the previous owner of the car. Ford gets the buyer's money only when it sells a new car. Similarly, companies get stockholders' money only when they sell new common stock. According to figures from the Federal Reserve, in recent years about one in one hundred dollars trading on public markets has been reaching corporations. In other words, ninety-nine out of one hundred "invested" dollars are speculative.[1]

That's today. But the past wasn't much different. One accounting study of the steel industry examined capital expenditures over the entire first half of the twentieth century and found that issues of common stock provided only 5 percent of capital.[2]

So what do stockholders contribute, to justify the extraordinary allegiance they receive? Very little. Yet this tiny contribution allows them essentially to install a pipeline and dictate that the corporation's sole purpose is to funnel wealth into it.

The productive risk in building businesses is borne by entrepreneurs and their initial venture investors, who do contribute real investing dollars, to create real wealth. Those who buy stock at sixth or seventh hand, or one-thousandth hand, also take a risk—but it is a risk speculators take among themselves, trying to outwit one another, like gamblers. It has little to do with corporations, except this: public companies are required to provide new chips for the gaming table, into infinity.

❧

It's odd. And it's connected to a second oddity—that we believe stockholders *are* the corporation. When we say that a corporation did well, we mean that its shareholders did well. The company's local community might be devastated by plant closings. Employees might be shouldering a crushing workload. Still we will say, "The corporation did well."

One does not see rising employee income as a measure of corporate success. Indeed, gains to employees are losses to the corporation. And this betrays an unconscious bias: that employees are not really part of the corporation. They have no claim on wealth they create, no say in governance, and no vote for the board of directors. They're not citizens of corporate society, but subjects.

We think of this as the natural law of the market. It's more accurately the result of the corporate governance structure, which violates market principles. In real markets, everyone scrambles to get what they can, and they keep what they earn. In the construct of the corporation, one group gets what another earns.

The oddity of it all is veiled by the incantation of a single magical word: *ownership*. Because we say stockholders own corporations, they are permitted to contribute very little, and take quite a lot.

What an extraordinary word. One is tempted to recall the comment that Lycophron, an ancient Greek philosopher, made during an early Athenian slave uprising against the aristocracy. "The splendour of noble birth is imaginary," he said, "and its prerogatives are based upon a mere word."[3]

~

A mere word. And yet the source of untold trouble. Why have the rich gotten richer while employee income has stagnated? Because that's the way the corporation is designed. Why are companies demanding exemption from property taxes and cutting down three-hundred-year-old forests? Because that's the way the corporation is designed. "A rising tide lifts all boats," the saying goes. But the corporation functions more like a lock-and-dam operation, raising the water level in one compartment by lowering it in another.

The problem is not the free market, but the design of the corporation. It's important to separate these two concepts we have been schooled to equate. In truth, the market is a relatively innocent notion. It's about buyers and sellers bargaining on equal footing to set prices. It might be said that a free market means an unregulated one, but in today's scheme it really means a market with one primary form of regulation: that of property rights.

We think of this as inherent in capitalism, but it may not be. It is true that throughout history capitalism has been a system that has largely served the interests of capital. But then, government until the early twentieth century largely served the interests of kings. It wasn't necessary to throw out government in order to do away with monarchy—instead we changed the basis of sovereignty on which government rested. We might do the same with the corporation, asserting that employees and the community rightfully share economic sovereignty with capital owners.

What we have known until now is capitalism's aristocratic form. But we can embrace a new democratic vision of capitalism, not as a system *for* capital, but a system *of* capital—a system in which all people are allowed to accumulate capital according to their productivity, and in which the natural capital of the environment and community is preserved.

At the same time, we might also preserve much of the wisdom that is inherent in capitalism. If we go rummaging through its entire basket of economic ideas—supply and demand, competition, profit, self-interest, wealth creation, and so forth—we'll find most concepts are sturdy and healthy, well worth keeping. But we'll also find one concept that is inconsistent with the others. It is the lever that keeps the lock and dam functioning, and it is these four words: *maximizing returns to shareholders.*

When we pluck this notion out of our basket and turn it over in our hands—really looking at it, as we so rarely do—we will see it is out of place. In a competitive free market, it decrees that the interests of one group will be systematically favored over others. In a system devoted to unconscious regulation, it says corporations will consciously serve one group alone. In a system rewarding hard work, it says members of that group will be served regardless of their productivity.

Shareholder primacy is a form of entitlement. And entitlement has no place in a market economy. It is a form of privilege. And privilege accruing to property ownership is a remnant of the aristocratic past.

❧

That more people own stock today has not changed the market's essentially aristocratic bias. Of the total gain in marketable wealth from 1983 to 1998, more than half went to the richest 1 percent.[4] Others of us may have gotten a few crumbs from this feast, but in their pursuit we have too often been led to work against our own interests. Physicians applaud when their portfolios rise in value, yet wonder why insurance companies are ruthlessly holding down medical payments. Employees cheer when their 401(k) plans post gains, yet wonder why layoffs are decimating their firms. Their own portfolios hold the answer.

Still, decrying the system's ills is not the same as saying the stock market is devoid of value or that it should be eliminated. The stock market does have its worthwhile functions. Stock serves as a kind of currency with which companies can buy other companies. A high share price can also be the basis for a good credit rating, making it easier for firms to borrow at favorable rates. Most vitally, public markets create liquidity, which is what makes genuine investment in companies attractive. Without an aftermarket for share trading, investors could cash out only when a company was sold or liquidated, which would make investing in a company like investing in a house. Money could be tied up for decades.

In making the value of companies liquid, the stock market has the effect of increasing that value. It's in part a function of auction. Because more bidders are available, a stock fetches a higher price, just as a first-edition Hemingway fetches a higher price on eBay than at a garage sale. But the auction function can get out of control when new wealth flows primarily to those already possessing substantial wealth. Because this wealth cannot fully be spent, it can only be reinvested, leaving more and more money to chase essentially the same body of stocks—causing them to artificially inflate in value. When that inflation becomes too large, the bubble bursts, often dragging the real economy down with it. Thus, while the stock market has its functions, it also has its dysfunctions.

Bubbles are one dysfunction. A second is the artificial overvaluation of financial capital and the devaluation of other forms of wealth. Progressive business theorist Paul Hawken describes it as a "worldwide pattern of decapitalization." "Capital," he wrote, "whether it be natural capital in the form of resources, or human capital in the form of low-wage workers, or local capital in the form of functional and healthy local economies, is being extracted and converted to financial capital at an increasingly accelerated rate."[5]

This process has accelerated dramatically in the last half-century, as the value of the stock market has increased over a hundredfold. But in that same period, forests have shrunk, water tables have fallen, wetlands have disappeared, soils have eroded, fisheries have collapsed, rivers have run dry, global temperatures have risen, and countless plant and animal species have disappeared.[6]

❧

This same half-century, not incidentally, has been the time when major public corporations have come to dominate the world. It is also a time when the shareholder primacy that drives them has become increasingly out of step with reality—due to a number of massive changes in the nature of major corporations:

1. *Increasing size.* Today, among the world's one hundred largest economies, fifty-one are corporations.[7] They have revenues larger than nation-states, yet maintain the guise of being the "private property" of shareholders.

2. *The shrinking of ownership functions.* While we still call stockholders the owners of major public firms, they do not—for the most part—manage, fund, or accept liability for "their" companies. Ownership function has shrunk to virtually one dimension: extracting wealth.

3. *The rise of the knowledge economy.* For many companies, knowledge is the new source of competitive advantage. To allow shareholders to claim the corporation's increasing wealth—when employees play a greater role in creating that wealth—is a misallocation of resources.

4. *The increasing damage to our ecosystem.* The rules of accounting were written in the fifteenth century, when to the Western mind nature seemed an unlimited reservoir of resources and an unlimited sink for wastes. That is no longer true, but the rules of accounting retain fossilized images of those ancient attitudes.

Major public corporations have evolved into something new in civilization—more massive, more powerful than our democratic fore-fathers dreamed possible. The major companies of their era, like the East India Company, were arms of the Crown. America was founded by similar, though often smaller, Crown companies. The founding generation in America seemingly felt that in bringing the Crown to heel, they had immunized themselves against corporate predation. This may be the reason that they left us few tools at the federal level for governing corporations: the word *corporation* itself appears nowhere in the Constitution.

At the state level, the founding generation did establish a system where corporations were chartered for purposes that served the public good—like constructing turnpikes—and were allowed to exist only for finite periods of time. But this system was overturned in the heyday of the Robber Barons, after the Civil War, when corporations became private, cut themselves free from government oversight, assumed eternal life, and began to see shareholder gain as their sole purpose.

Today, as the name itself implies, public corporations are no longer really private. The major corporation, as president Franklin D. Roosevelt observed, "represents private enterprise become a kind of private government which is a power unto itself."[8]

PART I: ECONOMIC ARISTOCRACY

If the stockholding class ruling these governments is a secular aristocracy, it functions like the secular monarchs that we call dictators functioned—attempting to reproduce aspects of privilege enjoyed in a previous era. Secular monarchs largely failed, because they lacked the sustaining myth of the divine right of kings. As fallen dictators from Mussolini to Marcos showed the world, power without myth does not long endure.[9]

The secular aristocracy today clings to its sustaining myths, for those myths provide the base of its legitimacy, without which the amassing of wealth begins to seem indefensible. The core myth—that shareholder returns must be maximized—is thus considered unchallengeable. It is a myth with the force of law. We might call it our secular version of the divine right of kings.

In tracing the roots of this myth, in part I, this book undertakes a venture into what French philosopher Michel Foucault would call an *archaeology of knowledge*: a foundational dig, examining the ancient conceptual structures on which aristocratic bias is built. The book explores six such structures—six principles—each serving to uphold the needs of property owners above all other needs.

1. *Worldview*: In the worldview of corporate financial statements, the aim is to pay stockholders as much as possible, and employees as little as possible.

2. *Privilege*: Stockholders claim wealth they do little to create, much as nobles claimed privilege they did not earn.

3. *Property*: Like a feudal estate, a corporation is considered a piece of property—not a human community—so it can be owned and sold by the propertied class.

4. *Governance*: Corporations function with an aristocratic governance structure, where members of the propertied class alone may vote.

5. *Liberty*: Corporate capitalism embraces a predemocratic concept of liberty reserved for property holders, which thrives by restricting the liberty of employees and the community.

6. *Sovereignty*: Corporations assert that they are private and the free market will self-regulate, much as feudal barons asserted a sovereignty independent of the Crown.

Myths take many forms. In essence, they are stories we tell ourselves, like the story that discrimination based on property ownership is permissible, even mandatory, which is examined in chapter 1. It looks at the story built into financial statements, which decree that corporations must give shareholders as much income as possible, while they give employees as little as possible. It's a story that can be likened to the ancient story of the great chain of being, which pictured the interests of some persons as naturally higher on the chain than others, because they were closer to God.

Chapter 2 turns to the notion of privilege, which in the predemocratic age meant legal rights reserved for the few and denied to the many. Foremost among aristocratic privileges, in the era before the French Revolution, were rights to endless streams of income, detached from productive contribution. We find this same privilege reserved today for stockholders and denied to employees. For while stockholder productivity today is negative, employee productivity is positive and climbing, and has far outstripped employee gains.

Stockholder privilege rests on the notion that corporations are not human communities but pieces of property, which means they can be owned and sold by the propertied class. We see in chapter 3 how this leads to the unconscious assumption that persons who work in corporations are, in a sense, property; the value of their presence is bundled into the value of the corporation when it is sold. This to some extent mirrors the ancient beliefs that wives belonged to their husbands, and vassals belonged to feudal lords.

In the predemocratic mindset, persons without property were not permitted to vote. And so it is with employees today, for stockholders alone govern corporations, as we see in chapter 4. The public corporation is a kind of inverted monarchy, with representatives of the share-owning aristocracy hiring and firing the CEO-king. It is a structure reminiscent of England after the Glorious Revolution of 1688, in which Parliament—which represented the landed class—first asserted power over the monarch.

That all of these myths and structures must be left in place, and not be tampered with by government, is a function of liberty. In chapter 5 we see that today's conception of the free market reserves liberty for property holders, even as it denies liberty to employees and the community.

In the final chapter of part I—chapter 6—we turn to the notion of sovereignty: the idea that stockholders are the corporation, which mirrors the ancient notion that the king was the state. The prerogative of the sovereign power is to have liberty within its own realm. Because the sovereign power is the source of law, it can do no wrong. It seems natural to us today that economic sovereignty rests with property ownership, because this once was true of all sovereignty, political and economic.

PART II: ECONOMIC DEMOCRACY

How do we begin to change such an entrenched and ancient system of discrimination? We begin first by seeing it for what it is, and naming it as illegitimate. For doing so allows us to reclaim our economic sovereignty—which means remembering that corporations are creations of the law, that they exist only because we the people allow them to exist, and that we create the parameters of their existence.

We begin also with imagination—with imagining a new framework—both institutional and conceptual—on which to ground a more democratic economy: new variations on financial statements, new property rights, strengthened human rights, new forms of citizenship in corporations, and enlarged corporate purpose. The first order of business is a new ideology to undergird these structures, for mechanisms are only effective to the extent that they find legitimacy in the public mind.

❧

Articulating an ideology for economic democracy is the aim of the second part of this book. It draws on varied efforts to reform corporations, but its aim is also to focus those efforts more effectively, by grounding them in the larger project of democracy—the great project of the Enlightenment, the historical project of moving society from monarchy to democracy. Because economic democracy will take different forms from political democracy, this venture draws also on market principles.

If we study the era of the Enlightenment, in which America was founded, we find it did not begin with crafting laws and structures. It began with challenging the principles on which the monarchy stood, and articulating new principles of democracy. In that spirit, I suggest six principles for economic democracy, mirroring the six principles of economic aristocracy:

1. *Enlightenment:* Because all persons are created equal, the economic rights of employees and the community are equal to those of capital owners.

2. *Equality:* Under market principles, wealth does not legitimately belong only to stockholders. Corporate wealth belongs to those who create it, and community wealth belongs to all.

3. *Public good:* As semipublic governments, public corporations are more than pieces of private property or private contracts. They have a responsibility to the public good.

4. *Democracy:* The corporation is a human community, and like the larger community of which it is a part, it is best governed democratically.

5. *Justice:* In keeping with equal treatment of persons before the law, the wealthy may not claim greater rights than others, and corporations may not claim the rights of persons.

6. *(r)Evolution:* As it is the right of the people to alter or abolish government, it is the right of the people to alter or abolish the corporations that now govern the world.

Intellectual principles like these may seem to be mere abstractions, airy things with little relevance to the real world. But as Michel Foucault observed, ideas are mechanisms of power. "A stupid despot may constrain his slaves with iron chains," he wrote, "but a true politician binds them even more strongly by the chain of their own ideas."[10] Ideas are the foundation of the social order. If we are to build a new order, we must build on the base of ideas.

⚘

The starting point is a change of mind, a process of enlightenment, which is the topic of chapter 7. It calls for collective agreement on the core problem of our economy: wealth discrimination. We might recall that battles against sexual harassment, unequal pay, and marriage inequality all gained power from recognition of their common source in sexism. In like manner, our separate economic battles—over issues like the environment, wealth inequality, and corporate welfare—can gain momentum from recognition of their common source in wealth discrimination. To help move us toward this awareness, we need new measurements of corporate success, new financial statements targeted not only at stockholders but at other stakeholders as well. Efforts now under way to develop these are explored in this chapter.

If equality is our aim, it takes tangible form in new rights, like the right of employees to share corporate wealth, a concept explored in chapter 8. Support for this view can be found in the theories of Adam Smith, John Locke, and Thomas Paine. This chapter looks at a few models of employee wealth sharing in progressive companies, and suggests how these might be furthered with new public policy initiatives. It also looks at another emerging economic right—the notion that community wealth belongs to all—and how it too can be furthered in public policy.

The legal barriers to such new rights are existing concepts of the corporation as the private property of shareholders, or the notion that shareholder rights derive from private contracts with which government must not interfere. These conceptions had their genesis in America's own process of feudalization in the nineteenth century, when power was privatized by the Robber Barons. The remedy may be an expanded notion of fiduciary duty, owed not only to stockholders but to other stakeholders as well. Chapter 9 shows that legal barriers to making this change are not as impenetrable as they seem, and small steps have already been taken with state stakeholder statutes.

Suggesting why we must move toward internal democratic corporate governance is the topic of chapter 10. If stakeholder theory commonly asks who is *affected* by the corporation, the more precise query is who is *governed* by the corporation. The answer is employees. This chapter makes the case that employees have a unique right to a voice in corporate governance, since the right to self-govern is one of the most fundamental human rights. Ultimately, this right must be recognized in law.

If we desire to make changes like this in the law, doing so will be difficult until we tackle the power of wealth in government, which is the topic of chapter 11, on the principle of justice. The "right" of wealth to govern is one of the most ancient aristocratic principles, intact even at America's founding, when governance by the rich and well-born still seemed natural. The privileges of wealth have arisen anew in recent decades, as corporations have increasingly claimed constitutional rights as "persons." A related concern is the mechanism by which much wealth concentration arises in the first place: inheritance.

In the final chapter of the book, chapter 12, we turn to the question of how to rouse public sentiment for reform by stirring up "a little rebellion," to use Thomas Jefferson's phrase. We look at the principle of revolution: the fundamental right of the people to alter or abolish the economic governments we call corporations. Corporate charter revocation, though little used today, is a right all states legally possess, and its very existence serves as a valuable reminder that citizens hold ultimate power over corporations. This raising of consciousness is imperative, and there are other ways it can be pursued by employees, business students, social investors, unions, activists, and even CEOs.

∝

Although it is a revolution we aim for, I suggest it will be a bloodless one, fought not at the barricades but in the press, the legislatures, and the courts. It will be (r)evolution—in other words, evolution. This means our ideal path to change should be both innovative and conservative, daring to build anew even as we preserve much of the old.

It may be that the only truly radical change we need is in our minds—in the collective pictures of reality we unconsciously hold. We accept that corporations are pieces of private property owned by shareholders, just as our ancestors believed that nations were private territories owned by kings. We live with these myths like buried shells, old bombs from an ancient war—the war we thought we had won, between monarchy and democracy.

To get at these deeper, unconscious ideas, a useful tool is metaphor. For that reason, this book employs the extended metaphor of aristocracy, which in another sense represents an ancient archetype—a set of archaic attitudes still alive inside our own minds. To begin to see those deep ideas, it helps to change the quality of our attention. To slow down a bit, become curious. See things we never thought to see, though they've always been there—right in front of our eyes.

❧

THE SIX PRINCIPLES OF
ECONOMIC ARISTOCRACY

1. **Worldview**
   In the worldview of corporate financial statements, the aim
   is to pay stockholders as much as possible, and employees
   as little as possible.

2. **Privilege**
   Stockholders claim wealth they do little to create, much
   as nobles claimed privilege they did not earn.

3. **Property**
   Like a feudal estate, a corporation is considered a piece of
   property—not a human community—so it can be owned
   and sold by the propertied class.

4. **Governance**
   Corporations function with an aristocratic governance
   structure, where members of the propertied class alone
   may vote.

5. **Liberty**
   Corporate capitalism embraces a predemocratic concept
   of liberty reserved for property holders, which thrives
   by restricting the liberty of employees and the community.

6. **Sovereignty**
   Corporations assert that they are private and the free
   market will self-regulate, much as feudal barons asserted
   a sovereignty independent of the Crown.

❧

The Six Principles of Economic Democracy

1. **Enlightenment**
   Because all persons are created equal, the economic rights of employees and the community are equal to those of capital owners.

2. **Equality**
   Under market principles, wealth does not legitimately belong only to stockholders. Corporate wealth belongs to those who create it, and community wealth belongs to all.

3. **Public Good**
   As semipublic governments, public corporations are more than pieces of property or private contracts. They have a responsibility to the public good.

4. **Democracy**
   The corporation is a human community, and like the larger community of which it is a part, it is best governed democratically.

5. **Justice**
   In keeping with equal treatment of persons before the law, the wealthy may not claim greater rights than others, and corporations may not claim the rights of persons.

6. **(r)Evolution**
   As it is the right of the people to alter or abolish government, it is the right of the people to alter or abolish the corporations that now govern the world.

PART I

Economic Aristocracy

1

The Sacred Texts

THE PRINCIPLE OF WORLDVIEW

In the worldview of corporate financial statements,

the aim is to pay stockholders as much as possible,

and employees as little as possible.

I grew up with bombs in the house. Two, actually. They were part of my father's collection of antique war implements: a motley assortment of swords, masks, rifles, and these two shells—tall as a two-year-old child, standing upright on the long brick hearth in our basement. It wasn't until my dad died and my mother moved out—after eight children had grown up wrestling near those bombs—that we discovered one shell was live. It could have gone off any time.

These days I collect tamer antiques than my dad: old magazines, cobalt blue Fiestaware. Mostly I collect antique ideas. I'm fascinated by the way an idea becomes antique, intrigued that a concept once considered ordinary can later seem absurd. I find it useful to keep antique ideas around, as a reminder that how we see things today is not how the world will always see them. And conversely, ideas we think of as dead may turn out—like old bombs—to have an unexpected, lingering power.

THE GREAT CHAIN OF BEING

In my antique idea collection, a prized artifact is my 1914 *Whitaker's Peerage, Baronetage, Knightage, and Companionage*—a fat little volume of royal blue, with a dozen gold crowns stamped on its cover (showing the king's crown as distinct from a duke's as distinct from an earl's, and so forth). It's a kind of phone book without phone numbers: a way for the British nobility to locate one another—in space (Winston Churchill residence: Admiralty House, Whitehall), and in order of noble precedence (grandson of Seventh Duke of Marlborough). I think of it as a souvenir from a lost world, not unlike a spent shell. Or a pot shard from Pompeii, dated the year of the eruption. For 1914 was the year World War I would break out, and it would leave five ancient imperial dynasties in its rubble.

The imperial descent began in 1908, when the Ottoman dynasty fell to revolutionary Young Turks. Within three years a revolution would topple the Ch'ing Dynasty in China. By the end of the war in 1918, three European dynasties lay in the dust: the hapless Romanovs in Russia, the Habsburgs in Austria-Hungary, and the Hohenzollerns in Germany. At war's end, as a member of the Reichstag put it, crowns were simply "rolling about the floor."[1] The British throne would stand, but its imperial possessions would soon break away to independence. Its aristocracy, as historian David Cannadine wrote, would continue its descent into "decline and decay, disintegration, and disarray."[2]

To the nobility in my 1914 *Whitaker's*, the coming devastation lay yet behind a veil. They were still "the lords of the earth," still "conscious of themselves as God's elect."[3] And they had *Whitaker's* to help them keep score among themselves—showing who had the greater nobility. When Americans think of the aristocracy—if we think of it at all—it is as a vague lump of important personages, in which we differentiate a viscount from an earl no more easily than we might tell a paper birch from a shagbark hickory. But *Whitaker's* Roll of the House of Lords was numbered in order of precedence: from 1. The Prince of Wales; 2.–8. Princes and Archbishops; 9.–29. the Dukes; 30.–54. the Marquesses; down through Viscounts, Bishops, and the long list of Barons, ending with 654. Baron Sumner of Ibstone.

The list was more than preening: it was the visible symbol of one's place in the cosmic diagram, a way of knowing who was above whom, and who below, for that was how they pictured all of life. It was a world based on a primary antique idea: the great chain of being. All life had its place in this chain, which stretched vertically from the lowliest peasants up through the gentry and nobility to the king, who was highest of all (His Royal Highness) because he was just below God.

This picture of reality held pride of place for centuries, wrote Johns Hopkins University philosopher Arthur O. Lovejoy in *The Great Chain of Being*. Like any idea that serves as a base for a society's worldview, it was less a formally expressed concept than an "unconscious mental habit." These beliefs, Lovejoy wrote, "which seem so natural and inevitable that they are not scrutinized," are most decisive of the character of an age. They are so deep as to be inaccessible, so pervasive as to be invisible.[4] For centuries, society accepted the great chain of being, not as an idea but as a description of reality itself.

℘

Today, we prefer the Forbes 400, ranking individuals from one to four hundred by relative worth. We may read in it the character of the corporate age.

Like aristocratic society, corporate society bases membership on property ownership. In Baron Sumner's era, land was the property that mattered. Today property takes varied forms and is called wealth, or financial assets. So that's the lens through which the corporation views the world: the lens of financial numbers, where it sees the numbers that belong to stockholders as the end point of the whole game. The financial statements are a lens focused on wealth holders, and that lens distorts what it sees—as did the lens of the great chain of being. *Whitaker's* lords did not see others as gentlemen like themselves. They saw commoners destined to be ruled. As CEO of Scott Paper, "Chainsaw Al" Dunlap did not see employees as members of the corporate society. He saw expenses to be cut.

Corporations believe their world of numbers is rational. They fail to see the irrational bias in the way the numbers are drawn—much as the lords failed to see (or chose not to see) the bias in the great chain of being. A primary bias built into financial statements is the notion that stockholders are to be paid as much as possible, whereas employees are to be paid as little as possible. Income for one group is declared good, and income for another group is declared bad.

UNPACKING BIASES IN FINANCIAL STATEMENTS

This decree is held in place by the structure of the financial statements, which we might think of as the conceptual foundation of the corporate worldview. These statements reveal, to a remarkable degree, the unconscious mental habits of the corporation. They merit a closer look.

The stripped-down structure of the income statement is this:

$$\text{Profit} = \text{Revenue} - \text{Costs}$$

We might begin by making a few things visible that are invisible here. In simple terms, there are two kinds of costs: labor costs and materials. People and objects. There are also two kinds of people: employee people and capital people. Instead of designating gains to one as costs and gains to the other as income—which contains an invisible bias—we might designate them both as income. So we may restate the equation:

$$\text{Capital income} = \text{Revenue} - (\text{Employee income} + \text{Cost of materials})$$

There's also something invisible on the capital side: retained earnings—profits not given out as dividends but retained for the corporation's use. Thus we have:

$$\text{Capital income} + \text{Retained earnings} =$$
$$\text{Revenue} - (\text{Employee income} + \text{Cost of materials})$$

Common algebra teaches us that we can draw an equation in different ways while retaining its essential meaning. We might, for example, draw it this way:

$$\text{Employee income} + \text{Retained earnings} =$$
$$\text{Revenue} - (\text{Capital income} + \text{Cost of materials})$$

Using this income statement, a corporation would define its purpose—its bottom line—as maximizing returns to employees. It would do so in part by driving capital income down as low as possible. That's the nature of the equation, to reduce costs, and to increase profit. Note that in this equation, capital income is relatively secure: it's a cost of doing business that must be paid. But it's also fixed, so if the corporation does well, capital doesn't share the gain. Employee income has been put at risk: if there aren't profits, employees don't get paid. But if the company does well, employees do well.

It might make more sense to draw income statements this way. If employees were given incentives to cut costs and increase revenues— knowing they'd pocket the gains—the company might become enlivened. Capital providers are in no position to increase revenues or cut costs, so giving them incentives to do so makes little sense. It's also simply more logical to lump capital providers with materials providers. Both are suppliers, people outside the daily workings of the company, providing resources for its use.

⁊

We might observe here the unconscious power of the equation, for by its structure it defines insiders and outsiders. Whoever gets lumped with materials becomes a commodity—an object conceptually outside the corporation, to be purchased at the lowest possible price, to be used to enrich the bottom line of the insiders. In our redrawn income statement, capital becomes the outsider. Employees become the insiders.

An equation is simply an equation. We can draw it any way we like. But the way we draw it says a great deal about our worldview—and it unconsciously locks us into that view. Drawing it as we do today represents a choice: to view capital providers as those who are the corporation—and to view labor as a commodity.

⁊

The balance sheet reveals a similar capital-centric bias. Its structure is this:

$$\text{Assets} = \text{Liabilities} + \text{Equity}$$

The balance sheet is a funny beast in that it must balance. The two sides must be exactly equal. But in a way it makes sense: every asset a company has is either owned outright (thus is represented by equity) or has debt against it (and is represented by liabilities). Thus liabilities and equity added together equal assets.

Stockholders are represented on the balance sheet by equity, which is supposedly a reflection of what they own (in truth they own far more—the value of the corporation as a whole). But employees don't appear on the balance sheet at all. They simply don't exist—much as commoners did not exist in the Roll of the House of Lords. When a corporation looks around and records everything it has of value (its assets), it doesn't see employees. It's commonly said, "Our employees are our greatest assets," but this isn't true in accounting terms. If it were true, layoffs would be portrayed as a wholesale destruction of assets, rather than as an elimination of pesky expenses.

In accounting terms, employees have no value. Money has value, objects have value, ideas (intellectual property) have value, even some airy thing called goodwill has value. Employees, by contrast, have a negative value: They appear on the income statement as an expense—and expenses are aimed always at a singular goal: to be reduced.

If it's the balance sheet that renders employees invisible, it's the income statement that turns them into an enemy of the corporation. The reason is simple: every dollar paid out to employees is a dollar that doesn't go to profits for stockholders. And common law (judge-made law) says public companies must maximize returns to shareholders. Every time an employee asks for overtime pay, or a raise, or benefits, he or she is acting as an enemy of the company's fundamental mandate.

CHANGING THE NARRATIVE

It doesn't have to be this way. For a moment, let's reimagine the income statement in a different design:

$$\text{Capital income} + \text{Employee income} = \text{Revenue} - \text{Cost of materials}$$

Instead of viewing either labor or capital as a commodity, we've made them both the bottom line. They're both insiders now—both considered full-fledged members of the corporate society, with a claim on profits. Now we have something that resembles a competitive internal market. We also have a natural partnership between stockholders and employees. Profit flows naturally to both—and the two parties must find a way to distribute it, presumably negotiating for it. The new design means employee income is put at risk. It also means employee gains are limitless. And it means employees are likely to start asking tough, market-based questions: Who contributed to the company's success recently? When was the last time stockholders put any real capital in? How much have they *already made* off their contribution?

Employees are not asking these questions today. The financial statements do not encourage them to do so. Nor does corporate governance allow them a voice in income allocation, because they are defined as outsiders.

This business of insiders and outsiders is key. As cultural historian Edward Said notes, the fundamental tool of an imperialist order is turning the natives into outsiders in their own land. "For the native," he wrote in *Culture and Imperialism*, "the history of colonial servitude is inaugurated by loss of the locality to the outsider." And because of that outsider's presence, "the land is recoverable at first only through the imagination."[5]

Stories are at the heart of how we view the world, Said wrote, for "the power to narrate, or to block other narratives from forming," is what defines culture. The great chain of being was the narrative of the old world, and implicit in it was the notion that all must accept their place, no matter how low. The financial statements are the narrative of the corporation, and implicit in them is the notion that employee income must be kept in its place, that is, as low as possible. The concept of divine right once kept other social narratives from forming. Our own version of divine right—the mandate to maximize profits for shareholders—blocks other corporate narratives from forming.

Financial statements are nothing more than a mental construct, a picture of reality that makes companies add and subtract in certain ways. But they exact a toll in flesh and blood. And that toll is rising. In the last decade and a half, the proportion of employees making poverty-level wages has climbed substantially, and in the mid-1990s it stood at an alarming

30 percent.[6] That's almost one in three working people, making wages that can't adequately feed and clothe their families.

The problem isn't limited to low-wage employees. For most Americans, wages have been falling for decades. Between the late 1970s and mid-1990s, income declined for a depressing three out of five Americans.[7] Ideas do have consequences.

WHY ENVIRONMENTAL DAMAGE IS INVISIBLE

Those consequences affect the community and the environment as well. That's a result of a second major bias built into the financial statements: *The corporation aims to internalize all possible gains from the community, and to externalize all possible costs onto the community.* Costs placed on the corporation show up on the income statement, and diminish the bottom line. That's bad. But costs placed on the community are invisible: the financial lens doesn't see them, so they are of no consequence in the corporate worldview.

Let's say Texaco drills in Ecuador—which it did for two decades. If Texaco had to pay to clean up the environmental mess, that would be bad. Environmental remediation is expensive. Thus the logic of the income statement dictated that contaminated "produced water" wastes (water brought up in the process of drilling) were dumped untreated into the Amazon's rivers and streams—in the astonishing amount of four million gallons *each day*. The same logic dictated that toxic drilling muds were buried untreated—though this virtually assured the destruction of groundwater aquifers.[8] Aquifers, rivers, and streams are not assets of Texaco. They do not appear on the balance sheet, so their destruction need not be written off. That destruction is invisible in the corporate lens.

That lens also fails to see the consequences for human and animal life: cattle dead with their stomachs rotted out, crops destroyed, streams devoid of fish, children with anemia because sources of protein have been destroyed. "All during the dry season," a clinic doctor in the region told *The Village Voice* in 1991, "[children] come in here with pus streaming from their eyes and rashes covering their bodies from bathing in the water."[9]

Damage to the fabric of life happens offscreen, as it were. This allows the corporate worldview to maintain the myth that social issues are *soft* (not businesslike, not important), while financial issues alone are *hard*. If something shows up on the financial statements, it matters. If it doesn't show up, it doesn't matter. Translated into human terms, this means that what affects stockholders is important; what affects everyone else is not important.

Saying this is the corporate worldview is not the same as saying everyone in business personally thinks this way. Individual managers might be very caring, and indeed many are. But the lens of the financial statements forces them to see, and to behave, in certain ways, regardless of their personal beliefs. The lens forces them to put aside their humanity and see in business terms—disregarding social costs if there are financial (that is, shareholder) gains at stake. It leads them to believe that it's natural and correct to discriminate in favor of shareholders, and against employees and the community.

❧

What is lost is at first recoverable only in the imagination, as Said noted. If we've never questioned the ideas implicit in the financial statements— never imagined we could (horrors!) add and subtract in different ways— it's because we don't think of these concepts as ideas. We think of them as reality.

The great chain of being, in its day, seemed like reality. It was a picture of reality that seemed so natural and inevitable that it was not scrutinized. Its bias was so pervasive as to be invisible—as the bias toward stockholders remains today. We see it not only in the corporation, but in treaties like the North American Free Trade Agreement, which puts financial concerns at the core and puts labor and environmental concerns into side accords. We see it in a business press that has trumpeted an era of great prosperity, while one in three workers made a poverty-level wage.

Our mental habits take many bizarre (indeed, dangerous) forms, once we think to notice them: that company assets matter, while community assets do not. That the people who work at the company every day are outsiders, while those who never set foot in the place are insiders. Most of all, that this is the only way corporations can see the world. That the corporation's current worldview is rational, natural, inevitable.

One hopes these notions turn out, some day, to be our own antique ideas. Today they retain their invisible, almost mythological power. We live with them like bombs on the hearth.

2

Lords of the Earth

THE PRINCIPLE OF PRIVILEGE

Stockholders claim wealth they do little to create,

much as nobles claimed privilege they did not earn.

What is at work in the corporate worldview is the principle of privilege. To the modern ear this is a word with an inescapable tone of belligerence—like a twelve-year-old's schoolyard taunt ("What makes you so *privileged?*"). But in an earlier age, it carried no such overtones. It represented what was a fact of life: some people had privileges, or legal rights, which others lacked. The word stems from the roots *privus*, meaning private, and *lex*, law, for in its antique sense it meant precisely that: a private law, a law that benefited (or harmed) one individual or group.

If equality under the law is the hallmark of democracy, privilege sanctioned by law is the hallmark of aristocracy. It is the great chain of being given tangible form: some persons are higher than others, and hence have more rights—as God himself intended.

The most fundamental right of an aristocracy is a right to income detached from productivity—in other words, to be free from labor. In America we believe we never had a class of nobles, but we simply called them by a different name: gentlemen. To our forefathers two centuries ago this was the most vital distinction in all of society. "The people, in all nations," John Adams wrote, "are naturally divided into two sorts, the gentleman and . . . the common people."[1] To be a gentleman was to be genteel—to be literate, well-dressed, and above all to live off one's property, on which others performed labor.

As Addison wrote in *The Spectator*, having a landed estate worked by others is "the only Gentlemanlike way of growing rich ... all other Professions have something in them of the mean and subservient; this alone is free and noble." Though America has often celebrated its Puritan ethic of hard work, this ethic did not apply to gentlemen. As historian Gordon S. Wood wrote in *The Radicalism of the American Revolution*:

> In the eighteenth century ... industriousness and hard work were everywhere extolled, and the Puritan ethic was widely preached— but only for ordinary people, not for gentlemen. .... Hard, steady work was good for the character of common people: it kept them out of trouble; it lifted them out of idleness and barbarism.[2]

Gentlemen, on the other hand, were all but forbidden to work. When they did, social norms forced them to pretend it was for pleasure, not necessity. To labor, for a gentleman, was to be disgraced.

PRIVILEGE IN THE FEUDAL ERA

In the European world of the feudal era, aristocracy was of course far more developed. Privileges then were manifold and ubiquitous, ranging from the minuscule to the horrifying. At the lighthearted end of the spectrum was the British aristocratic privilege described in *Whitaker's*—that a nobleman sentenced to be hanged "has the consolation of swinging by a silken cord."[3] In France before the Revolution, there was the notorious privilege of obtaining *lettres de cachet*, which, as historian C.B.A. Behrens noted, "were doled out, in the reign of Louis XV, like blank cheques, to ministers and other officials," who could fill in the name of anyone they wished imprisoned, and immediately it was done.[4]

More unsettling were the antique privileges involving hunting. Though hunting might be a matter of survival for the poor, commoners were forbidden to hunt even on their own land, because rabbits, doves, and other game were legally reserved for the sport of the upper classes. As historian Reinhard Bendix wrote, the laws "also allowed aristocratic hunting parties to follow the chase even if they trampled and devastated the peasants' fields."[5] One can imagine what this meant in reality: a poor family fleeing as a hunting party on horseback came thundering through, leaving the peasants' crops—their source of livelihood—a rubble. But for such destruction the nobles bore no responsibility.

It is much the same today, in the great hostile takeover hunt—a practice likewise reserved for the sport of the upper classes, who destroy the humble classes' livelihoods through layoffs and plant shutdowns.

❧

Another characteristic of aristocracy little changed today is the supposed right to be free from paying taxes. Before the French Revolution, the nobility was largely exempt from taxation. Today, our own upper classes say it is valid to eliminate the estate tax and to pay capital gains taxes lower than employment taxes paid by workers.

But of course the most vital privileges for any aristocracy are those involving income. As stockholders today enjoy both dividends and capital gains income, the French aristocracy also enjoyed rights to various streams of revenue. Their financial privileges were thus dual: little going out to the king, a good deal coming in from the commoners. Commoners, on the other hand, labored under a dual burden: paying taxes to the king and fees to the lord. In essence, they paid both public taxes and private taxes.

These took an ingenious variety of forms. As historian George Rudé described them, medieval French peasants paid a tithe to the church and various taxes to the state, including a direct tax on income or land, a "twentieth" tax on income, an income tax per head, plus a salt tax. To the lord of the manor they owed still more, such as forced labor on roads, toll charges, dues on fairs and markets, feudal rent in cash, rent in kind, and taxes on property transfer.[6] Even when a commoner purchased land, he still owed the lord perpetual rent—one of the first customs outlawed by revolutionary legislation.[7]

Whatever the peasant set out to do, there were the nobles, "consuming the produce of his toil."[8]

❧

If it seems odd that the French put up with all of this, it's instructive to recall that privileges once went hand in hand with functions. In the feudal era—after the collapse of the Roman Empire, when central government was weak or nonexistent—the manor house became a seat of private government. As Alexis de Tocqueville wrote in *The Old Regime and the French Revolution*:

> In the age of feudalism . . . the nobles enjoyed invidious privileges and rights that weighed heavily on the commoner, but in return for this they kept order, administered justice, saw to the execution of the laws, came to the rescue of the oppressed, and watched over the interests of all. The more these functions passed out of the hands of the nobility, the more uncalled-for did their privileges appear—until at last their mere existence seemed a meaningless anachronism.[9]

What's interesting is how long it took for society to notice, or care, that aristocratic functions had disappeared. One simply did not ask, Does the lord earn his keep? For to question the social order was taboo. Only after Enlightenment thinkers broke many such taboos did the French Revolution find its spark. "Abandon all privileges" became a rallying cry, and the antique meaning of privilege was changed utterly and forever.[10] What had seemed ordinary—this notion of endless income as recompense for doing nothing—began to seem absurd.

After the French Revolution, aristocratic titles were outlawed in France, as they were in America after its revolution. But aristocracy itself was not to die. As John Adams wrote to Thomas Jefferson in 1813: "Aristocracy, like waterfowl, dives for ages and then rises with brighter plumage."[11]

Financial Privilege Today

The financial plumage in our own time has been bright indeed—with the Dow Jones industrial average advancing between 1987 and 1997 by a majestic 300 percent.[12] Fate was less kind to the common folk in that decade, with average real hourly wages falling 7 percent.[13] And so we might ask, do the privileges of stock ownership—today so substantial—still go hand in hand with functions? Do the financial lords earn their keep?

It's a curiously overlooked fact today that, though we speak of stock market activities as investing, there is only the smallest bit of direct investment in companies going on. What is at work is *speculation*, the trading of shares from one speculator to another. Another word for it is *gambling*. But since these words have a less noble cast to them, we prefer the word *investment*, for it keeps us from confronting the stark reality.

Let's look at that reality in some detail. As we saw in the introduction, invested dollars reach corporations only when new equity is sold. In 1999 the value of new common stock sold was $106 billion, whereas the value of all shares traded was a mammoth $20.4 trillion.[14] So of all the stock flying around on Wall Street, less than 1 percent reached companies. We might conclude that the market is 1 percent productive and 99 percent speculative.

But we might also look at it another way, one more generous toward investors. We can examine only the *increase* in the value of exchange-listed stocks from year to year, and calculate the proportion that came from new investments. Take 1998 to 1999, for example. The value of stocks in that period increased $1.1 trillion, while sales of new common stock were $83 billion, or about 7 percent of the increase.[15] Thus we might conclude that the market is 7 percent productive; its increased value comes 7 percent from real money going in.

Yet this leaves out a crucial piece, stock buybacks, which in the aggregate are important. We must figure these in, just as a retail store must look at sales minus returns. Luckily the Federal Reserve has done the heavy lifting. It publishes a figure for net new equity issues (new issues minus buybacks) each year. For 1998, the figure was a negative $267 billion.[16] Thus equity issues were ultimately a negative source of funding for corporations. The stock market, in reality, is not 1 percent or 7 percent productive, it is *less than 0 percent productive*. (See Figure 1.) And that's not even including dividends, which in 1998 extracted an additional $238 billion from corporations.[17]

Figure 1. Stockholder Productivity Versus Gains

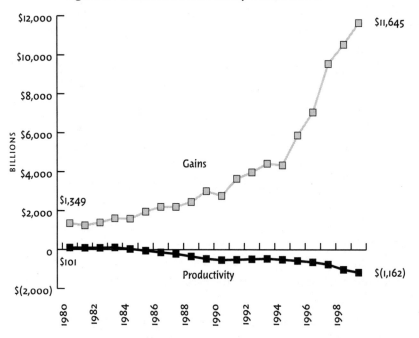

Note: Gains represent cumulative dollar change in value of exchange-listed stocks. "Productivity" represents cumulative net new equity issues. The 1980 starting figure represents the sum of all net new equity issues from 1946 through 1980. *Source for equity issues figures:* Board of Governors of the Federal Reserve System. Flow of Funds Accounts of the United States. www.federalreserve.gov. *Source for value of stocks on exchanges: 1999 Annual Report of the Securities and Exchange Commission.*

Now, we might pause a moment and let this sink in. This business of equity sales as a negative source of funding is today the dominant reality of the stock market, and has been for decades. New equity sales were a negative source of funding in fifteen out of the twenty years from 1981 to 2000. In other words, when you look back over two decades, you can't find any net stockholder money going in—it's all going out. The net outflow since 1981 for new equity issues was negative $540 billion.[18]

During roughly those same twenty years, not incidentally, we saw the largest bull market the stock market has ever known.[19] The fact is, stockholders did not fund that rising market. *Companies pumped massive amounts of money into it, to prop it up.*

As this book goes to press in 2001, the technology bubble has burst and the bull market is no longer charging ahead. Trillions of dollars of value have evaporated, but companies are left holding massive amounts of debt—debt incurred on behalf of that evaporated value. As Floyd Norris noted in *The New York Times*, stock buybacks used up so much cash that companies had to resort to borrowing for investment in their businesses. The result, he wrote, was that "during a period of unparalleled corporate prosperity, the debt of corporate America grew substantially." [20]

The net outflow has been a very real phenomenon—not some statistical conjurer's trick. Rather than capitalizing companies, the stock market has been decapitalizing them. Stockholders for decades have been an immense cash drain on corporations. They are the deadest of deadwood.

It's inaccurate even to speak of stockholders as *investors*, for more truthfully they are *extractors*. When we buy stock we are not contributing capital: we are buying the right to extract wealth.

؇

This isn't new. If stock buybacks are a phenomenon largely of the last twenty years, stock sales have been a minuscule source of corporate funds for more than fifty years. Prominent business theorist Adolf Berle made the observation as early as 1954, and he made it again in the preface to the 1967 edition of *The Modern Corporation and Private Property*—a book that management consultant Peter Drucker called "arguably the most influential book in U.S. business history." [21] Originally published during the Depression, the book is famous for noting the separation of ownership and control in the modern corporation. It was the first to observe that company owners had dropped their management function. By the time of its 1967 revision, Berle was observing that stockholders had dropped yet another function: that of providing capital. He wrote:

> Stock markets are no longer places of "investment". . . . [They are] only psychologically connected with the capital gathering and capital application system on which productive industry and enterprise actually depend. . . . The purchaser of stock does not contribute

savings to an enterprise . . . he merely estimates the chance of the corporation's shares increasing in value. The contribution his purchase makes to anyone other than himself is the maintenance of liquidity for other shareholders who may wish to convert their holdings into cash.[22]

Now, this is a striking statement: that stock markets are only *psychologically connected* to real capital gathering. It was a statement made in one of the most important books in business history, yet it seems not to have been heard.

As Berle wrote, the primary purpose of stock trading now is liquidity— that is, liquidating one's investments to turn them into cash. This is certainly a useful function, because stocks aren't worth a great deal if you can't sell them. But liquidity is a function of *extraction* rather than *investment*. In the aristocratic analogy, it's about collecting one's dues and fees without fuss.

The point is not that direct investment never occurs, because it does. Companies do occasionally sell stock to raise actual cash for operations. The obvious example is the initial public offering, in which a (usually young) company goes public, and shareholder dollars do reach corporate coffers. These newly public companies also often return to the markets with secondary offerings of new stock.

Even older, established corporations occasionally sell new common stock—as American Telephone and Telegraph did in 1964, General Motors did in 1992, and Conoco did in 1998. But the sale of common stock by large companies is often an ephemeral reality, as we can see in the GM case: in 1992 it sold $2.2 billion worth of common stock—and within six years had bought back three times that amount.[23]

The point is that productive sales of common stock represent, in Berle's words, an insignificant percentage of stock trading. He wrote memorably, "Stockholders toil not, neither do they spin."[24] We might add that they manage not, neither do they accept liability. Society long ago acknowledged that stockholders as owners had dropped these functions. What we've yet to acknowledge is that, in the last half-century, *stockholders have largely dropped their final productive function: providing capital.* Economic texts still speak of capital inputs, but with most public corporations there is precious little inputting going on.

Evidence of this phenomenon can be dug out from reams of Fed statistics, but one is hard-pressed to find people today tracking it or commenting on it. Check stock tables in the *Wall Street Journal*, and you'll find no column showing capital contributed. Search the *Value Line* investment books at your local library, and you'll find no tables showing the history of capital input for individual companies. The figure for paid-in capital is there on company balance sheets, but it's impossible to tell when it was paid in: Last year? Thirty years ago? Fifty years ago?

Though no one acknowledges it, the truth is clear. In most major companies today stockholders serve about as many functions as an eighteenth-century French marquess, which is to say almost none. Except collecting their own income.

THE NEW PEASANT CLASS

That income is the produce of someone else's toil. If stockholder productivity has been negative, employee productivity has been positive and rising. But employee rewards have not kept pace. Stephen S. Roach, chief economist at Morgan Stanley & Co., points out that the rise in employee productivity over the last decade has been *three times* the rise in compensation. Even with the pickup in real wages starting in the mid-1990s, he emphasizes, "we still have fifteen years of an enormous gap between worker rewards and worker contribution."[25] (See Figure 2.)

In human terms, this benignly named rising productivity often means crushing workloads and punishing hours. Unions fought one hundred bloody years to win the right to a forty-hour week, only to have it lost in a fraction of that time. In the last twenty years, the proportion of employees working fifty hours or more each week has jumped by 50 percent. More than one in three employees now struggles under this load.[26]

As recompense, aggregate wages have dropped: in 1998, the median real wage was lower than a decade earlier.[27] Benefits have also decreased: between 1979 and 1997 the share of workers receiving employer-provided health care dropped 8 percent.[28]

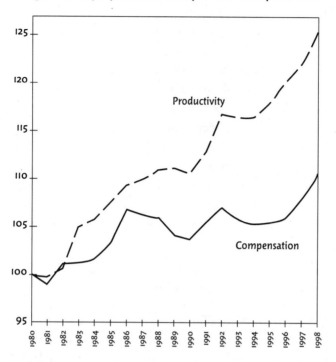

Figure 2. Employee Productivity Versus Compensation

Note: Cumulative increase in nonfarm productivity and real hourly compensation, as represented by an index set to 100 in 1980.
Source: Morgan Stanley Dean Witter, Bureau of Labor Statistics.

Like their peasant forebears, employees labor under a dual burden: doing more yet making less. Stockholders, like French aristocrats, enjoy dual privileges: doing less and making more.

ॐ

What's at work is indeed a private law—a privilege—because the rules for employees are quite distinct from those for stockholders. Employees contribute more and more to companies, year after year. Yet they are paid as little as possible. If they slack off, they are let go. Stockholders make a onetime investment when a new share of stock is purchased, and beyond that contribute nothing. Yet the company aims to create maximum income for them forever.

If we rarely speak of this phenomenon in such terms, it may be because we have few words for it. The phrase *stockholder productivity* is strangely missing from the capitalist vocabulary, perhaps because it points to a reality we would rather ignore. We do not say stock ownership is about extracting wealth. Instead we say it is about *creating* wealth. As a columnist for the financial magazine *Barron's* wrote, an "amazing $4 trillion in wealth *has been created in the stock market* since the end of 1994" (italics added).[29]

Hence we are led to believe stockholder wealth is legitimate, for shareholders "create" it through "investing." Such a manner of speaking diverts our attention from the reality—that like the French aristocracy before the revolution, stockholders as owners have discarded virtually all productive functions they once had, but still retain their privileges.

The French eventually awoke to the absurdity of it all—this business of endless income as recompense for doing nothing. One wonders when we will awake.

3

The Corporation as Feudal Estate

THE PRINCIPLE OF PROPERTY

Like a feudal estate, a corporation is considered a

piece of property—not a human community—so it

can be owned and sold by the propertied class.

*I*n searching for the source of stockholder privilege, we come around again to the incantation of that single, magical word: *ownership*. Because we say stockholders own corporations, they are permitted to contribute very little and take quite a lot. This word *own* is deceptively small and worth unpacking.

Since stockholders own corporations, implicitly (1) the corporation is an object that can be owned, (2) stockholders are sole masters of that object, and (3) they can do as they like with "their" object.

It's an entire worldview in three letters. And as a result of this tiny incantation (like the *Shazam* that turns a boy into Captain Marvel), stockholders gain omnipotent powers: they can take massive corporations, break them apart, load them with debt, sell them, shut them down, and drive out human beings—while employees and communities remain powerless to stop them.

Power of this sort has an unmistakable feel of the ancient. Ownership, that bundle of concepts we also label property rights, is another antique tradition that has remained impressively intact. It comes down to us from that time when the landed class was the privileged class, by virtue of its wealth in property. To own land was to be master. And in the master's view, what was owned was subordinate, as in the imperial presumption that India was a possession of the throne of England. Or the feudal presumption that lords could own serfs, like so much livestock.

Ownership, according to British law, conferred upon the owner a right to "sole and despotic dominion." The phrase is from William Blackstone's influential eighteenth-century *Commentaries on the Laws of England*. It is a phrase worth lingering over, for *dominion* shares the same root as *domination*. And *despotic*, the *Oxford English Dictionary* tells us, means tyrannical rule of those who are not free.

ANCIENT RELATIONSHIPS OF OWNERSHIP

Blackstone's chilling phrase is one I encountered in a 1993 scholarly article by Teresa Michals, who at the time was completing a Ph.D. at Johns Hopkins University. The piece was titled "'That Sole and Despotic Dominion': Slaves, Wives, and Game in Blackstone's *Commentaries*," and it was something I stumbled on serendipitously—on a day I had abandoned myself to the random, as one does in antiques collecting. I rummaged upon this particular volume of the *Eighteenth Century Studies* journal on a dusty lower shelf—one among acres of shelves—in the Book House used bookstore in Minneapolis. Pulling up a chair there in the cluttered aisle, I sat transfixed as Michals described the ancient aristocratic mind, that antique perspective that saw virtually all human relationships as varieties of ownership.

Eighteenth-century England, she wrote, was a world of "land-based hierarchy," in which social standing rested on ownership of land, or "real property." "Blackstone seems to assume that one either owns real property or becomes real property oneself," she wrote. "Although the common law did not support the buying and selling of persons, it did support the general principle that one person could own certain kinds of property in another."[1]

There were, in effect, three categories of persons: the property owner with full rights, the slave as a piece of property with no rights, and, in between, a mixed category: "that of a right-bearing subject who is also the property of another." In this third category she noted that we might find a man's wife, or his servant, whom he owned though was not able to sell.

The element of ownership went one way. The "inferior hath no kind of property in the company, care, or assistance of the superior," Blackstone

wrote. And because ownership was one way, loyalty was also one way. Thus a servant owed loyalty to the master, but the master owed no loyalty to the servant. The husband could claim damages for trespass if his wife was abducted or seduced, but she had no reciprocal right.[2] Curiously—or perhaps appallingly—the law of master and servant remains the law in employer-employee relationships today, as a living fossil of the notion of ownership. Employees still owe a common-law duty of loyalty to the corporation, but as massive layoffs demonstrate, the corporation owes no loyalty to them.

In Blackstone's era, those without property lacked voice in the legal process. Blackstone justified this by saying that only those who owned property possessed an independent will; hence only they could vote. Those without property were "under the immediate dominion of others," meaning they had "no will of their own" and were incapable of casting a valid vote.[3]

⅌

In this ancient property-based world, a whole range of relationships—not only with wives and servants, but also with children, even with God— were considered relationships of ownership. And this view made its way to America. In colonial times, a widely read American advice manual stressed that "children are so much the goods, the possessions of their Parents, that they cannot without a kind of theft, give away themselves" without permission.[4]

Even in *Two Treatises of Government* by John Locke—the seventeenth-century British theorist whose book is considered a founding document of democracy—God is conceived of as the Great Property Owner. Locke wrote: "For Men being all the Workmanship of one Omnipotent, and infinitely wise Maker; All the Servants of one Sovereign Master, sent into the World by his order and about his business, they are his Property, whose Workmanship they are."[5]

This notion of one sovereign master extended to the marriage relationship, where only men were permitted to own property. In early American law, a husband became owner of his wife's property upon marriage.

He had sole right to administer it, claimed its profits, and was required to render his wife no accounting. In the 1764 case of *Hanlon v. Thayer*, a Massachusetts court said a husband owned even his wife's clothing—though she'd brought it with her at marriage.[6] As Michals described the marital relationship:

> At marriage a woman not only loses her property, which passes into her husband's possession; more fundamentally, she also loses her very ability to own property, becoming instead the property of her husband. Her consent to the loss of her property is taken to imply a free consent to the disappearance of her own legal personality into that of her husband.[7]

Husband and wife were one legal person, and that person was the husband.

MODERN OWNERSHIP

Today, the corporation is considered one legal entity, and that entity is equated with stockholders. Like wives, employees "disappear" into the corporation—where they have no vote. The property of the corporation is administered solely in the interests of stockholders, who, like husbands, claim the profits, and are required to render employees no accounting. We have thus a corporate marriage in which one party has sole dominion. The reason is property.

Stockholder dominion today primarily means extracting wealth. This is done less directly than indirectly, through mechanisms that are worth understanding.

The property stockholders have in corporations is represented by two numbers. The first, *stream of income,* is called profit or earnings. It's the bottom line, what is left over from revenue after all expenses are paid. Stockholders are theoretically said to have a right to all of it, and in an earlier age this was apparently true; all profits were at one time customarily paid out to stockholders. But today stockholders get only a piece of earnings (about a third) in dividends.[8] The rest is kept as retained earnings, to be used by the corporation. That retained portion is booked on the balance sheet as stockholder equity, in a kind of nod to the old tradition. It's a way of saying this equity "belongs" to stockholders.

Even though earnings are no longer entirely paid out to stockholders, those earnings are still often considered the basis of company value, for company worth can be measured as a multiple of its earnings. This is the meaning of the term *price-earnings ratio*. If a company has earnings of *x*, and a total market value of 25*x*, its p-e ratio is 25—meaning the company is worth 25 times its earnings.[9]

So earnings are one part of stockholder property. The second part is the *value of the corporation itself*—called market value, or capitalization (in Wall Street lingo, market cap). This is simply the value of all shares added together. Stockholders receive their portion of market value when they sell stock and pocket capital gains, if the stock has gone up. By analogy with a rooming house, you might say stockholders own the stream of rent coming in, and they own the house itself.

The key to it all is profits. This is the wealth—the property—the corporation creates each year. If earnings go down, the value of the corporation will often go down. Hence maximizing profits means working in the stockholder's interests—and if necessary, working against employee and community interests.

One way or another—through direct payout or increased firm value—the benefits of profit flow to shareholders. Attorney and employee-ownership specialist Jeff Gates, in *The Ownership Solution*, calls this the "closed loop" of wealth creation. Stockholders are by definition those who possess wealth. And in the design of the corporation, most new wealth flows to those owning old wealth, in a closed loop.

This closed loop functions in a literal way on the balance sheet. Equity represents the actual capital stockholders contributed when they purchased new shares. And the retained earnings portion of profits is added to that equity each year. Thus by the magical closed loop of accounting, equity grows year after year, while stockholders never contribute another cent.

THE QUESTION OF INTANGIBLES

One might debate the legitimacy of this arrangement. One might question the rationality of infinite payback for a onetime hit of money. (Even credit cards let you off the hook at some point.) But let us sidestep that debate.

Let us assume, for the sake of argument, that all profits legitimately belong to stockholders. Let us assume they own all tangible corporate assets, so the book value of the corporation is theirs. (Book value means everything you own minus everything you owe. It's what would be left, theoretically, if you sold everything and paid off debts.) Even granted this, stockholders are still running off with 75 percent of corporate value that's arguably *not* theirs.

Consider: at year-end 1995, book value of the S&P 500 accounted for only 26 percent of market value. Intangibles were worth *three times* the value of tangible assets.[10] Thus, even if S&P stockholders owned the companies' tangible assets, they got off scot-free with other airy stuff worth three times as much.

Included in intangibles are a lot of things, like discounted future value, patents, and reputation. But also included is a company's knowledge base, its *living presence.* Or to call it by a simpler name: employees.

❦

In owning intangible value, stockholders essentially own employees—or at the very least, they have the right to sell them, which amounts to the same thing.

Take the case of the Maryland company in Chapter 11 bankruptcy, which in 1997 sold itself to Space Applications Corp. (SAC) in Vienna, Virginia. The company's real assets were its one hundred scientists. So it sold them. As Edward Swallow of SAC told the *Wall Street Journal,* "The company wasn't worth anything to us without the people."[11]

Such human capital acquisitions happen all the time. Through 1997, Cisco Systems in San Jose, California, had made nineteen of them—mostly acquisitions of small software companies with little revenue but fifty to one hundred employees, for which it paid premium prices, up to $2 million per employee.[12]

It's revealing when the accountants go to record such purchases on the balance sheet. If you pay $100 million for a company with, say, $25 million in tangible assets, what's the other $75 million of stuff you bought? How do you record it? Well, what you *don't* record is "one hundred scientists." In post–Civil War America, we recoil from the notion that human beings might be bought and sold. So we say a company has purchased goodwill. That's how it's booked: as a line item on the balance sheet called goodwill.

The parallel to Blackstone is telling. Our law does not support the literal buying and selling of persons, but it does support the principle that stockholders can own certain kinds of property in employees. We allow company owners to sell company assets, even when the primary assets are one hundred scientists. This doesn't make these scientists property in the sense that slaves were property, because the scientists are free to leave. But neither are they property *owners*, with a right to vote on the sale and a right to pocket the proceeds. Their status is akin to the third category Michals described: "that of a right-bearing subject who is also the property of another."

PROPERTY IN THE KNOWLEDGE ERA

Employees-as-property is a troubling concept. But evidence of it is widespread—as in the commonplace observation that "employees are our greatest assets." Assets, of course, are something one owns.

Companies can take this quite literally. Consider the case of Evan Brown. This computer programmer claimed to have dreamed up a concept that would fix outdated computer codes, and he wanted to develop it on its own. But his employer, DSC Communications in Plano, Texas, said the idea was company property, because Brown had signed an agreement granting DSC rights to inventions "suggested by his work." Brown never made notes for his concept. So when DSC sued him, it wasn't for ownership of his papers. It was for ownership of his thoughts.[13]

Through the lens of ownership, one either owns property or becomes property. There is nothing else. It's an attitude that says, if I own the assets of a firm, I own everything created on top of those assets. All new wealth flows to old wealth. This is inherently a feudal assumption—and we can see this more clearly if we make an analogy with land:

> Say a landowner pays a tenant to farm some land, and the tenant builds a house there. Who owns the house? The landowner or the tenant?

In feudal England, the landowner legally claimed the house. But as legal scholar Morton Horwitz points out, American courts rejected this—beginning with the 1829 case *Van Ness v. Pacard*, where Justice Story wrote: "What tenant could afford to erect fixtures of much expence or value, if he was to lose his whole interest therein by the very act of erection?" Under democratic law, the rule became that "the value of improvements should be left with the developer."[14]

Refusing to bow to ancient property rights, democratic law articulated a new precedent: the house belongs to the person who built it. New wealth flows to those who create it.

In this tradition, employees who "build" atop the corporation (creating new products or new efficiencies) have a legal right to the value of their improvements. But in *corporate* law that isn't the case. Corporate law says stockholders own everything the corporation now has and everything it will create into the perpetual future. Hence the increasing value of the corporation will flow forever to shareholders, though they won't lift a finger to create that value. The presumption is literally feudal.

⚘

Tied up with it is the notion that property owners *are* the corporation. Employees are incidental: hire them today, get rid of them tomorrow; they're of no consequence. Sell the company; maybe employees will come along, maybe they won't. It doesn't matter. They're not on the balance sheet, so they don't exist in the tally of what matters.

Yes, well. We might puncture this fantasy with a simple question: What is a corporation worth without its employees?

This question was acted out, interestingly enough, in London, with the revolutionary birth of St. Luke's ad agency, which was formerly the London office of Chiat/Day. In 1995, the owners of Chiat/Day decided to sell the company to Omnicon, which meant layoffs were looming, and Andy Law in the London office wanted none of it. He and his fellow employees decided to rebel. They phoned clients and found them happy to join the rebellion. And so at one blow, the London employees and clients were leaving.

Thus arose a fascinating question: What exactly did the "owners" of the London office now own? A few desks and files? Without employees and clients, what was the London branch worth? One dollar, it turned out. That was the purchase price—plus a percentage of profits for seven years—when Omnicon sold the London branch to Law and his cohorts after the merger. They renamed it St. Luke's, and posted a sign in the hall: *Profit Is Like Health. You Need It, But It Is Not What You Live For.* All employees became equal owners. Ownership for St. Luke's is a right that is free, like the right to vote. Every year now the company is re-valued, with new shares awarded equally to all.[15]

❧

Thus we see how the presumptions of property hold up in the knowledge era: The fiction that outsiders can own a company, which is nothing but a network of human relationships, is a house of cards. Employees themselves are the cards, willingly holding the place together, even as stockholders walk off with the wealth that the employees create.

How long this will be sustainable remains to be seen. But for the time being, employees remain hypnotized, believing themselves powerless, and accepting (*Shazam*) that stockholders have sole and despotic dominion.

We accept this because we operate from the unconscious assumption that corporations are objects, not human communities. And if they're objects—akin to feudal estates—then they're something outsiders can own, and the humans working there are simply part of the property. Either you own property or you become property; there is nothing else in a property-based world.

We're not aware that we're holding such a picture of reality until someone like Andy Law or Evan Brown stands up to stockholders and says, "We are not your property." Such gestures are reminiscent of the founding fathers standing up to Great Britain and saying, "America is no longer your property." What seems solid melts under challenge. In the heat of confrontation, the notion of owning human beings slips away— like ice melting. Or like an incantation fading, once we have broken its spell.

4

Only the Propertied Class Votes

THE PRINCIPLE OF GOVERNANCE

Corporations function with an aristocratic governance structure,

where members of the propertied class alone may vote.

*T*he notion of ice melting is something I've had on my mind lately. I've been chipping a good deal of it on my sidewalks these days, as penance for my lazy habits as a Minnesota homeowner. But there's a secret ice teaches: that the seemingly impenetrable isn't. The trick is to hit on a seam—hit it just right—and witness the miracle of an entire chunk breaking away. Attack under the exposed edge, and another chunk can be loosed effortlessly. Before long the unyielding has, in fact, yielded.

What seems impenetrable, isn't. This is a useful maxim for tackling the topic of corporate governance.

FROM MANAGERIAL CAPITALISM TO INVESTOR CAPITALISM

Corporate governance is a field where stockholders reign supreme, because they are considered owners rather than mere investors. It's a curious field. In poring over corporate governance materials recently, I've come away with the feeling that, as author Gertrude Stein once put it, "There's no there there." In theory, boards of directors are elected by shareholders, but in reality they're handpicked by the CEO and the previous board, and rubber-stamped by shareholders. Again in theory, boards govern in shareholders' interests, but mostly they choose a chief executive officer, who does the rest. Once in a while they vote on a takeover or merger offer. That's pretty much it.

As an indication of how little governance goes on, consider that in 1998 Vernon Jordan sat on ten boards at once.[1] And that was in addition to his full-time job as a lawyer. Imagine someone serving in the senates of Iowa, Illinois, Indiana, Kansas, Michigan, Minnesota, Missouri, Nebraska, Ohio, and Wisconsin while also holding a full-time job. How much governance could actually be going on?

Stanford University professor Joseph Grundfest makes this point by proposing to his law students a simple test. Imagine that the board has been abducted by aliens. Would anyone notice? How much would the company pay to get the board back? How much would it pay the aliens *not* to bring them back?[2]

There's not a lot of governance going on in corporate boardrooms. And the first thing that's not going on is that boards are not establishing the purpose of the corporation. Board members believe their only choice is to follow the prime directive, which is to maximize returns to shareholders.

The genesis of this directive is worth exploring a bit. It may have a feeling to it of long-settled and inviolable law, but it does not arise from either federal or state constitutions, nor is it in any solid sense found in state statutes. Indeed, it contradicts America's early tradition of chartering corporations to serve the public good—to construct bridges, for example. Shareholder primacy emerged from the ether in the midnineteenth century, when it was articulated by the courts. (Chapter 9 discusses these issues in depth.) The basis of shareholder primacy is thus primarily common law, judge-made law. In state statutes, directors have a duty of loyalty to the *corporation*. But in common law, this is interpreted as a loyalty to shareholders alone.

Common law can be overturned in a heartbeat by legislation. And legislators have in fact attempted to make changes in thirty-two states, with stakeholder statutes that give directors leeway to serve the interests of employees and the community. But because enforcement tools for these laws are nonexistent, the myth of shareholder primacy remains solid in the business mind.

This myth found its most forceful articulation in the 1919 Michigan Supreme Court case of *Dodge v. Ford Motor Co.*, which established that "A business corporation is organized and carried on primarily for the profit of the stockholders. The powers of the directors are to be employed for that end." There are exceptions, but this basic design has been affirmed in various ways over the years—particularly in Delaware, where over half the Fortune 500 is incorporated and hence where the most significant precedents are now set. Thus we have a handful of conservative Delaware judges setting economic policy for the nation. And that policy remains tethered to two sentences a state judge wrote eighty years ago. "To this day," as George Washington University law professor Lawrence Mitchell has written, "*Dodge v. Ford* remains the leading case on corporate purpose."[3]

Shareholder primacy may have a firm grip on us because it in fact is an ancient tradition, predating the founding of America. It stems from the seafaring age, when persons jointly financed ships and sought to hold the operators accountable, so money would not be wasted (from which we have the old adage, "When my ship comes in"). As Minneapolis corporate attorney Richard Saliterman told me, it's part of the "unwritten law for cooperative investment," which precedes even the ancient law of Greece.[4]

One might add, parenthetically, that the custom of investor primacy once permitted piracy—as seafaring vessels were legally permitted to attack other ships and seize their cargo. Things are little different today, as corporations loot pension funds, degrade public resources, and demand corporate welfare. The world might be laid waste in the interest of not wasting investor money. One might suppose even modestly civilized thinking would have led us by now to carve out a "piracy exemption," saying corporations should maximize returns to shareholders, except they should avoid piracy. But we haven't gotten even that far yet.

Protecting the interests of the monied class seems the only moral value the corporation fully recognizes. We often refer to it by the benevolent term *fiduciary duty*. In its simplest form, this means that if I take your money for an investment, I shouldn't be careless with it. I am acting as your fiduciary, your financial representative, and thus have a responsibility to be loyal to your interests. This is a reasonable rule. But there are other rules that might be seen as equally reasonable: If I take your full-time labor, I have a duty to pay you enough to live on. If I am a member of a community, I have a duty to pay taxes and protect that community's well-being.

Corporations in a sense are fiduciaries of employees and the community as much as of shareholders. But none of this seems to have taken firm root in our collective thought or our law. The courts continue to insist that maximizing returns to shareholders is the sole aim of the corporation. And directors who fail to do so can be sued.

⨳

In fundamental ways, then, boards don't really govern, except to protect shareholder return. For this goal is the sun around which corporate governance revolves.

Enforcing the mandate of shareholder primacy, outside the courts, relies primarily on three tools. If wealth holders (stockholders) wish to force boards to honor the directive, they have the blunt instrument of the hostile takeover bid: buy up shares in an "underperforming" company, and take it over against the company's will. When boards force CEOs to honor the prime directive, they use two instruments, slightly less blunt: the carrot of CEO pay (primarily stock options) and the stick of firing the CEO.

It's no accident that all three tools—hostile takeovers, stock options, and CEO firing—have been used generously in recent years, at the same time that corporations have grown ruthless in profit seeking, turning to layoffs, overseas sweatshops, corporate welfare, tax avoidance, and the like. This brutality is due, in large part, to a recent mini-revolution in corporate governance, much talked about in governance circles, but missed by much of the rest of the world.

In the half-century preceding this revolution, corporate directors had been like sleeping bears. They were first spotted napping in 1932, when Adolf Berle and Gardiner Means famously observed that stockholders as owners no longer held control, for it had passed to management.[5] Board hibernation lasted another fifty years—through the early 1980s, when the stock market languished at levels *below* those reached two decades earlier.[6] Seeing opportunity in this state of affairs, corporate raiders bought up large holdings and started knocking on boardroom doors, forcing boards to sell underperforming corporations to the highest bidder or be sued by stockholders. This meant companies had to start wringing every dime from operations (sending jobs overseas, selling off weak divisions, laying off thousands), or be taken over by someone who would. The assault grew to gargantuan proportions. In 1990, fully one-third of the companies in the Fortune 500 were targeted for hostile takeovers.[7] The rest lived in fear of the knock at the door. While the 1980s were considered the hostile takeover years, the trend has in fact accelerated since then.

Unsolicited bids exploded in 1999 to one hundred bids valued at $364 billion, triple the total for 1988, the previous record year. This recent hostile trend "has gone all but unnoticed," Laura Holson wrote in *The New York Times*, because "haggling in court has all but disappeared." CEOs and boards simply stopped fighting the takeovers, and started embracing them.[8]

The stark reality of takeovers—plus calls from newly mammoth institutional investors, making similar profit-maximizing demands—is what woke boards from their slumber. Alarmed, the bears proceeded to lumber about and whack CEOs for not being ruthless enough. In one legendary period from 1991 to 1993, activist boards fired CEOs at two dozen behemoth companies, including General Motors, IBM, American Express, Kodak, Westinghouse, and Borden.[9] Those CEOs who were not fired were given stock option packages worth multimillions if stock prices climbed. Thus CEOs faced a clear choice: pledge allegiance to shareholder value and become fabulously wealthy, or be fired.[10]

Under these pressures, the corporate world made a swift—if largely invisible—passage from an era of *managerial capitalism* to one of *investor capitalism*. As Michael Useem summed it up in the book that named the new era, "Managerial capitalism tolerated a host of company objectives besides shareholder value. Investor capitalism does not."[11]

◌

Serving shareholders meant cutting costs, and in the lens of the financial statements, employees were strictly costs. So like great threshing machines, corporations mowed down row after row of employees in layoffs. If one in five Americans had been employed by large firms in the early 1970s, by the early 1990s it was one in ten.[12] Part-time, temporary, and contingent work soared to close to 30 percent of all jobs.[13] Health benefits and traditional pensions declined. Left in the dust, like chaff in the wake of the machine, was that old value, loyalty. At General Electric, CEO Jack Welch launched what staff members termed the "campaign against loyalty." At a company where employee careers had traditionally spanned forty years, *loyal* became a bad word.[14]

A similar attitude was displayed by the president in 1982, when Ronald Reagan fired striking air traffic controllers and authorized the hiring of replacements. That kind of move had been considered illegal for decades, ever since the passage of the 1953 Wagner Act. But after Reagan's gesture, the hiring of scabs during labor disputes became commonplace. Union representation, already declining, took a steep dive.

Labor had been put in its place. And so, in many ways, had government. Its power to tax was sharply curtailed in the era of investor capitalism, as wealthy individuals and corporations cut their tax obligations dramatically. In 1960 corporate income taxes provided nearly a quarter of government revenue, but by 1997 that contribution had been cut in half.[15] Similarly, the top marginal tax rate on personal income plunged from 70 percent in 1982 to about half that today. Capital gains taxes went even lower, to around 20 percent. Although government lost power to tax corporations, corporations gained power to tax governments, increasing demands for public subsidies. In Minnesota, to take one example, "needy" corporations in 1994 got $1 billion in corporate welfare, *seven times* what needy families got.[16]

THE INVERTED MONARCHY

It was, you might say, an economywide palace coup. Having in an earlier era lost control, financial interests had reclaimed power over corporations— and by extension, over CEOs, over employees, and in many ways over the economy itself. Capital had come to reign supreme.

❧

It's interesting how often social activists and business ethicists fail to understand this. Shareholder resolutions take aim against sweatshops and sky-high CEO pay, while business school courses teach ethical decision making—both imagining that executives could choose differently, both supposing that individual greed or individual ethics is the prime moving force in corporations. What is in fact the prime force is *systemic pressure*, pressure that comes from the design of the system itself. The pressure to "get the numbers" (generate profits for shareholders) is felt by CEOs or managers—and enforced by them—but it *originates* with the financial interests behind corporations. If executives are newly ruthless in seeking profits, it's because stockholders are yanking their chains. It could be a simple call from a pension fund manager. But from this flapping of butterfly wings, hurricanes come. Stockholder governance may indeed be perfunctory. But make no mistake; stockholder power is very, very real.

This power remains all but invisible, because in daily corporate operations, CEOs hold the reins of power. Under the business judgment rule, an observation Berle made decades ago is still true today: "Managements act in their 'discretion'—which is merely a lawyer's way of saying that their power is uncontrolled." And as Berle further observed, this offers "a striking parallel to the classic political doctrine that the king could do no wrong."[17] Public corporations thus function like monarchies, with power concentrated in the hands of one individual. But as the boardroom coups of the 1990s demonstrated, corporations are in fact inverted monarchies, with the financial aristocracy above the CEO-king. For the CEO serves only at the board's pleasure. And the board exists only to maximize gains for shareholders.

The inverted monarchy is an arrangement not without precedent. In the financial aristocracy's revolution—when boards tossed out dozens of powerful CEOs—we can find a telling parallel to the Glorious Revolution of 1688 in England, when aristocratic revolutionaries tossed out James II and brought in William and Mary.[18] It was a watershed event in British history, when Parliament for the first time asserted power over the king. Though the main event seemed to be the exchange of kings, this was actually incidental. The revolutionary event was the assertion that Parliament *gave the Crown*. As political theorist Lord Acton wrote,

"The king became its servant on good behaviour, liable to dismissal."
Since Parliament at the time represented the landed class, the revolution
installed propertied interests as the supreme power. Acton wrote:"For the
divine right of kings, it established . . . the divine right of freeholders."[19]
(A freeholder was a landowner who owned the land free of encum-
brances.) In our own Glorious Revolution in the boardroom, a similar
change occurred. In place of the divine right of CEOs, the revolution
established the divine right of capital.

In the case of England, the Glorious Revolution was an important
step on the road to democracy. But it was only a step, for it claimed sovereignty on behalf of the wealthy alone, not on behalf of all. Over time this
did change as the voting franchise was extended. But what's curious is
that today, more than three hundred years later, corporate governance has
not yet made that change. Public corporations are still governed in the
name of the propertied class alone.

At root, what really governs corporations is an idea that is the intellectual descendant of the great chain of being: the notion that only those
who possess wealth matter. Implicitly, they are a higher class of persons
who alone are considered real members of corporate society; hence only
they have a vote.

In spirit, this mindset retains the bias of seventeenth-century British
society, which believed only the aristocracy mattered. That society was
effectively governed not by its parliament, but by the ideas that Parliament
embodied: (1) the interests of the aristocracy are paramount, and (2) the
aristocracy alone has a voice in governance. The parallel to public corporations today is precise: (1) stockholder interests are paramount, and
(2) stockholders alone have a voice in governance.

≪

There's a reason why boards of directors could be abducted by aliens and
no one would notice: all essential governance happens before the board
meets. There's no there there in corporate governance, because corporations are governed not by boards but by the ideas that boards embody.
And by the ideas, one might add, that the stock market embodies.

If truth be told, the stock market is the real governing force in corporate society, for if a stock price falls too far, both board and management can be ousted in a takeover. The stock market in turn is governed by a single, impersonal imperative: *more*. Not more for everyone, but more for stockholders, which if necessary means less for employees and less for the community. We have thus a seamless unity of purpose in the stock market, the boardroom, and the courts. Shareholder primacy is the center of the corporate universe.

THE MYTH OF EMPLOYEE STOCK OPTIONS

It's often said many employees have stock options these days, so when corporations serve shareholders, they're serving employees too. The truth is, stock options go mostly to the top.

A 1999 Federal Reserve survey found stock options were extended to nonmanagement employees by *only 7 percent* of companies. Top managers, by contrast, got 279 times the number of options awarded to other employees, according to a 1998 Financial Markets Center survey. And these lavish management options actually reduced the money available to pay nonmanagers—by an estimated $500 per employee.[20]

Furthermore, options have not been widespread but have been overwhelmingly concentrated in the technology sector. A 2000 study by UBS Warburg economist Joseph Carson found in adding up the entire net-gain value of all outstanding S&P company options at June 30, 2000, that nearly 60 percent was in technology firms. And nearly a third of the total net-gain value was at just six firms: Microsoft, Cisco, Yahoo!, America Online, Sun Microsystems, and Broadcom.[21]

The notion that employees are getting rich from stock options is a figment of the media's imagination. Even the few employees who get stock or options aren't all that lucky, compared to the really lucky folks: the wealthy. As an illustration, imagine an exceptional employee, Tom, who at XYZ Corp. makes $70,000 a year, and owns $35,000 of his company's stock. If his stock returns, say, 10 percent a year, he gets $3,500 as a shareholder. But he makes twenty times that as an employee. He is twenty times more an employee than he is a stockholder. If the company holds down wages to drive up its share price, he can lose more than he gains.

Again, the real winners in this scenario are the 1 percent wealthiest families. Although most do not work, they reap a major windfall from our friend's labors. If XYZ Corp. has a $1 billion market cap, Tom's $35,000 in stock represents an infinitesimal fraction. The wealthiest families own about half of all stock, so they hypothetically own half of XYZ stock.[22] When its $1 billion value goes up 10 percent, they gain $50 million, while our friend gains $3,500.

Wealth concentration is found even in pension funds, reputed to be the great democratizing force. In 1992, the wealthiest 10 percent of families held 62 percent of all value in pension accounts.[23] If a pension fund does better than expected, employees don't get a bigger pension. The money goes to the corporation, where it adds directly to the bottom line, as at USX in 1999, where pension gains represented 108 percent of operating income. For many companies today, overfunded pensions have become a new profit center. And profit benefits shareholders, who are predominantly the wealthy.[24]

൭

There's no avoiding the reality: the people who gain the lion's share from the stock market are not ordinary people. With half of all corporate stock owned by the top 1 percent, it is striking how little changed this is from the medieval era, when, as historian Reinhard Bendix noted, "between 1 or 2 percent of the population . . . appropriated at least one-half of the society's income above bare subsistence." Equally striking is how quietly this disparity has been accepted, both then and now.

In the medieval era, Bendix wrote, "the vast mass of people acquiesced in the established order out of religious awe," for "the rule of the privileged few appeared to the many as if it were a force of nature."[25] Today, we acquiesce out of financial awe, believing the wealth of the few is a natural consequence of economic forces too complex for ordinary mortals to comprehend.

DISTINGUISHING BETWEEN NATURAL
AND NORMATIVE LAWS

Impenetrable is a good word for such a system.

But that very impenetrability offers a clue that what we are dealing with is a predemocratic system: a closed society, to use Karl Popper's phrase. In his book *The Open Society and Its Enemies*, he noted that the archetypal closed society is the tribal aristocracy. These ancient civilizations equated the fate of society with the fate of the ruling class, just as we equate the fate of corporations with the fate of stockholders. In the closed society, this basic premise is not questioned, for the tribe dwells "in a charmed circle of unchanging taboos, of laws and customs which are felt to be as inevitable as the rising of the sun."[26]

Governance by taboo—by norms not open to discussion—is characteristic of closed societies, Popper wrote. Such cultures make no distinction between natural and normative laws, like the distinction between, say, the law of gravity and the divine right of kings. These societies believe their customs have the same force as natural law, and may never be altered.[27]

The art of ruling in such a society, Popper observed, is a kind of "herdsmanship, . . . the art of managing and keeping down the human cattle." These are the workers and servants, "whose sole function is to provide for the material needs of the ruling class." No one questions this social order, Popper wrote, for "everyone feels that his place is the proper, the 'natural' place, assigned to him by the forces which rule the world." In such a society, even slavery fails to create social tension, because slaves are no more part of society than cattle— "their aspirations and problems do not necessarily create anything that is felt by the rulers as a problem within society."[28]

If the ancient closed society was the tribal aristocracy, Popper saw its modern variant in the totalitarian state. He published *The Open Society and Its Enemies* in 1943, in an era when Hitler, Mussolini, and Stalin stalked the world stage, and he intended the book as a critique of totalitarianism. In the "totalitarian theory of morality," he wrote, "good is what is in the interest of my group; or my tribe; or my state." Thus it is permitted to attack other states, or to do violence to one's own citizens, if it benefits the ruling tribe. The closed society is explicitly amoral.[29]

❧

As is the corporation. Nobel Prize–winning economist Milton Friedman famously wrote that the only social responsibility of the corporation is to make a profit.

In corporate society, good is what is in the interest of stockholders. That is the primary criterion of morality. It means the corporation has the right to do financial violence to its employees or the environment (conducting massive layoffs, clear-cutting forests), or to attack other corporations (brutal competition, hostile takeovers), if that increases the well-being of the ruling tribe, the stockholders.

Haitian contract workers sewing Disney garments might be paid starvation-level wages (28 cents an hour), but this isn't considered a corporate problem—unless it erupts as a public relations problem, which threatens earnings (that is, stockholders' interests). And this is so, even when paying a living wage would have a negligible effect on earnings. In Disney's case, *doubling* the contract wage would still leave it at *less than 1 percent* of the cost of the garment.[30] But no matter. Worker income must be minimized.

❧

The real forces at work in corporate governance—as in any closed society—are in the negative spaces. Not in the gestures of governance, but in the empty space around them. Not what boards vote on, but what they *never* vote on. What is taboo, like the question of why employees have no vote. Or why they must necessarily be paid as little as possible.

In any rational picture of reality, employees *are* the corporation. If you call the company, they answer the phone. If you buy from a company, you buy from them. Companies would grind to a halt without them. Yet in corporate governance, employees are largely invisible. As Kent Greenfield of the Boston College Law School wrote in the *Boston College Law Review*:

Workers have no role, or almost no role, in the dominant contemporary narratives of corporate law. Corporate law is primarily about shareholders, boards of directors and managers, and the relationships among them. . . . Only rarely . . . does a typical corporate law course or a basic corporate law text pause to consider the relationship between the corporation and workers.[31]

Employees not only lack voice in governance, they are actively suppressed when they attempt to gain voice through unions. One recent study found that unions were aggressively opposed by 75 percent of employers.[32]

The resulting silence among employees is reminiscent of the silence of commoners in predemocratic society. As Reinhard Bendix wrote in *Kings or People: Power and the Mandate to Rule*:

Until the revolutions of the seventeenth and eighteenth centuries, European rulers assumed that the general population would quietly allow itself to be ruled. Popular uprisings were regarded as violating the divine order and were suppressed by force. Kings, aristocrats, and magnates of the church made claims against one another. In these conflicts, each manipulated appeals to the transcendent powers without fear of seriously undermining the exclusive hold on authority they all enjoyed. The general populace was excluded from the political arena.[33]

That stockholders dominate governance today seems to us a natural law, but it is in fact a *normative* law: it expresses a norm, a belief about who should matter. It is, in short, a bias. We fail to grasp this when we view stockholder primacy as a natural outcome of free markets. In classic closed society thinking, we fail to distinguish between natural and normative laws.

We unconsciously accept what Lord Acton called "the ancient doctrine that power goes with land," that ownership confers a right to govern.[34] This in turn relies on assumptions that the corporation is a piece of property, and that stockholders own it. Because, of course, no one properly thinks of governing a piece of property. If it's yours, you do with it as you will.

WEALTH DISCRIMINATION

What is at work here is property bias, or wealth bias. It is one of the few forms of discrimination that remain largely unconscious. And completely legal.

It's instructive to recall that at America's founding, the voting franchise was limited by three biases then considered legal: race, sex, and wealth. All three restrictions on the vote have since been removed. But only the first two have been recognized as unfair forms of discrimination, which we term *racism* and *sexism*. The third, discrimination based on wealth, hasn't yet been fully recognized. We might begin by giving it a name. I suggest *wealthism*.

We could with equal validity call it discrimination against labor. For it is a bias favoring those who possess wealth, and disfavoring those who work for a living. It is as ancient as racism and sexism, and bound up with them. Historian Don Herzog makes this point in *Poisoning the Minds of the Lower Orders*, which shows that conservatism began as an ideology defending the monarchy against democracy, and that its central aim was to keep the lower orders in their place. The lower orders were women, blacks, Jews, and workers.[35]

Wealth bias has gone historically by the name *class*. But the vertical structure this implies—upper, middle, and working classes—is offensive, for it retains the bias of the great chain of being, that some persons are naturally higher than others. The term *wealth discrimination* places all on an equal plane, and implies that the wealthy are irrationally favored over others. Instead of envisioning a working class struggling against all those "above" it, it turns the middle and working classes into allies. It thus focuses on the real battle: the one between the wealthy and everyone else.

The notion of wealth discrimination also elucidates the core issue more precisely. Class is amorphous. Wealth lurks in its background, but in the foreground are family of origin, mode of dress, mode of speech, schools attended, and so forth—which may be only tangentially related to wealth.

Wealth and class are in many ways distinct concepts. For example, in his 2000 movie, *Small Time Crooks*, Woody Allen depicts a working couple who accidentally strike it rich, and seek out an art dealer to teach them about painting, sculpture, music, and language. The central gag is that they have money but no class.

In social status, it may be class that matters. But in the economic and political realms, it's money that confers power. The voting franchise was not restricted based on how people spoke. The corporate financial statements do not discriminate based on mode of dress. These structural forms of discrimination find their basis in wealth. Thus the notion of wealthism or wealth discrimination has a precision that the notion of class lacks, and it also ties this bias more closely to racism and sexism. Indeed, wealth discrimination may well be the primary form of discrimination, for other forms of bias were historically rooted in property. There was a master class of white, wealthy men who owned black slaves and claimed their wives and servants as a kind of property. Race, sex, and labor discrimination were knitted into one.

⚭

Naming wealth discrimination is vital, for when we fail to do so, we fail to see how it functions (how many people understand financial statements?)—and we fail to claim its history. How many of us could say when or how wealth restrictions on the vote were removed?[36] How many of us remember Thomas Dorr?

Dorr was a hero in the fight for white male suffrage in Rhode Island, where property restrictions once kept *more than half* of adult males from voting. In the Dorr Rebellion of 1842, the disenfranchised rose up and created their own "People's Constitution"—mandating universal suffrage for white males—and elected Dorr as their governor. This put Rhode Island in the awkward position of having two governors, until President Tyler stepped in to crush the rebellion. Dorr was sentenced to life imprisonment (which lasted one year). But his cause was soon triumphant: in 1843, state suffrage provisions in Rhode Island were liberalized. By the 1850s, wealth restrictions on the vote were abolished in virtually all states.[37] Thomas Dorr ought to be as well known as Elizabeth Cady Stanton. But he's not, because the history of wealth discrimination is lost in collective amnesia.

CRACKING THE ICE

Wealth bias is articulated—quite brazenly—in the corporate mandate to maximize returns to shareholders. It is given institutional form in the denial of corporate voting rights to employees. It is right in front of our eyes. And we fail to see it.

The 1919 date of *Dodge v. Ford Motor Co.*—the case that articulated corporate purpose—is worth noting, because it anchors the notion of shareholder primacy in the era to which it belongs. At that time, when only white men were considered full members of society, it seemed natural that only wealth holders would be full members of corporate society.

Corporations still live in the charmed circle of this taboo. They see their customs as beyond change, and we buy into those customs. With our tiny stashes of stock, we think the system is working for us, even as wages are sluggish, working hours are increasing, layoffs are rampant, and benefits are declining. Even as our children study in poorly funded schools, while corporations elude the property taxes that once supported those schools. Even as the wealthiest 1 percent run off with 40 percent of the nation's wealth.

There are seams of vulnerability here, once we think to look for them. Great seams of illegitimacy, of a creaky antiquity. One day, when there's been a bit more of a thaw in the climate of opinion, the time will come to strike at a few of these seams. As one finds in chipping at ice, rigid structures can be dislodged more quickly than we imagine. Roosevelt enacted his most transformative New Deal laws in just one hundred days. This kind of opening for change may come again. For if the system design is unsustainable (and it is), crisis becomes likely. If the corporate governance system in the meantime seems impenetrable, it's because all closed soci-

eties seem impenetrable. The monarchy in its day seemed eternal. But democracy, like Minnesota winters, teaches us that useful maxim: what seems impenetrable, isn't.

Liberty for Me, Not for Thee

THE PRINCIPLE OF LIBERTY

*Corporate capitalism embraces a predemocratic concept
of liberty reserved for property holders, which thrives
by restricting the liberty of employees and the community.*

W hat seems eternal rarely is, and what calls itself freedom may not be freedom at all. I think, for example, of the make-believe games of my childhood, where we were free to make up whatever rules we wanted, but somehow we always ended up with rules making the neighborhood bully the winner. When we played at being horses, she was the golden stallion, I was the old gray mare. When we played cowboys and Indians, she was the cowboy, I was the Indian tied to the tree (with pretend ropes). But whenever I dared to find my voice and protest, she told me I was "breaking the rules."

It's much the same with our economy, where the wealthy somehow always end up the winners. When wealth interests seek government protection, we're told that property rights are vital to a free market. When labor or environmental rights need government protection, we're told about the danger of infringing on the free market.

We've seen in earlier chapters how the myth of property functions, but that's just one of the two bedrock values of the capitalist idea structure. The second is liberty—often referred to as freedom of contract or the free market. These ideas likewise are worth taking apart.

FREEDOM OF CONTRACT

We'll start with freedom of contract, which is based on the theory that in economic matters, we're all free to make any arrangements (or contracts) that we choose. The government supports these contracts by making them legally binding, and by generally refusing to interfere in setting terms. In the Constitution, we find this principle embodied in Article 1, Section 10, stipulating that no state shall make any law "impairing the Obligation of Contracts."

This represents a legal loophole that corporate governance has been ducking into in recent decades. In legal circles it's become outmoded to say stockholders "own" corporations, but legal scholars manage to establish the same body of rights in a roundabout way—using the notion of contracts.[1] Following the work of R. H. Coase, later developed by University of Chicago legal theorists Daniel Fischel, Frank Easterbrook, and others, corporate governance scholars now speak of the corporation as a "nexus of contracts."[2] They conceive of it as a place where various parties come together and contract for their rights, rather than a thing that someone owns.

The shift dates back to the 1932 publication of *The Modern Corporation and Private Property*, when Berle and Means noted that as a result of the separation of ownership and control in the public corporation, stockholders were no longer active owners but passive recipients of capital returns. This revolution in the nature of property meant we were "no longer dealing with property in the old sense," they wrote, and the "traditional logic of property" no longer applied. Because of the additional facts of perpetual life and increasing corporate size, Berle and Means asserted that the corporation had "ceased to be a private business device and had become an institution"—a means of organizing economic life—informally, "an adjunct of the state itself."[3]

These were genuinely revolutionary assertions. But in the nexus-of-contracts view that developed in later decades and that in recent years has become virtual dogma,[4] the sharpness of their impact was blunted, like a dart absorbed into pudding. Contract theorists argue that there is still good reason to focus on shareholder value, because stockholders are "residual claimants": they get only what remains when other claims have been paid. Maximizing the value of common stock thus ostensibly means maximizing the total wealth generated by the corporation.[5]

The difficulty, as progressive corporate law scholar Margaret Blair points out, is that the old notion of ownership has never really been supplanted but has retained a subliminal hold. In legal journals today, for example, there is much discussion of the "agency" problem in corporate governance—a formulation that views stockholders as principals, and managers or directors as their agents, with the problem being how to keep the agents loyal to the principals' interests. But as Blair explains, "Why are shareholders the 'principals' in the relationship? Because they are the 'owners.' And why do we call them 'owners' and we don't call other contracting parties owners? Because they have residual income and residual control rights. But why do they have residual control rights? Because they are the 'owners.'" In short, she adds, there is a "gaping flaw in the logic of the Chicago School way of thinking about corporations." Scholars may acknowledge in footnotes that stockholders no longer own corporations, but they proceed to treat the stockholder contract as the only one that matters.[6]

There are other problems with the nexus-of-contracts theory. The term *residual* implies that stockholder income takes second place to other income, when in fact maximizing stockholder income is the fundamental aim of the corporation. And in truth stockholders today don't really get the residual—instead they *get the whole thing,* the entire market value of the corporation. They have the right to demand that the corporation be sold to the highest bidder, and the right to pocket the proceeds—which certainly represents ownership. In addition, the stockholder contract contains an element that cannot be contracted away, which is fiduciary duty. But still, we're told, it's a freely negotiated contract, so it's legitimate.

⤙⤚

When this contracting occurred, no one says; it was presumably in the distant past, like the time the British were said to have contracted with their king to rule them forever. As Kent Greenfield of Boston College Law School notes, the contract theory doesn't involve actual contracts, which even Fischel and Easterbrook admit. They say instead that their theory explains the "logic of corporate law," and stockholder rights are rules that "people would have negotiated" if they could have. "Perhaps the corporate contract," they write, "is no more than a rhetorical device."[7]

But still, this airy contract is said to give stockholders their ironclad rights—for the state is not to interfere in contracts. In like manner, employees are said to have freely contracted for their wage, so that's all they get. They are believed to have freely consented to an arrangement where they have no property rights and no governance rights—much like wives of old, who were believed to have freely consented to the loss of their property rights upon marriage.

If this idea of freely agreed-upon contracts seems like sleight of hand, we might note that it serves a vital purpose. As Francis Fukuyama wrote, "All regimes capable of effective action must be based on some principle of legitimacy."[8] And in a democracy—whose twin principles are liberty and equality—there is no better foundation for the capitalist economy than liberty.

The Free Market

If freedom of contract is the legal variant of liberty, its economic variant is the free market. Here we find the notion of an invisible hand guiding individual actions to work out to the benefit of all, which is the doctrine of the self-regulating free market. Although the invisible hand is commonly attributed to Adam Smith, it was an idea pervasive in the early eighteenth century, related to the theory popularized by the philosopher Leibniz that postulated a preestablished harmony of the universe—making this the best of all possible worlds. As historian Robert Anchor described it in *The Enlightenment Tradition*, the theory was that a "hidden hand" led to "a basic harmony of interests among men in the long run." Hence it was "only necessary to release everyone to pursue freely his own self-interest in order to realize a harmonious social order."[9]

By the end of the eighteenth century, philosophers had pretty much abandoned the idea of the hidden hand and basic harmony, after the violence of the French Revolution had made clear that harmony was not the order of the day. But the idea is still found in economics classes today, where it is taught not as philosophy but as science. It's no accident that it had its genesis in the aristocratic age. That era may indeed have been the best possible world for the nobility, but it was decidedly not best for everyone else. This point was made hilariously by Enlightenment philosopher Voltaire in his satiric novel *Candide*.

❦

It's a satire worth remembering, for it comes from the same cultural milieu as *The Wealth of Nations*, published in 1776. *Candide*, published in 1759, chronicles the tale of the sweetly named Candide, who is thrown out of a baron's castle and subjected to outlandish perils—until the end, when he becomes a nobleman himself (via an invented pedigree), and lives happily ever after. In his wanderings in between, he is nearly frozen to death, has his leg cut off, is cast into a dungeon, is shot, caught in an earthquake, and cast adrift in a shipwreck, to name but a few of his calamities. In one scene, he encounters a fire where three thousand people have perished, and he discusses it with the ever-present philosopher Pangloss.

> "What a shocking disaster!" cried Candide.
> "All for the best," said Pangloss: "these little accidents happen every year. It is very natural that fire should catch wooden houses, and that those houses should burn. Besides, it delivers many honest people from a miserable existence."[10]

All these misfortunes, Pangloss explains, are indispensable, for "private misfortunes constitute the general good; so that the more private misfortunes there are, the whole is the better."[11] All things are for the best in this best of all possible worlds.

One can imagine a similar lampoon today, of an individual sweetly named, say, Lucky, who loses a vast inheritance and is subjected to endless economic perils—until the end, when he wins the lottery and lives happily ever after. In his wanderings in between, he might be forced to take a temporary job without benefits, spend all his money on credit card interest and late fees, finally land a back-breaking factory job, only to be laid off, whereupon he would be sent overseas to a garment sweatshop, where he might be fired for trying to unionize, and would at last be thrown into a stream polluted by Texaco. At various points, he would be visited by an economist, lecturing about how the invisible hand of the free market leads events to work out to the benefit of all.

⚭

I do not mean to be unkind to Adam Smith. The truth is, he published *The Wealth of Nations* in a time of innocence, before the effects of industrialization had fully arrived. But as historian Karl Polanyi observed in *The Great Transformation*, those effects came swiftly. A few short years after Smith's book was published, it became clear that pauperism was rising even as wealth soared. Riots were occurring more frequently. Industrial towns were becoming wastelands.[12] By 1817, Robert Owen lamented that laborers were "infinitely more degraded and miserable than they were before the introduction of these manufactories." Industrialists, meanwhile, were amassing great fortunes.[13]

At work was something Polanyi termed "the two nations" effect: the tendency of capitalism to uplift some even as it degraded others. There was perhaps only one unique era, historian Eric Hobsbawm noted, where the two nations effect was not in evidence. This was the quarter-century following World War II, when a rising tide actually did lift all boats, bringing luxuries like the refrigerator, the private washing machine, and the telephone to the masses. But as Hobsbawm observed in *The Age of Extremes*, postwar industrialization was "backed, supervised, steered, and sometimes planned and managed by governments."[14] The free market was remarkably successful in that era when it was notably not free.

The two nations effect offers an apt parable for capitalism. But it is a story of conflict—like democracy itself. Aristocratic capitalism prefers the parable of the invisible hand, which (Pan)glosses over the system's imperfections. Little things, like the Great Depression. Like the Asian crisis of 1997–1998, when stock markets crashed around the world. Or like 30 percent of workers today making a poverty-level wage.[15]

⚭

In reality, if the invisible hand does not always function very well, the free market does not always extend its freedom very far. When economic texts and the business press trumpet phrases like *free enterprise, free trade,* and *the free market,* there is a contradiction staring us in the face: that free enterprise is in the business of trampling freedom.

The police would need a court order to do what corporations do routinely: tape conversations, install cameras, and monitor computers. Employee surveillance like this occurs at nearly three-quarters of major companies—more than double the number of just two years ago, according to a recent American Management Association survey.[16]

More pervasively, 86 percent of major corporations do drug testing.[17] It's so commonplace, we fail to see how horrific it is. Imagine that agents of the federal government showed up at your door and said they were conducting a drug screening, so would you please pee in the jar? And when you went to the bathroom, they trailed you and watched, to make sure you didn't cheat. You would be justified in screaming about police state tactics. Free enterprise does the same thing daily, and no one screams.

It's chilling to see how intimate the corporate invasions of privacy can be. A Nabisco plant in Oxnard, California, refused to allow female employees the simple freedom of deciding when to go to the bathroom, forcing some to wear diapers to work. The women filed a class action in 1995—citing "bladder and urinary tract infections . . . from being forced to wait hours for permission to use the rest rooms." The company settled in 1996 on undisclosed terms.[18]

What incidents like this point to is the fact that there are virtually no mechanisms within companies to ensure employee freedom. At progressive companies, white-collar workers might find management sympathetic to their personal needs. But in the legal construct of the corporation itself, employees generally have no due process, no right to privacy, no protection against unreasonable search and seizure, no representatives to take their side, no say in governance, no free speech, no jury to hear their case. Those are democratic freedoms, and they stop at the company door.

Inside the corporation, there is one primary legal freedom: to maximize profits for shareholders. Liberty is the value invoked to legitimize this pursuit of gains for the wealthy. It's the pursuit of self-interest in a free market, we're told. We rarely stop to observe that the corporation's "self" is equated with wealth holders. The liberty that capitalism invokes is thus a medieval notion of liberty. It is *liberty of property*: freedom as the right to the undisturbed possession of property. In the days of the feudal barons, this meant freedom from the king's interference. The lord of the manor could do what he liked within the bounds of his own estate, and his serfs had no recourse.

In the democratic era, we recognize a different concept of liberty, *liberty of persons*: the right to full personhood, no matter how low one's station. All human beings have the right to dignity and freedom. This is a liberty we turn to government to protect. But where liberty of property is paramount, liberty of persons does not exist.

For the community, democratic freedom means the right to make laws. But this freedom, too, is trampled by financial interests—often via the World Trade Organization (WTO). In the *Oxford English Dictionary*, one definition of freedom is "exemption from arbitrary, despotic, or auto-cratic control." But the autocratic WTO allows nations no such freedom.

Consider patents, for example. India's Patent Act once kept all foods and medicines in the public realm, to assure broad access. But the WTO said this offered insufficient protection for corporate property rights and demanded the law be changed, which it was in 1999. Thus we see that in the global economy, what is at work is not free trade but protection for property rights. Similarly, inside corporations, what is at work is not free-dom of contract but protection for wealth holders—again in the name of property rights.

In this repetitive invocation of freedom, we see what John Kenneth Galbraith calls "innocent fraud." It may well be innocent, because it is largely unconscious. But it is nonetheless fraudulent, because it conceals structures of power. Galbraith made this point in his article "Free Market Fraud" in *The Progressive* magazine, where he remarked that the word *cap-italism* had fallen out of fashion. "The approved reference now is to the market system," he wrote, and this is a shift that "minimizes—in-deed, deletes—the role of wealth." Instead of capital owners in control, "we have the admirably impersonal role of market forces," he wrote. "It would be hard to think of a change in terminology more in the interest of those to whom money accords power. They have now a functional anonymity."[19]

In like manner, free trade grants corporations a functional anonymity. Instead of corporations dominating the world economy, we have the admirably impersonal role of free trade.

ॐ

But with this concept "freedom," corporations and the wealthy have their hands on the tail of a tiger. And that tiger is likely to turn on them. It has done so before, when it turned on the aristocracy that once claimed freedom as its exclusive prerogative. Liberty was memorably invoked at Runnymede in 1215, when King John of England affixed his seal to the Magna Carta, formally limiting the divine right of kings. At the time its protections extended only to the upper classes, staving off encroachment on their liberty from above, from the king. But eventually it would open the way for new encroachments from below, as commoners claimed liberty for themselves.[20]

The spirit of capitalism, in an unconscious way, remains tethered to that field at Runnymede. For it still claims liberty as the exclusive right of the wealth-holding class. It does so in a clever way, with a free market ideology that conceals two assertions, not each equally valid. First, there is an assertion that *natural processes are self-regulating.* And this is undoubtedly true. We see it in nature, where the renewal of life in spring comes on its own, or in our own lives, where the drive to make money brings us to do our part in holding the world together. Our economic drives are part of the natural order and are trustworthy.

But the second assertion is less true, and it is this: that *the corporate governance structure embodies the natural order.* This does not follow logically from the first, for it glosses over the institutionalized power of wealth.

ॐ

We might note that while employees and the community are left to the protection of the invisible hand, wealth is protected by the *visible hand* of government and corporation. But this is something, it is hoped, that will be overlooked.

To help us begin to see it, we might, for a moment, imagine a different arrangement of institutional power. Picture a free market in which labor rights are enthroned in law, and property rights are left to the invisible hand. This would be a world in which we believe employees *are* the corporation. They are, after all, the ones running the place. Hence only employees could vote for the board of directors, and the purpose of the corporation would be to maximize income for employees. In theory, stockholders would receive income they negotiated through contracts. In practice, the corporation would dictate those contracts with little real negotiation, and stockholders could accept the terms or go elsewhere, only to find other corporations offering nearly identical (and dismal) terms.

In this world, stock would be sold in a manner controlled entirely by the corporation, much as wages are set today. Stockholders would appear alone at the company, where they would be taken into a room and made an offer. There would be no reliable way to compare current stock price to past price, to compare the price one person receives to what others receive, or to compare prices from one corporation to another. Wage and benefit data would be published daily in the *Main Street Journal*, and the movement of the Dow Jones wage index would of course be tracked nightly on the news. But returns to shareholders would be considered proprietary information and would not be given out.

If stockholders tried to improve their negotiating position by organizing into mutual funds, corporations would threaten to cut off payments altogether. The companies would talk about replacing stockholder money with funds from people overseas who were willing to accept lower returns.

And of course overseas, stockholders would have even less power. Although free trade agreements would provide intricate protections for labor and environmental rights, they would offer capital no protections. "What does capital have to do with trade?" pundits might ask. "Trade is about goods and services and the people who create them, it's not about capital."

When the newspapers said "the corporation did well," they would mean that employees did well. Stockholders might have seen no dividend increases in years. Some might even have seen their income terminated in "capital layoffs." But whenever anyone dared to suggest changes in this economic order, they would be said to be "tampering with the free market."

⚘

That's what we're told now. But we don't have to buy it. We can begin to see through the sleight of hand of the free market and the nexus-of-contracts corporation, just as our ancestors saw through the sleight of hand of the divine right of kings.

As it turned out, it wasn't necessary to abandon belief in God in order to change the monarchy. And it is not necessary to discard belief in the free market in order to change corporate structures. There is indeed a natural order to our economy, and it is an order where *competing* self-interests can at times work out to the benefit of all. But that is a far cry from the existing order, where the self-interest of capital is given exalted standing.

In moving toward freedom, societies move in stages, German philosopher G.W.F. Hegel believed. Early monarchical societies "knew that *one* was free," he wrote, "the Greek and Roman world only that *some* are free; while *we* know that all men absolutely . . . are free." The movement from one stage to another was an evolution Hegel saw as virtually inevitable. As he wrote: "The boundless drive of the World Spirit, its irresistible thrust, is toward the realization of these stages."[21] In the flow of history, the middle stage—where only some are free—is not likely to be sustainable.

We are not likely to suffer forever bullies who make up rules that suit only themselves. One day, surely, we will wake up, as I finally did in my childhood games, and see that the ropes binding us are only pretend.

6

Wealth Reigns

THE PRINCIPLE OF SOVEREIGNTY

Corporations assert that they are private and the free market

will self-regulate, much as feudal barons asserted

a sovereignty independent of the Crown.

*I*f economic liberty today remains the province of the few, the reason is a concept we might term *economic sovereignty*. Democratic freedoms stop at the company door, because inside the corporation the democratic polity is no longer sovereign. Here we see how private property and liberty combine into economic sovereignty: the sovereign power has liberty in its own private realm. Stockholders are sovereign because we believe they are the corporation, much as the medieval world believed the king was the state (*L'état, c'est moi*, in Louis XIV's memorable utterance). Benefiting the sovereign power is the purpose of the state—just as making the king rich was once the point of society. The sovereign power is the source of law, and thus can do no wrong.

While stockholder sovereignty is largely an unconscious assumption, we can see it manifest in corporate legal theory when mainstream scholars fret about managerial self-dealing, implying that managers' self-interest is illegitimate. Similarly, in discussing the stakeholder statutes enacted in thirty-two states, scholars likewise fret about the "mischief" these laws can do, as though employee and community interests are also illegitimate. (We'll look at these laws in more detail in chapter 9).[1] The only ones who can legitimately pursue self-interest in the corporation, presumably, are stockholders. We do not see mainstream scholars fretting about stockholder self-dealing, or the mischief shareholder primacy can do.

PROPERTY RIGHTS THROUGH HISTORY

If the exalted rights of wealth holders are beginning to be challenged today, it's not the first time. Property rights have repeatedly and successfully been challenged throughout history. Indeed, the history of democracy is a history of little else.

As Julie Andrews might admonish, let's start at the very beginning, a very good place to start. When you sing you begin with do, re, mi. In history we begin with sovereignty. The king's, that is.

As we saw earlier, royal sovereignty originally had its source in land. As historian Reinhard Bendix wrote in *Kings or People: Power and the Mandate to Rule*, "In theory, the ruler owned the whole realm."[2] The king was sovereign over the entire nation, because he owned it. Ownership conferred a right to govern. Hence political and economic sovereignty were entwined. Since granting the right to property meant granting power, the king was reluctant to do so. Initially he extended the right to tenancy only, through an intricate network of leases and subleases, which was the basis of feudalism.[3]

Turning land owned at the king's pleasure into land owned absolutely was a step away from absolute monarchy and a step toward democracy. It was a way of limiting the king's power. When this was done with the Magna Carta—which limited the king's right to take others' property—it was not only a seminal moment in the history of democracy but also an encroachment on the king's property rights.

A more decisive encroachment occurred with the Glorious Revolution of 1688, when the landed class switched kings and in the process made itself the sovereign power. Property and sovereignty were still linked but now had devolved from the king to the aristocracy. In tossing out a king, the aristocracy not only took his sovereign power but also took his property.

The American Revolution was more of the same. Businesspeople may shudder to recall this, but America was founded by nationalizing the assets of the eastern seaboard. Those assets—which today we call states—were originally the property of companies chartered by the British Crown to settle colonies. In these initial company-colonies, sovereignty and property again were linked. The 1609 charter of the Virginia Company of London, for example, made Virginia literally a corporation, where company "adventurers" governed the state and its trade. With the Massachusetts Bay Company, the General Court of the Stockholders likewise governed, because stockholders owned Massachusetts.[4]

By the end of the seventeenth century, the king had dechartered these companies and converted them into royal colonies.[5] He took away company property. The founding fathers of America, in turn, took it from him.

Gandhi did the same when he led India to break from British colonial rule. For perhaps the greatest country-company was the British East India Company, which ruled India. As colonial historian James Morris wrote, in the midnineteenth century this company "no longer had mercantile functions at all":

> In 1833 it had surrendered its monopoly of the India and China trades, except in opium, and it was now a kind of sovereign agency, administering its Indian possessions on behalf of the Crown, and only incidentally paying its stockholders their guaranteed 10 percent dividend. Its governing Court of Directors was subject to an official Board of Control, and with its own civil service, its own fleets and armies, its own military academy and its own administrative college, it was not exactly a company any more, nor exactly a ministry, nor quite a Power, but rather, as Macaulay said of it, "the strangest of all governments."[6]

Like American colonies, this company too was dechartered by the Crown, when the king took away company property. And the people of India took it from Great Britain.

❦

ECONOMIC SOVEREIGNTY OF THE WEALTHY MINORITY

If we wonder why it seems natural to us that economic sovereignty today is centered on property, it's because this once was true of *all* sovereignty, both political and economic. There was no difference between the two. In the age of democracy, political and economic power have been split asunder. Exclusive political sovereignty has (theoretically) slipped from the hands of the propertied class. But that class clings fast to the economic power it retains, a living fossil from the aristocratic age.

Although the custom of linking property and sovereignty originated with property in land, it was extended to other forms of wealth as they arose. Companies were one such form of new wealth. As economic historian Fernand Braudel wrote in *The Wheels of Commerce: Civilization and Capitalism 15th–18th Century*, the earliest joint stock companies were associations of capital only, in which "capital or stock formed a single mass, identified with the firm itself." Hence the firm was governed by its stockholders.

Scholars may justify stockholder governance rights today by their status as residual claimants, but this is a fabrication out of whole cloth. The link between share ownership and sovereignty is a tradition at least seven centuries old. It dates as far back as the thirteenth century, when "one could buy shares in a silver mine near Siena," Braudel noted, "or in a French copper mine."[7] Holders of these shares *were* the company.

In these economic entities, as in society at large, laborers—those without property—lacked sovereign power. The lower orders did eventually gain power politically, when we recognized as a society that sovereignty was not a fixed and eternal possession, as kings had claimed, but rather an evolving concept. The growth of democracy thus advanced on multiple fronts: expanding liberty, widening property rights, and extending sovereign power—from the king, to the aristocracy, to propertied white males, to unpropertied white males, to black males, and finally to women.

But if political power has fully devolved, economic sovereignty remains arrested at an intermediate stage. The financial aristocracy has wrested it from the government, but has not yet extended it to the lower orders. In accepting legal scholars' notion that stockholder sovereignty is an unbreakable contract, we might as well accept that white male sovereignty is an unbreakable contract, which is of course absurd. But it is no more absurd than believing employees and the community must forever be excluded from sovereign corporate power.

❧

The notion of economic sovereignty is worth examining a bit, for there's more to it than voting rights. We might note, for example, that it has both an internal and an external component, as masculine political sovereignty once did. In an earlier age, men held power both inside the family and outside it, in society—their sovereignty was internal and external to the family. In like manner, economic sovereignty is internal and external to the corporation. Internally, stockholders are sovereign because the corporation is said to be private. Externally, they are sovereign because the free market must self-regulate.

Inside the corporation, stockholder sovereignty is manifest in the notion that rising income for stockholders is good, while rising income for employees is bad. Externally, capital sovereignty is manifest in, for example, Federal Reserve policy, which similarly views wage gains as bad (that is, inflationary), while it views stock market gains, for the most part, as good (they are not counted directly in measures of inflation). As long as stock market gains don't overheat the consuming economy, they are limitless. But labor must be kept in its place. If wages were to triple, the Federal Reserve would go berserk. But the stock market tripled in a matter of years, and the Fed considered the economy healthy. That's economic sovereignty. It's a question of whose interests are considered one with the health of the economy.

❧

Unlike political sovereignty today—where each person has an equal vote—economic sovereignty resides not in persons but in dollars of wealth or shares of stock. The wealthy thus have more votes. The wealthiest 10 percent of households own about half of all stock—so that minority has a virtual economic majority.[8]

This is the source of the real mischief in economic matters today. Because corporate revenues represent the bulk of GDP, and the wealthiest own the bulk of corporate equity, running corporations to serve stockholders means running the economy to benefit the wealthy. Thus, in service to the wealthy majority, corporate profits have been eating a larger and larger share of the economic pie—growing by 10 percent a year from 1991 to 1999, even as U.S. GDP grew by only 3 percent a year.[9] Now, if one group's slice of the pie is growing three times as fast as the pie itself, the result is obvious: the slices of other people are being devoured.

If profits are growing at a rapid clip, the growth of internal corporate equity is even more rapid, about 15 percent a year.[10] An average 15 percent return on equity requires profits to quadruple every decade. It's a bit like the plant in *The Little Shop of Horrors,* which ate everything in sight. Quadrupling in size is one thing for a houseplant and quite another when the plant gets as big as the house. But today, the plant is larger than the house. In 1999, stock market capitalization was 160 percent the size of GDP. That's something new in history, and a startling change from the early 1940s, when the market was only 20 percent of GDP.[11] We're no longer feeding a houseplant. It's eating us for lunch.

Hence we saw Mercedes-Benz in 1993 receiving $200 million in incentives from Alabama for building a plant there, even as schools remained underfunded.[12] Or in the early 1990s we saw the Stillwater Mining Company appropriating $43 *billion* worth of platinum and palladium from Montana public resources, while paying only $10,000 for it.[13] As public wealth is being devoured, little is being put back into the public pantry. Corporate income tax revenues have dropped from over 25 percent of total tax revenue in the 1960s to under 9 percent today.[14]

CORPORATION AS KING

We pretend we cannot change this state of affairs because we have ceded our economic sovereignty to the wealthy. How this has happened, in a democracy, deserves some attention. It was not done openly. It wasn't done as an election is done, where Senator X says "Vote for me." It was done as things are done in a monarchy, where terms are defined—*L'état, c'est moi*—and we're unaware a choice has been made. Private property owners have assumed sovereign power economically, not by vote, but by ancient prejudice. Since we don't recognize how or when this choice was made, or even that it was made, we feel helpless to change it.

We believe it is natural that our economic system serves wealth holders. This allows the power of wealth to grow, unchecked, and to become unnaturally potent. It escapes all societal bounds as it crosses national boundaries in global free trade. In the process, the only rules that come along are rules that protect property. Thus NAFTA required Mexico to give up its habit of nationalizing foreign industry before it was considered a fit partner for trade. The power of the economic sovereign—property owners—must be protected from encroachment. The rights of labor and the environment are of no consequence, for economically they are not sovereign rights.

◈

The notion that stockholders *are* the corporation is of course a legal fiction. That stockholders must be endlessly acquisitive is a related fiction. However generous and productive stockholders might be as individuals, in the system design they are an absent, passive, largely unproductive body of shifting speculators whose sole aim is to extract wealth. The corporation, by contrast, is a relatively stable community of persons engaged in making things and meeting human needs. That we equate stockholders with the corporation is thus clearly a fiction, a fiction so bold as to be breathtaking.

At least some legal scholars have recognized this. Lon Fuller in his 1967 work, *Legal Fictions*, made the point that corporate law is founded on fiction. "The very strangeness and boldness of the legal fiction has tended to stifle [the layman's] criticisms," he wrote.[15] Similarly commenting on the unreality of corporate law, in the 1970s John F. Lubin of the Wharton School of the University of Pennsylvania observed that it is "unrealistic to manage the affairs of a company as specified in most legal statutes," for the board "simply cannot perform the functions" required. Further, he said, "It is just as unrealistic to expect the board to be a policy making body and to really participate in strategy making function." Our fiction of stockholder governance, in other words, doesn't match reality.

In a more recent work, Minneapolis attorney Richard Saliterman observed that corporate law today is governed by "a highly theoretical and, arguably, a nonreality-oriented framework," where "hotly debated topics amount to counting angels on pinheads."[16] Thus we see governance experts pondering the importance of independent directors or social investing activists counting the number of women on boards—while neither questions the central fictions: that stockholders are the corporation, that they elect the board, that the board supposedly governs the corporation, and that employees have no vote.

Maintaining the fictions of corporate law, in light of the facts, requires some conceptual contortions. And these contortions are reminiscent of those used on behalf of the earlier fiction that the king was the state.

The cascading series of monarchical fictions was outlined delightfully by medieval historian Ernst Kantorowicz in his book *The King's Two Bodies*. The first problem faced by royal theorists was that the king was mortal, while the state went on forever. This was solved with the fiction that "the king is immortal because legally he can never die," as British legal scholar Blackstone put it. A second issue was that, as the sovereign power, the king could not be challenged. Thus Blackstone wrote that the king "is not only incapable of *doing* wrong, but even of *thinking* wrong: he can never mean to do an improper thing: in him is no folly or weakness."

The king could do no wrong because he himself was the source of law. As Johannes de Deo wrote in about 1245, "The Prince is not subject to laws: He himself is the animate Law on earth." And this was so because the king was not an ordinary man. Thus arose "a belief in certain royal qualities and potencies dwelling in the blood of kings and creating, so to speak, a royal species of man," Kantorowicz wrote. Since royal power had to be present throughout the kingdom, the king became invisible and ubiquitous: "His Majesty in the eye of the law is always present in all his courts, though he cannot personally distribute justice."[17]

Knitted together, these fictions found expression in the doctrine of the king's two bodies. In one legal case in the sixteenth century, Crown lawyers wrote:

For the King has in him two Bodies, *viz.*, a Body natural, and a Body politic. His Body natural . . . is a Body mortal, subject to all Infirmities that come by Nature or Accident . . . to the natural Bodies of other People. But his Body politic is a Body that cannot be seen or handled, consisting of Policy and Government . . . and this Body is utterly void of Infancy, and old Age, and other natural Defects and Imbecilities, which the Body natural is subject to, and for this Cause, what the King does in his Body politic, cannot be invalidated or frustrated by any Disability in his natural Body.[18]

When the mortal aspect of this immortal being died, lawyers applied the fiction of the migration of the soul. Thus it was said, upon the king's death, that "there is a Separation of the two Bodies, and that the Body politic is transferred and conveyed over from the Body natural now dead . . . to another Body natural."[19]

Indeed.

❧

This curious batch of ideas seems irretrievably antique to the modern mind. But it's useful to recall that these ideas once bore the full force of law. And this was true even though, as Kantorowicz wrote, this kind of "man-made irreality—indeed, that strange construction of a human mind which finally becomes slave to its own fictions—we are normally more ready to find in the religious sphere than in the allegedly sober and realistic realms of law."[20]

Yet here's the unsettling point: that we find a similar man-made irreality in our own allegedly sober and realistic realm of corporate law and economics. Thus we have the fictions that stockholders are the corporation, and that the corporation itself is a person, or an individual.

We see this second fiction at work in economic theory, for example, where the corporation is viewed as just another individual, competing for its own self-interest in a free market. This might be a valid concept if a company were little more than the entrepreneur who ran it, which was true to some extent in our past. But as major corporations have evolved, economists, in effect, simply substituted the word *firm* for the word *entrepreneur*, and pretended nothing fundamental had changed. Where once we had individuals, we now have firms and individuals, but still each is simply competing for its own self-interest. As economist D. Gordon wrote, for example, "Smith's postulate of the maximizing *individual* in a relatively free market . . . is our basic paradigm . . . economics has never had a major revolution" (italics added).[21]

The same fiction—that economics is all about individuals—is similarly at work in public policy debates. Consider, for example, the recent best-selling book *The Commanding Heights: The Battle Between Government and the Marketplace That Is Remaking the Modern World.* In it, authors Daniel Yergin and Joseph Stanislaw posit a debate between government control of the economy and "the dispersed intelligence of private decision makers and consumers in the marketplace."[22] These authors likewise somehow miss the gigantic fact of globe-spanning corporations, and see only private decision makers. The corporation, one might conclude, is like the pink elephant at the free market cocktail party. Everyone pretends not to see it.

In the legal realm we find the fiction that the corporation is a person, as the Supreme Court declared in its 1886 decision in *Santa Clara County v. Southern Pacific Railroad.*[23] Thus it is afforded free speech protections and can participate in the political process through lobbying and political contributions. Although society itself creates the corporation, its control over the corporation is limited—because it has, voilà, become a person.

The corporation is of course a very strange kind of person: larger than you or me, and dwelling across national borders, ubiquitous. While real persons live where they live, the corporate person can reside anywhere it likes, choosing its own legal regime. The corporate person is also immortal, for it enjoys perpetual life. Like the king, it likewise has two bodies: the buildings and employees of the corporation itself (its body natural), and its body of stockholders (its body politic). This body politic practices "migration of the soul" regularly, as shares trade hands.

Stockholders, as the body politic, can do no wrong. Certainly they bear no responsibility for what the corporation does wrong, due to the doctrine of limited liability. And however ruthless the actions they require—closing

factories, clear-cutting forests—those actions are right. The stockholder body politic "is not only incapable of *doing* wrong, but even of *thinking* wrong." Like fictions about the king, corporate fictions serve a single purpose: to protect current arrangements of power.

We can learn to see through the absurdity. We can embrace the implicit solution of allowing economic sovereignty to evolve, to include employees and the community. And this begins by rejecting the notion that we have already attained the ultimate end point of history, as Francis Fukuyama suggests in *The End of History and the Last Man*. He wrote of "a universal evolution in the direction of capitalism," which he said had been proven superior to the centrally planned economies of the Soviet Union and China.[24] This is a valid observation, as far as it goes. Capitalism does indeed seem to represent a universal economy toward which the world is evolving. Yet we can discern that *capitalism itself is evolving*. And it is evolving in the same direction in which all of society has been evolving: toward new structures that serve the many rather than the few.

We see the beginnings of such structures in employee ownership, for example, or the growing use of employee stock options. We see it in the German practice of codetermination that guarantees board seats to employees. We see it in the market dominance wielded by employee pension funds, which represent at least potential employee voice in corporate governance.

We see it in the growing strength of socially responsible investors, who urge corporations to focus on social welfare as well as profit. We see it in growing corporate concern for environmental stewardship. We see it in the rising practice of cause-related marketing, where community interests and corporate interests to some extent converge. We see it even in corporate purpose itself, at companies like Medtronic, the Minneapolis-based manufacturer of pacemakers and other medical devices, whose mission is to produce devices that work for "man's full life."

But corporations today have a limited freedom to pursue such nonfinancial aims, for they are beholden—by the structures of governance, by the design of financial statements, in some measure by the courts, and above all by the fiction of stockholder sovereignty—to pursue shareholder gains above all else.

Shareholder primacy is the wrench in the gears of evolution. It is shareholder primacy that thwarts corporations from their natural movement toward wider economic sovereignty for all.

What free enterprise represents today is only the middle chapter in the history of sovereignty, not the ultimate chapter. The final chapter is called *economic democracy*, and it holds out the promise of economic liberty and justice for all. That chapter remains to be written, whenever we, the people, decide to take up the pen.

PART II

Economic Democracy

7

Waking Up

THE PRINCIPLE OF ENLIGHTENMENT

Because all persons are created equal, the economic rights

of employees and the community are equal

to those of capital owners.

We can help corporations become a more humane presence in our society, but to do so we must first update our internal economic maps. The danger in working with antique maps, as we do today, is illustrated by a story my friend Zanryc tells—a story of going camping in Canada's Boundary Waters, using an old map he'd been given for free. Traversing a trail on foot, he and his camping party found themselves unexpectedly facing an enormous swamp. As they studied and restudied their map, trying to find where they'd gotten lost, it suddenly dawned on them: they actually were on the trail. But that trail had been covered by a swamp. Their old map described a reality that no longer existed.

Our antique model of the corporation likewise describes a reality that no longer exists. Our model pictures the corporation as a tangible object, like a factory, built with shareholders' money and thus owned by them. This may have been a valid picture at the turn of the last century, for as late as 1900 three-quarters of American corporations listed on the New York Stock Exchange were railroads.[1] Today, corporations are far less tangible; they are in large part human communities, which can't be owned in the way a bunch of engines are owned.

But our maps haven't changed. The courts still use the old map of *Dodge v. Ford*—involving the tangible factories of Ford Motor Co., only a few years earlier literally funded by shareholder investments. Corporations are still governed by shareholders, though there is something inherently irrational about shifting speculators being said to govern a distant human community. It's like England presuming to govern America. As Thomas Paine memorably put it, "There is something very absurd, in supposing a continent to be perpetually governed by an island."[2] In our case the island is Manhattan, where Wall Street resides, and the continent is virtually our entire economy.

At a certain point, exclusive stockholder governance may have made some sense. But at a certain point, it stops making sense. Again as Paine said of America's governance by England: "There was a time when it was proper, and there is a proper time for it to cease."[3]

RECOGNIZING THE ECONOMIC RIGHTS OF ALL

The time has come to recognize that all human beings have equal economic rights. The time has come to recognize that corporations are not just pieces of property but are something more complex and alive, requiring a more nuanced set of human rights. Shareholder property rights can remain in some measure, but they must take their place alongside property rights for employees and the community. Aristocratic privilege must give way to economic equality, in a new corporate order that recognizes a constellation of economic rights. This is the fundamental principle of enlightenment: *Because all persons are created equal, the economic rights of employees and the community are equal to those of capital owners.*

Enlightenment is a matter of seeing old customs with new eyes. The Enlightenment was the era that sought to ground institutions anew in reason—in contrast to the Old Regime, which grounded the monarchy and aristocracy in "tradition, custom, and convention."[4] Enlightenment is about questioning tradition.

In our own era, it is a tradition of long standing to link free markets with the property rights of capital. Yet the great majority of citizens rely for the great bulk of their income on labor. Perhaps it's time to ask: Why are the rights of working persons inferior to those of wealthy persons? Why does the corporate board have a fiduciary duty to wealth holders, but not to employees?

Similar questions are being asked today about community rights. If it is the essential right of a democratic community to write its own laws, why can the WTO overturn those laws? Why do trade treaties see property rights as essential, and all other human rights as peripheral?

In a truly democratic economy, this would not be so. The purpose of a body like the WTO would be to protect all economic interests, and the purpose of the corporation would be to enrich all who are part of it. Employees and the community would not be seen as means to create wealth for others, but as ends in themselves.

This was the principle articulated by Immanuel Kant, a leading German philosopher of the Enlightenment. In the era of the great chain of being, he dared to declare that no person is higher than others; none are born to rule, and none are born to submit. Kant offered a new imperative: that "every rational being, *exists* as an end in himself, *not merely as a means* for arbitrary use by this or that will" (italics in original). We must treat all humanity, he wrote, "never simply as a means, but always at the same time as an end."[5]

We should recall Kant's imperative when we as reformers find ourselves telling corporations, "Treat employees well because then stockholders will prosper." Or when we find ourselves saying, "Practice environmental stewardship, because then profits will increase."

These, unfortunately, are the arguments often made by social investing professionals, and my own publication *Business Ethics* is as guilty as any other. All of us in social investing repeatedly assert that socially screened investments can outperform other investments (which they can: on an annualized basis, the socially screened Domini Social Index over ten years has brought higher shareholder returns than the S&P 500).[6] But this argument in a sense is self-defeating, for it implies that stockholder gain is the only measure that matters. Ultimately, we must assert that other measures of prosperity matter too—like wage increases, or well-funded schools, or a healthy environment. Until we begin asserting this, we will not have fully claimed our power.

☙

And claiming our power is key. Economic texts obscure the issue when they tell us our economic system is about liberty or freedom. In truth it is about power—the concentrated, unaccountable power of corporations and of wealth.

This problem is reminiscent of what America confronted at its founding, which was concentrated power in the hands of the monarchy and the aristocracy that controlled Parliament. In pre-Revolutionary America, as historian Bernard Bailyn wrote in his Pulitzer Prize–winning *The Ideological Origins of the American Revolution*, the specter of power was "what lay behind every political scene"; it was "the ultimate explanation of every political controversy." And power, our forefathers believed, meant "the dominion of some men over others."[7] In reviewing pre-Revolutionary literature, Bailyn traced this focus on power and the language used to describe it:

> Most commonly the discussion of power centered on its essential characteristic of aggressiveness: its endlessly propulsive tendency to expand itself beyond legitimate boundaries. . . . Sometimes the image is of the human hand, "the hand of power," reaching out to clutch and to seize: power is "grasping" and "tenacious" in its nature; "what it seizes it will retain."[8]

If early Americans recognized the core issue was power, we have yet to do so. We have yet to see that capitalism suffers not from countless social problems but from one problem: the power of wealth. It will benefit us to come to agreement on this, just as feminism benefited from agreement about the power of men. It would not have been enough to see poor funding for girls' athletics as one problem, unequal wages for women as a separate problem, and harassment in the workplace as still a different problem. These battles became one when their common source in sex discrimination was recognized. Yet today we chase after corporate pollution as one problem, low wages as another problem, and corporate welfare as still a third problem. They're all manifestations of wealth discrimination—the insistence that more wealth for the wealthy is the single greatest need. When we recognize this core issue, our separate battles will become one. And that battle will gain momentum.

RESPECTING THE RIGHT TO ATTAIN WEALTH

If the power of wealth is the central issue, that is not to say the wealthy are the enemy, for the revolution—evolution—we seek will be without enemies.

The wealthy, for the most part, are no more evil or greedy than anyone else. Most are not literally "demanding" greater wealth, for they don't have a clue what's being done with their money. They've most often left it in the hands of investing advisers. If the wealthy are not the enemy, neither are their advisers, for they're simply fulfilling their duty to serve clients. Even CEOs aren't the enemy, because they have no real power: their marching orders are to get shareholder wealth or get out. All of these actors are to some extent *complicit* in the system, and do have an ethical duty to resist. As the Nuremberg trials established, following orders does not ultimately excuse injurious behavior. But the aim of activists should not be to demonize anyone, but to open people's eyes.

We fool ourselves if we think we can find the enemy somewhere. Our anger at the system leaves us like the farmer in *The Grapes of Wrath*, who when his farm was repossessed couldn't find anyone to shoot. There isn't anyone to shoot.

The problem is in our internal maps, and rethinking these can require some vilification of outmoded views. But we must remember that we're vilifying the value system of wealth discrimination—not the wealthy themselves. Respect for the right to attain wealth is integral to the American psyche. Many of us would like to acquire wealth one day, and the possibility of doing so should remain open—though it should become broadly open, to employees as much as entrepreneurs, to community members as much as stockholders. And as we broaden the potential to attain wealth, we should also change the mechanism by which much concentration of wealth arises, which is inheritance.

Wealth should not be dispersed entirely, as communism attempted to do. Communism aimed for equality of outcome, when the more proper remedy is equality of opportunity. Communist theory did correctly identify property (wealth) as the source of the problem, but in seeking to eliminate private property altogether, it eliminated incentive. Without the engine of self-interest, the system foundered.

The point is not to do away with wealth but to change the system design that gives illegitimate power to wealth—just as in the fight against sexism, the point was not to do away with men but to change the system that gave illegitimate power to men.

We might recall that sexism has trapped men as much as women. In the system of wealth discrimination, most of us are likewise trapped—we focus on a misleading map, believing that economic health is defined by the rise and fall of the Dow Jones industrial average.

LANGUAGE ISSUES

Attention to language is vital. There was a time when we had no words for sexual harassment, recalls Patricia Ireland of the National Organization for Women. "If someone hadn't wrapped words around these ideas, I never would have seen," she told *The Progressive*. "If you don't have words to describe something, it's really hard to conceptualize it."[9]

We might remember, for example, how people once said rape victims "asked for it," or how lawyers asked women in rape trials if they "enjoyed it." Feminists countered with talk of "blaming the victim." We blame the victim today in economics, when pundits suggest that low wages can be cured with training—as though it's the employees' fault they're underpaid, because they're not educated enough. We should insist, to the contrary, that employees are *worth more*, that they're not being paid in proportion to their productivity. Instead of blaming the victim, we must question the system design that allocates labor less than its due.

Similarly, as feminists protested sexist ads, we should protest when financial writers claim that the stock market creates wealth. As feminists objected to the word *mankind*—which implied that men represented the human race—we should object to suggestions that stockholders represent the corporation.

We should likewise object when stockholders are called *owners*—which is a claim of dominion—and instead call them *investors*, or more precisely, *speculators*. In place of the term *property rights*—which invokes manorial privilege—we might talk about *wealth rights*.

As feminists objected to terms like *honey* and *baby*, we should object when insulting terms are used for employees—as in the book title *Contented Cows Give More Milk*, which suggests that employees-as-cows should be treated well because they will yield more "milk" for stockholders. We should write letters to the editor when we see outrageous articles like *The New York Times* interview with iPrint.com CEO Royal Farros, where he suggested that managing employees is like "having pets." As he put it, "Creating a loving, affectionate home for pets is similar to fostering an active environment where employees feel important and influential"—not to mention degraded.[10]

Language reveals unconscious attitudes. At one time, women were routinely identified by their marital status, as Mrs. or Miss. The term Ms. established a female identity independent of men. In like manner, employees are referred to as assets of the corporation, when an asset is something owned. And since stockholders are called owners, the implication is clear—and outrageous. We should express that outrage whenever CEOs say, "Employees are our greatest assets."[11] Employees might instead be referred to as colleagues, co-workers—even investors, for they invest ideas and energy and time. "Employees are our greatest investors" has a very different ring.

❧

The most powerful language a corporation uses is the language of financial statements. Here we find not rhetoric but power that determines income. If the standard income statement focuses on shareholder gains, we might begin to see corporate activity in a different light with an *Employee Income Statement.*

It's useful, for many purposes, to have employee income scattered into different lines of costs—such as production costs or marketing costs. This helps determine cost of goods produced. We might leave this entirely unchanged, and simply produce a supplemental statement where employee income is aggregated together in one line at the bottom. Thus we would have:

Employee income + Capital income = Revenue − Cost of materials

Nothing fundamental in accounting practices would change. But we might begin to see that corporate activities are really directed toward supplying two streams of income: one for employees, another for capital providers. It would be interesting to compare how employee income changes from year to year, and to see how that change is related to employee productivity.

Useful in this regard would be an *Employee Productivity Report*, showing how much revenues went up in a given year and how much employee income went up. If revenues are up 15 percent and wages are up 2 percent, why the difference? Who created those revenues?

Lear Corporation's annual report does something along these lines. It shows sales per employee, and total income per employee—yielding a "people-asset-productivity" measure that has steadily increased.[12] The problem with Lear's approach is that, presumably, it retains the old bias: productivity should go up much faster than employee income, thus siphoning off employee-created wealth for shareholders. But employees might use such a report as a bargaining tool, arguing that productivity gains should lead to wage gains.

A further point might be made with a *Stockholder Productivity Report*, laying out how much capital was contributed by stockholders, when it was contributed, and how much stockholders have since gained. It might list stock buybacks and dividends as a cost against income from stockholders. The bottom line would be an enormous loss to the company, which increases every year. Such a report might help reconceptualize stockholders not as owners but as investors—with the implication that they do deserve a return, but that it's reasonable to ask how much. Boards might use such a report to question whether it is a misallocation of resources to continue booking all retained earnings as stockholder equity.

They might consider a new entry: employee equity. A portion of profits could be allocated to employees, and those who defer taking it out as cash might receive stock instead—with the amount booked as employee equity.

Another possible report is a corporate cost-internalization audit, which can be called a *Market Efficiency Audit*, to highlight its source in market principles. This is the concept suggested by author David Korten, who holds a Ph.D. in business from Stanford University. In any socially efficient market, he wrote in *Business Ethics*, "producers must bear the full cost of the products they sell," because when costs are not internalized, "a firm's profits represent not an addition to societal wealth, but an expropriation of the community's existing wealth." Externalized costs would include items like public subsidies, costs borne by injured workers, the depletion of the earth's natural capital, or the $54 billion annual cost of the health consequences of cigarettes.[13]

Another approach would be to create a *Community Income Statement*, showing corporate taxes received as income, or jobs created as another measure of benefit, weighed against the expenses of tax abatements, infrastructure, subsidies, and externalized costs. These might prove useful tools in the hands of groups working to control corporate subsidies.

The lack of such reporting leads to abuses. In Minneapolis, for example, the state put together an $838 million aid package for Northwest Airlines in return for a promise to create 1,500 jobs. There was no accounting to the community for how money was spent. Within two years, the company announced plans to shed 3,000 jobs. And after five years, only 150 new jobs had been created.[14] A Community Income Statement could serve as a basis for challenging such corporate malfeasance.

New Maps Being Developed

If most of these reports today remain conceptual, tangible work is advancing on the broader front of measuring community health in new ways—an approach championed for the last quarter-century by evolutionary economist Hazel Henderson, among others. She reports that in 1995, the World Bank issued a *Wealth Index*, redefining the wealth of nations as going far beyond built capital, which contains the items our current measures focus on, like factories and financial capital. In the bank's model, this form of capital represents only 20 percent of real wealth. It estimated that 60 percent of real wealth was in human capital like social organizations and knowledge, and the final 20 percent was in environmental capital.[15]

A related approach is represented by the *Calvert-Henderson Quality of Life Indicators*—developed by Henderson and the Calvert Group of social investing funds—which measure U.S. socioeconomic health using twelve indicators, including health, education, public safety, and environment, as well as more traditional indicators like employment and income. While that approach uses multiple measures, a single measure has been developed by economist Herman Daly, and John and Clifford Cobb—the *Genuine Progress Indicator*, which deducts many environmental and social costs from Gross Domestic Product, and adds nonmonetary items like household and volunteer work, to arrive at a more accurate overall figure of genuine progress.[16]

The recognition of a need for such new indicators is growing, and they are supported by nearly three out of four Americans. As Henderson put it, alternative indicators—along with new approaches like full-cost pricing and environmental economics—together represent "the greatest revolution in accounting and statistics since the invention of double-entry bookkeeping."[17]

⁂

In the area of company reporting, tangible work is also under way to develop new financial statements, and to require more social disclosure from corporations. As Stetson University legal scholar Marleen O'Connor has observed, reform of disclosure practices might be more politically acceptable than other reforms, "because the United States has strong cultural norms that favor transparency."[18] Disclosure might help cleanse the system of abuses. In the words of Supreme Court Justice Louis Brandeis, "Sunlight is the best disinfectant."[19]

The best example of new disclosure is the environmental annual report, which 35 percent of the world's largest companies, particularly in Europe, now issue.[20] Standardizing the measurements in these reports is an important step, and it's a project being pursued by the Global Reporting Initiative (GRI), a multidisciplinary group involving environmentalists, social investors, and major accounting groups—including the Association of Chartered Certified Accountants, KPMG, and PricewaterhouseCoopers—as well as groups like the U.N. Environment Program.[21]

Although it began with environmental concerns in 1997, the GRI expanded its focus in 1998 to include other social measures, such as compensation, diversity, community investment, and philanthropy. Its guidelines have been used by at least thirty international companies, including U.S. firms like AT&T, Bristol-Myers Squibb, and GM, as well as foreign firms like NEC in Japan, Electrolux in Sweden, and Shell in the United Kingdom. Most significantly, the GRI is on its way to creating a global social accounting body.[22]

※

While GRI seeks voluntary disclosure, a different group is lobbying the SEC for mandatory disclosure: the Corporate Sunshine Working Group (CSWG), an alliance of social investors, environmental organizations, community groups, and labor unions. "The SEC already has congressional authority to require more disclosure," notes legal scholar Cynthia Williams from the University of Illinois at Urbana-Champaign. The Securities and Exchange Act of 1934 empowers the SEC to require disclosure "as necessary or appropriate in the public interest or for the protection of investors," she points out.[23]

Because legislation is already in place, all that's needed is rule-making by the SEC. For several years, organizations and individuals in the CSWG have been lobbying the SEC, asking it to write social disclosure rules. If the commission doesn't do so, the group plans to file a petition for rule-making, to force the SEC to create rules. Williams suggests a variety of data be disclosed, including equal employment statistics, safety and health data, environmental penalties, the ratio between highest and lowest paid employees, total lobbying budget, and information on handling dangerous chemicals.[24]

A rule-making petition is winnable, Williams argues—particularly if the SEC sees this as an investor-led movement. It may be in pushing for greater social disclosure that the social investing community can be most valuable. This is a crucial first step. "There is no social change without knowledge," says Amy Domini, namesake of the Domini Social Index. As she put it, "You create data, then knowledge, then social change."[25]

Disclosure reform efforts might be strengthened by broader participation from labor unions and community groups, because new accounting measures are effective only when they're used. Tools are useful only when someone picks them up. We should note that social accounting had an earlier heyday in the 1970s, but died when recession hit. As former accounting professor Ralph Estes observed, "We went from over 90 percent of large corporations engaged in social reporting to a trickle." This was because social accounting was a top-down initiative, Estes wrote, coming from corporate executives, CPAs, and professional accounting bodies, without "strong participation by grassroots stakeholders."[26]

The point is to create new tools for concrete action, new maps to guide our steps. We've lived so long with the tradition that stockholder profit is the measure of health that we've come to think of it as a law of the market. But we might just as validly speak of employee profit or community profit. The question is, From whose viewpoint do we view money moving around?

Seeing differently is what enlightenment is about. For change begins in the mind—just as the American Revolution began in the minds of Americans. As John Adams once wrote to Thomas Jefferson, "What do we mean by the Revolution? The war? That was no part of the Revolution; it was only an effect and consequence of it. The Revolution was in the minds of the people."[27]

Today, we again need a revolution of the mind. We must realize again that some persons do not matter more than others. The economic rights of employees and the community are equal to those of capital owners. Fully internalizing this truth is not only the starting point of change. It is indeed change itself.

8

Emerging Property Rights

THE PRINCIPLE OF EQUALITY

Under market principles, wealth does not legitimately

belong only to stockholders. Corporate wealth belongs to

those who create it, and community wealth belongs to all.

*I*f change begins in the mind, it consists not only of seeing differently but of conceiving of new rights—conceiving of ourselves as fully empowered. In this spirit, we might turn to a second principle of economic democracy: corporate wealth belongs to those who create it and community wealth belongs to all. As we thus enter the terrain of new economic rights, we might remember what Thomas Paine wrote upon entering the terrain of the common man's new political rights:

> Perhaps the sentiments contained in the following pages, are not *yet* sufficiently fashionable to procure them general favor; a long habit of not thinking a thing *wrong,* gives it a superficial appearance of being *right,* and raises at first a formidable outcry in defence of custom. But the tumult soon subsides. Time makes more converts than reason (italics in original).[1]

Thus began Paine's most famous pamphlet, *Common Sense,* which was widely credited with solidifying public resolve for American independence from the Crown. In those memorable pages, Paine wrote, "I offer nothing more than simple facts, plain arguments, and common sense." And he asked of the reader only "that he will divest himself of prejudice and prepossession, and suffer his reason and his feelings to determine for themselves."[2]

Like Paine, we might invoke plain arguments and common sense in the face of custom—the custom, for example, that public companies manage for profits, and that these profits (at least conceptually) belong to shareholders. Even if only a portion is paid out directly, earnings are generally the basis for company value, and that value is pocketed by shareholders. Yet in the knowledge era, much corporate wealth arises not from assets purchased with shareholder dollars but from the knowledge in employees' minds. As the foundation of wealth creation has changed, the allocation of gains should change also.

The principle is simple: efficiency is best served when gains go to those who create the wealth. Thus, instead of aiming to pay employees as little as possible, corporations should distribute employee rewards based on contribution—while recognizing that in any humane social order, a living wage is the basic minimum. Likewise, corporations might aim for a decent minimum stockholder gain but drop their focus on maximum gain. The legitimate goal is reward based on contribution. Since the contribution of stockholders has shrunk dramatically, their gains should shrink also. It simply defies market principles to continue giving speculators the wealth that employees create.

To use again the terminology of Jeff Gates, we must look at opening the closed loop of wealth creation. Instead of allocating wealth only to wealth, we need a greater emphasis on mechanisms that allocate wealth to merit. We must recognize new principles: First, that infinite and increasing flows of wealth for a onetime hit of money are artificial, aristocratic, and absurd. Second, that wealth flows more naturally to those who create it. As Thomas Jefferson put it, the "artificial aristocracy founded on wealth" must make room for the "natural aristocracy" of talent.[3]

THE PROPERTY RIGHT OF LABOR

We can rest our argument for this principle on natural law—and by that I mean not scientific law, but the naturally just order that Thomas Jefferson invoked when he wrote of principles we hold to be self-evident. As we saw in chapter 3, it was this kind of natural law that American courts appealed to in articulating a democratic law of real property: the value of improvements are to be left with the developer. Wealth belongs to those who create it.

It makes little sense today that corporate law remains feudal, with stockholders supposedly owning a firm's assets and thus everything created on top of those assets. If we divest ourselves of prejudice and allow reason to determine for itself, it's natural that employees have a right to much of the value they help to create.

Market principles, at their best, are about self-reliance, hard work, and competition. Free market theorists are always urging nations to open themselves to competition, to let down protectionist barriers. We might make the same argument to stockholders, urging them to let down the protectionist legal barriers guarding shareholder primacy, to open themselves to free competition with employees. If the contribution shareholders make to the corporation is so vital, it will be regarded as such by market forces. If their contribution is not so vital—and in many cases, clearly it is not—then why protect them? Economic theorist Joseph Schumpeter said the free market is about "creative destruction." Perhaps it's time for a little creative destruction of the privileges reserved for wealth.

∝∾

Perhaps it's time to replace archaic privileges with democratic economic rights—like new property rights for employees. A property right accruing to labor may seem like a new idea, but in truth it is a very old idea. In our best political and economic traditions, it is labor that creates the right to property in the first place.

John Locke in *Two Treatises of Government* was one of the first to articulate this principle, in the late 1600s. "Justice gives every Man a Title to the product of his honest Industry," he wrote.[4] "As much land as a man tills, plants, improves, cultivates, and can use the product of, so much is his property."[5]

Writing nearly a century later, Adam Smith echoed this philosophy in *The Wealth of Nations*, writing, "The property which every man has in his own labour . . . is the original foundation of all other property."[6]

We find the same principle scattered throughout democratic history. Thomas Paine wrote, for example, that a key issue was the status of the common man, and "whether the fruits of his labour shall be enjoyed by himself."[7] Thomas Jefferson, in the same vein, defended a right "to the acquisition of our own industry . . . resulting not from birth, but from our actions."[8] As a slave owner himself, Jefferson's actions of course fell short of his ideals. But it is to the ideal that we must constantly return, as Abraham Lincoln did in challenging the institution of slavery. He observed: "Labor is prior to, and independent of, capital. Capital is only the fruit of labor, and could never have existed if labor had not first existed. Labor is the superior of capital, and deserves much the higher consideration."[9]

Some might argue that it is the labor of the entrepreneur that creates title to corporate wealth, and that this wealth—in the form of corporate stock—rightfully passes to one's descendants. We think of this as economic democracy: that anyone may start his or her own company and run for the top. We fail to see our unconscious aristocratic assumptions: that there is a top, that wealth should flow to the top, that those who reach it will rule their own commoners like feudal lords, and that their privileges will pass intact to the next generation. If this system favors entrepreneurs, it also favors CEOs, who likewise benefit from a system where wealth flows upward. We may think of this "openness" at the top as democratic, but it's really about allowing a chosen few entry into the aristocracy.

The alternative, in a democratic era, is Thomas Jefferson's vision of all citizens owning productive assets and enjoying the fruits of their own labor. Similarly, Thomas Paine's vision was of "every man a proprietor."[10] It's a worthy ideal, to own one's place of work. But in the corporate era, most citizens are necessarily employees, and always will be. We need a new economic vision for a new era: not every man a proprietor, but every employee an owner.

All of us have the capability of working on our own, but many choose to deposit this capability with a corporation. The corporate contract thus works much like the social contract. As Paine described it in *Rights of Man*, the citizen deposits his rights and capabilities "in the common stock of society, and takes the arm of society, of which he is a part." This makes him or her a full citizen, by natural right. "Society *grants* him nothing.

Every man is a proprietor in society, and draws on the capital as a matter of right"(italics in original).[11]

In similar manner, every employee is a natural owner of the corporation, and draws on wealth created as a natural right. This is not something the corporation *grants* the employee, as in the gift of a few stock options.

In believing that property rights spring not from all labor but only from the labor of entrepreneurs and CEOs, we value aristocratic rights over natural rights. The point is not that the skills of a CEO aren't scarce and valuable but that they realize their value only in conjunction with the skills of others. The point is not that the property rights of the entrepreneur are illegitimate but that they have been stretched beyond reasonable bounds—much as the property rights of kings were once stretched beyond reasonable bounds. Entrepreneurs are like the original warrior-kings, for whom it is legitimate to own territory they themselves have conquered. But when their rights pass to descendants or speculators, we have others claiming wealth they did little to earn.

If our centuries-long battle with kings has taught us anything, it is that property rights are an evolving concept. And they must continue to evolve. They must conform to natural principles of justice, which means having some reasonable relation to productivity and reflecting some concern for a decent minimum income. In our own era, this may well mean emerging property rights for employees. It may also mean that a living wage is as important a right as the right to a reasonable return on investment.[12] And it certainly means that granting exclusive and increasing privileges to those who live off wealth that others create is no longer legitimate.

RECLAIMING LOCKE AND SMITH

If we find hints of these principles in many sources, we find their best elaboration in John Locke, who is often claimed as a champion of property rights. When his writing is viewed in full, we find him expressing contempt for "the idle, unproductive, and Court-dominated property owners," the "court parasites" and "pensioners" who lived off their property but no longer worked it. In terms that might be used to attack poverty-level wages paid today, Locke called it an offense "against the common rule of charity" for one individual to "enrich himself so as to make another perish." To thus exploit someone because of his necessity Locke said was robbery.[13]

This radical criticism of property detached from labor is a point often missed in Locke, but University of California–Los Angeles political science professor Richard Ashcraft draws it out persuasively in his book *Revolutionary Politics and Locke's Two Treatises of Government.* In his analysis, Ashcraft upends the common interpretation of Locke—an interpretation seen in Isaiah Berlin, for example, when he proclaims Locke to be "the spokesman of unlimited capitalist appropriation."[14] This interpretation is likewise seen when conservatives defend property rights by citing Locke's famous statement that government "has no other end but the preservation of Property." But for Locke, we must recall, property did not mean merely wealth: it meant one's life, liberty, and possessions. In modern terms, it means everything that is one's own, including family, dignity, and the right to a decent life.[15]

Ashcraft emphasizes that Locke did not exalt property rights in general but favored only those rights stemming from honest industry. In his own time, Locke was a revolutionary. In his *Two Treatises of Government*—which was, in effect, the political manifesto of Britain's Glorious Revolution—Locke attacked the absolute property rights of the king and his court, and was thus among the first to intellectually undermine eternal property rights, to assert that property was an evolving concept. As Ashcraft writes, Locke's essential political message was that the productive members of society ought to unite against "an idle and wasteful land-owning aristocracy."[16]

ॐ

We might summon the spirit of Locke in uniting against the idle stock-owning aristocracy. Using Locke in this way is more significant than it might seem at first blush. Although he is not as well known today as Jefferson or Paine, his ideas permeated the air of Philadelphia when the American Revolution began. Locke was a founding theorist of democracy.

By allowing wealth-rights absolutists to claim him as their own, we allow them to claim the mantle of democracy. In reclaiming Locke, we capture the guns of the opposition and turn their own weaponry against them. In the process, we seize the legitimacy once claimed by wealth privilege—just as Locke seized the legitimacy once claimed by monarchical privilege.

Ideas provide every regime's base of legitimacy, without which the amassing of wealth seems indefensible. Reclaiming Locke is thus much more than an intellectual nicety; it is, in the most profound sense, a coup.

We might execute a similar coup by reclaiming Adam Smith—placing alongside his ubiquitous notion of the invisible hand his other, more revolutionary principle: that high corporate profits represent an "absurd tax." Here again we find a thinker used as an apologist for "unlimited capitalist appropriation" whose own writing contradicts that usage.

What's often overlooked in Smith is that he believed profits should naturally be low. They are "always highest in the countries which are going fastest to ruin," he wrote. Such a state of affairs enriches only the few, he continued. For "by raising their profits above what they naturally would be," wealth holders in effect "levy, for their own benefit, an absurd tax upon the rest of their fellow-citizens."[17]

This is intellectual ammunition of the most potent sort. We might pull out both cannons of our canon at once, and invoke Smith and Locke together as we depict corporations levying an absurd tax on employees and the community in order to benefit an idle, speculative, stock-owning aristocracy.

What we gain from these thinkers are principles for challenging the legitimacy of the system design. We gain from them the grounding to assert that current wealth allocation relies not on natural principles but on artificial principles: the courts' insistence that corporations maximize returns to shareholders. We gain the audacity to say this mandate no longer makes sense.

The time is coming when we must replace today's archaic mandate with a more humane law: individuals have a right to the acquisition of their own industry.

⚭

The principle is so simple—yet so often neglected. Economists some-times dismissively refer to it as the "labor theory of value," and like to say it has been discredited. But the labor theory of value, usually attributed to Karl Marx, stipulates that *"only* human sweat and skill is the true source of all value" (italics added).[18] And that is clearly not the case. Human skill becomes more effective when combined with financial resources.

But we might turn the argument around and note that the stock mar-ket today embraces a "financial theory of value," which stipulates that financial capital is the true source of all value. If we allow our reason to determine for itself, we see that corporate wealth is a joint creation of cap-ital and labor, and by right belongs to both.

Employees are deprived of their rightful share when productivity goes up much faster than wages and the surplus is directed to stockholder gains. Citizens of communities are deprived of their rightful share when corpo-rations evade taxes or are given billions of dollars of "property rights" in the public airwaves. It's not the market that directs those gains to corporations and their stockholders. It's the *corporate power structure,* a structure that tramps on democratic right and violates economic laws.

RESTORING NATURAL ECONOMIC LAW

It's a common tenet of mainstream economics that agents of production are paid in relation to their marginal productivity. We see this, for exam-ple, in the work of American economist John Bates Clark—one of the initial developers of marginal productivity theory (and the namesake of a prestigious award for economists under forty). In the first sentence of the preface of his *Distribution of Wealth,* he wrote: "It is the purpose of this work to show that the distribution of the income from society is con-trolled by a natural law, and that this law, *if it worked without friction,* would give to every agent of production the amount of wealth which that agent creates" (italics added).[19]

The problem is, corporate wealth distribution is not without friction. It is controlled by a feudal law—a privilege—that says new wealth be-longs to those already possessing wealth. This friction is built into the

current structure of corporations. Because of their size and economic dominance, corporations systematically undermine the natural law of wealth allocation throughout our economy—as Clark himself recognized. In his *Essentials of Economic Theory*, he wrote that corporations "are building up a semi-public power—a quasi-state within the general state—and besides vitiating the action of economic laws, are perverting governments."[20]

If we are to restore the operation of natural economic law, we must acknowledge an employee right to a substantial portion of corporate wealth—as some of our most successful business leaders already do.

One of the most elegant structures for recognizing employee economic rights is the arrangement devised by Roberto Eisanman, founder of Brazil's *La Prensa*—an arrangement whereby the publication's profits are split evenly with employees, after capital draws its "wage." "Capital should make a wage," Eisanman explains, based on where else it might be invested, and at what rate. (And this, I might add, seems to me a reasonable proposition.) Thus at the beginning of each fiscal year, the company determines the proper salary for capital. If it is 10 percent, then the first 10 percent of profits that year go to capital. Additional profits are split with employees, fifty-fifty. "It creates extraordinary efforts that create extraordinary profits," he said at the 1998 Business for Social Responsibility conference. The previous year, for example, the lowest-paid employee had taken home profit sharing equal to six months in wages. And shareholders got a cash dividend of 36 percent. "It didn't cost us anything," he added. "It's good for everybody." And this system has been in place for thirty-five years.[21]

La Prensa's plan is striking in its simplicity. Employees and stockholders together create wealth, and since it's impossible to determine who created how much, they split it evenly, after each draws a wage.

Profit sharing has of course been around for a long time. It's one sign that our system is naturally trying to evolve toward a more democratic economy. But the fact that profit sharing with lower-level employees remains so rare—it's practiced at only about 10 percent of companies—is a sign of how far we have to go.

THE PROS AND CONS OF EMPLOYEE OWNERSHIP

If profit sharing on a large scale (not the tiny scale in force at many companies) is one way to move toward an employee property right, direct ownership in the company is another. Here we might look to the example of Robert Beyster, founder of Science Applications International Corp. of San Diego. With 1999 revenues of an impressive $5.5 billion, SAIC was dubbed by *Red Herring* magazine "the giant that moves like a startup." A good deal of that nimbleness is due to the fact that employees own 90 percent of the company.[22]

Beyster's philosophy is simple: "Those who contribute to the company should own it," he has said. And as the company's ownership philosophy puts it, that ownership "should be commensurate with employee contribution and performance as much as feasible."[23]

In this spirit, two hundred among the firm's forty-one thousand employees—identified as future leaders—get $25,000 in stock annually, through a trust vesting over seven years. Others are eligible for stock purchase, bonus, and option programs. And everyone can participate in the Employee Stock Ownership Plan (ESOP). Through these various means, about 91 percent of employees own stock. And many hundreds have already become millionaires.[24]

As a consulting firm, SAIC offers a nearly pure example of the principle that employees create company wealth. Apparently recognizing that, Beyster made an early pledge never to own more than 10 percent of the company. Today he owns just 1.3 percent, which is estimated to be worth $90 million. As he told *Forbes*, "How much money can you spend anyway?"[25]

∞

Employee ownership is a valuable tool of economic democracy, though it is not without flaws. It retains the principle that economic sovereignty rests in property and that with property ownership comes a right to have one's interests considered paramount. In an ultimate scheme of reform, we should make the claim for a legitimate employee stake quite apart from property ownership, based on the notion that corporations are not objects but human communities. Because these corporate communities exist inside a democratic order, all their members should have a right to a voice in governance—even if they don't own property.

A second problem with employee ownership is that it implies that if the "right" people own stock, corporate focus on shareholders alone is somehow justified. We thus run the risk of simply elevating a new body of feudal lords.[26] What economic democracy also requires is a broad recognition that corporations must serve the common good—a topic to which we'll turn in chapter 9.

That said, the concept of employee ownership is fruitful because it taps directly into market forces. The whole idea of profit is that it spurs owners to manage efficiently, because they know they'll pocket the gains. Absentee ownership works against this natural economic law, as it can force corporations to lay off productive employees in order to siphon wealth to idle speculators. Employee ownership begins to put incentives back in their proper place.

What's also promising about employee ownership is that it could be almost immediately viable politically. Asset-based policies are popular today, in part because they're often acceptable to both liberals and conservatives. This is a sign that new principles are indeed emerging: rewards should be related to productivity; wealth should flow to those who create it; and financial assets should be broadly owned.

The time may be ripe to create new public policy initiatives for employee ownership. In prior decades—the 1970s and 1980s—we had government policies promoting employee ownership, and we can rejuvenate them. Though it's little noticed today, a large-scale experiment in employee ownership has been under way for the last twenty-five years. The National Center for Employee Ownership in Oakland, California, estimates there are over 11,500 partially or wholly employee-owned firms in the United States, covering more than 8.5 million employees, and holding assets of more than $650 billion. About one in four of these firms are majority-owned by employees—which gives them a real chance to become models of genuine economic democracy.[27] These companies are laboratories of change. They deserve far more attention than they currently receive from writers, theorists, think tanks, and legislators.

As John Logue of the Ohio Employee Ownership Center at Kent State University observes, research and experience show that employee ownership can not only broaden asset ownership but also avert plant shutdowns, reduce absenteeism, decrease the risk of capital flight, and increase productivity. Research also shows, Logue wrote in *Business Ethics*, that employee ownership works best when it's combined with employee involvement in decision making at all levels. Put another way, it works best when it follows natural economic law: gains go to those who are actively empowered to create them. The benefits from genuine employee empowerment flow not only to employees but to the entire economy. If American companies broadly implemented employee decision making and wealth sharing, one study for the New York Stock Exchange estimated that productivity in the United States would increase by 20 percent.[28]

There's still another benefit of employee ownership. It's a way to defer (or eliminate) taxes for founders who sell to employees, thus enabling them to pass the company on to its rightful heirs: those who helped build it. Unfortunately, some of the tax advantages of employee ownership have been eliminated over the years, and they should be reinstated and broadened—perhaps on a sliding-scale basis, so companies with more substantial employee ownership would receive more substantial tax benefits.[29]

❧

We might devise other policy options for tackling a major challenge of employee ownership: share repurchase obligations. When firms place stock in an Employee Stock Ownership Plan—a kind of retirement trust—they are obligated to buy the shares back when employees leave or retire. Companies in effect must liquidate themselves, paying out the entire value of the company, over and over again, from cash flow.

Some firms—like SAIC—get around the obligation to buy back shares by creating an internal market, allowing employees and retirees to sell shares among themselves. On a public policy level, we might do something similar by creating special financing vehicles that allow employee-owned firms to become "semipublic"—to have access to equity investments without giving up control. As we now promote home ownership with institutions like Fannie Mae and Freddie Mac—which repurchase home loans from lenders—we might promote employee ownership with a similar federally chartered institution, say, a Federal Employee Ownership Corporation (FEOC).

Such an entity could purchase shares, perhaps only from majority-employee-owned firms, and hold them like a mutual fund. As part of the charter of both the FEOC and the firms themselves, it might be stipulated that firms may not be sold to the highest bidder but can trade hands only with majority employee approval. Firms might write further democratic terms into charters, and FEOC participation could be open only to those meeting certain minimal requirements—like employee voice in governance or substantial profit sharing. Through an institution like this, employee-owned firms would gain the advantages of being public—increased liquidity and decreased share repurchase obligations—while remaining safe from hostile takeovers.

One possible objection to this approach is that founders may be reluctant to see shares trading in a relatively faceless venue and prefer to keep ownership close to home with their own employees. Part of the pride (and effectiveness) of ownership might also be diluted if employees' holdings are not directly in their own company.

These problems may not be insurmountable, however. Experience shows that public financing for employee ownership can work. Canada's Crocus Fund, for example, is a regional venture capital fund sponsored by the Manitoba Federation of Labor and the provincial government, which pools Canadian-style IRA accounts to invest in equity stakes in local firms. The fund uses social screens, including a preference for employee-owned firms. Crocus today provides about two-thirds of Manitoba's venture capital, and it has invested $100 million in forty-seven companies, creating thirty-five hundred new jobs and maintaining fifty-two hundred—in a province with only one million inhabitants. Notably, Crocus has been the top performer in its class of funds in Canada.[30]

❧

Still another method of moving toward employee ownership, for public companies, is stock options. The very existence of these options is an acknowledgment of the principle that if employees help increase the value of the firm, they get to keep some of the gains. But options are only a small step in the right direction. Employees generally have no voting rights with options. And they benefit only upon exercise of the options and sale of the stock, so long-term ownership is discouraged. Indeed, as employee ownership attorney Deborah Groban Olson points out, employees who have acted as long-term owners may have suffered in the recent volatile market. If they exercised when share price was high but failed to sell, they may have found themselves holding stock worth less than the taxes owed on the exercise price.[31]

Another problem with options is that so few are given to employees. Even in widespread option plans—which are relatively rare—employees often get only a hundred shares. If the value of a share goes up $10, which is a lot, an employee gets $1,000, and it can take five years to earn even that.

An additional drawback with options is that employees still must buy the stock, and artificially low wages make that difficult. The result is that nine out of ten employees sell shares as soon as they exercise their options. We might begin to solve this problem with new policies on employee stock options: instead of allowing firms to discount shares only a modest amount, we could allow discounts of, say, 50 percent. Employees might be allowed to purchase shares at this discount only if they held them for perhaps five years. Gains could be taxed not as employment income but as capital gains, for which taxes are lower.

Existing stockholders will no doubt complain about dilution, but dilution is actually the aim, and it is legitimate—for it's the easiest way to reduce the gains of noncontributing shareholders and move gains to those who make a productive contribution. It is, after all, a time-honored principle of capitalism that new capital dilutes old capital. And much new capital these days is the intellectual capital of employee knowledge.

❧

A more innovative path to employee ownership is the ownership transfer corporation, a concept promoted by Australian employee ownership theorist Shann Turnbull, as well as by Deborah Groban Olson and Alan F. Zundel, associate professor at the University of Nevada, Las Vegas—all three of whom are active in the Capital Ownership Group, a global online think tank focused on ideas for broadening capital ownership. As Olson and Zundel described it in a paper published in *Business Ethics*, the concept involves reducing the corporate tax rate to make it feasible for stockholders to transfer some equity each year to employees. If the corporate tax rate were cut in half, they say it would provide incentive to transfer 5 percent of equity annually, so that all ownership would be in employee hands in twenty years.[32]

A related example can be found in the Zimbabwe Enterprise Development project, which requires foreign investors to have a local partner for 30 percent (in some cases 65 percent) of ownership in local firms.[33] Similar requirements for foreign investors to transfer shares to indigenous persons have been created in Malaysia and Australia. And a related arrangement was used in the Chrysler Loan Guarantee Act of 1980, which as part of a government loan guarantee required the company to set up an Employee Stock Ownership Plan and contribute $163 million in stock to it by 1984.[34]

What's particularly attractive about the ownership transfer concept is that by making transfer financially palatable, it ingeniously solves the problem of eternal ownership by absentee shareholders. We might make a conceptual argument for such an approach by noting that other forms of ownership, like patents or copyrights, are often limited in time. Even imperial ownership was limited, as we saw when Great Britain recently ceded control over its colonial possession, Hong Kong.

We might try floating a "Hong Kong rule" with corporate ownership that says stockholders may own corporations no longer than 158 years—the amount of time Great Britain held Hong Kong.[35] Ten or fifteen, even thirty years might be more reasonable. But the point is to raise the issue, Is there any length of time—even a century and a half—after which return on investment legitimately ends? Must it necessarily go on into eternity? I might note that conceiving of stock as expiring does not mean anyone buys out shareholders in the end. It simply means their time of extraction has gone on long enough to recover both principal and return, and ownership should therefore revert to the company. It might then be issued to employees, whose ownership would in turn also eventually expire.

❧

For the time being, that's a conceptual argument. There is a more direct way to demonstrate employee property rights immediately—with a St. Luke's maneuver. St. Luke's, you will recall, was the London ad agency purchased by employees during a buyout of Chiat/Day by Omnicon, and it offers an intriguing model that might be replicated, like this:

Imagine a hostile takeover. When a company goes into play, let's say employees decide they're not coming along—all employees, from the CEO to the janitor (or perhaps all employees except the CEO, who is amply bribed by stockholders). Employees might tell the buyer, "You can certainly buy this company, but you can't buy us. Let's see what the company is worth without its employees." Valuation specialists could be called in to draw up relative values.

Let's say a $1 billion company—stripped of all human knowledge—is worth half as much: $500 million. Then the value of the employee presence is $500 million. Should employees change their minds and decide to come along, that's the amount of stock they would get. They wouldn't take stock away from anybody, but would do what CEOs routinely do for themselves: issue new stock. If there are 10 million shares outstanding, employees would be issued an additional 10 million shares, so they end up with half the company. They could decide among themselves how to distribute it.

Or should the buyer turn tail and run, employees might sit down with the board and make the same demand: "We have now seen that employee knowledge is worth $500 million, so we demand that much in stock, or we're leaving tomorrow." Faced with this choice or the choice of governing a pile of lifeless assets—files no one can find, machines no one knows how to run, customers no one has heard of—a board might come to a decision rather quickly.

Imagine what would happen if this occurred at one major company, even at a branch of a major company. What tremors would run through boardrooms nationwide? And since this tactic would be inappropriate for a company with substantial employee ownership, what mad dash might we see to put stock in employee hands?

A St. Luke's maneuver might have drawn the approval of John Locke, the first major theorist to say that governance rights can be forfeited when the governing power breaks the social contract—which it does when the ruler delivers "the people into the subjection of a foreign power." This marks "a dissolution of the government," Locke wrote, and once the government is dissolved, the people are free to erect a new government.[36]

A corporate merger or takeover is literally a dissolution of the old corporate contract. It can mean collective bargaining agreements will be broken, layoffs made, benefits cut, offices closed, and charitable giving gutted. When such destruction of old agreements is in the offing, Locke said the people "have not only a Right to get out of it but to prevent it."[37] Far from being a theoretical right, this principle was enacted in practice by revolutionaries in both Great Britain and America, when they believed the king had broken the social contract.

In the economic realm, even conceiving of such a move as an imaginary exercise makes the point—without laws, without endless debates—that employees have a natural right to ownership, if they choose to claim it. A St. Luke's maneuver makes another point as well: stockholders have no right to sell employees in the market as though the corporation were a feudal estate. Stockholders get away with such acts today because, as Paine said, "a long habit of not thinking a thing *wrong*, gives it a superficial appearance of being *right*."

What is more naturally right is recognizing employees' emerging property rights. In the knowledge era, it's time to dedicate our economy to a new proposition: that corporate wealth belongs to those who create it.

PROPERTY RIGHTS FOR THE COMMUNITY

Related to this is another principle of economic equality: community wealth belongs to all. Although such a concept seems intuitively right, it is just now beginning to take tangible form in laws and lawsuits invoking community property rights.

One example of the dollar value of such rights can be seen in a 1997 lawsuit in California, which established a public property right to the use of public beaches. After a 1990 oil spill closed beaches for six weeks, a jury ordered a tanker company to pay $18 million to the community. Other companies involved paid an additional $11 million in settlements. Since that verdict, lost recreational value has been a part of other significant settlements, including a $215 million settlement in 1998 for the restoration of the Clark Ford River basin.[38]

A more powerful example of community property rights is the Alaska Permanent Fund, created by Governor Jay Hammond in 1978 to share revenues from public oil reserves. As Peter Barnes described it in *The American Prospect*, "Hammond felt strongly that Alaska's oil wealth belonged to its people, not its government (he described Alaskans as 'stockholders in Alaska, Inc.')." In a unique design, the fund pays an annual cash dividend to state residents, which in 2000 brought a household of four an impressive $7,855. Other portions of the fund go to schools and infrastructure, and are invested in a stock and bond portfolio, so when the oil is gone the dividends will continue. Though the fund was initially controversial and faced a Supreme Court challenge, today Alaskans love it.[39]

Barnes advocates giving every American a share in the sky, so that polluting it would require corporations to pay individual Americans (he estimates the windfall could reach a trillion dollars).[40] A similar proposal has been offered by Olson and Zundel, who suggest creating a Fair Exchange Fund, so that any business must provide a fair exchange to the public whenever it extracts natural resources, uses up clean air or water, receives tax abatements, or enjoys other public subsidies and contracts. The idea might be more palatable to business, they say, if payment were made in stock rather than cash. A trust could be established to reinvest in the community and to pay a portion to citizens. "At one blow," Olson and Zundel wrote in *Business Ethics*, "this structure would deter local governments from competing for corporate location, build a diverse stock portfolio for every citizen, and secure a vote in corporate decisions by a diverse citizenry."[41]

Making payment in stock rather than cash carries an additional benefit, Olson points out. In an era when corporations are becoming major global powers, broad stock ownership secures economic voting rights for the citizenry. To secure these rights, Olson has written, "we must use the current power of existing nation-states before it diminishes further."[42]

But as with many solutions, devices like a Fair Exchange Fund could bring a new set of problems. They may mean citizens actually come to favor pollution and resource extraction because such acts bring direct financial benefit. We can already see this as a side effect of the Permanent Fund in Alaska, where in some quarters there is strong support for opening the Arctic National Wildlife Refuge to oil drilling, even though such a move could be environmentally disastrous.[43] But such problems might be solved with strong enforcement of environmental protection laws.

No solution will be perfect, but citizen and employee property rights are worth developing in law because they have the potential to create a countervailing force to the growing global power of finance. They may ultimately help create a more broadly grounded economic governing power. But in the meanwhile, they can also help create a *broad constituency for change*. If self-interest must never be allowed to run rampant, it still can serve as an engine of change. We are rarely so moved to fight for something as when we stand to gain from it.

As Thomas Paine might have said, granting property rights to the common folk simply makes sense. It may be radical, but it is no more radical than the notion of granting political voting rights to all. Of course, citizen and employee property rights are principles that will no doubt meet at first with a formidable outcry in defense of custom. But that tumult will soon subside. Time will make more converts than reason. And time, one suspects, will be on our side.

9

Protecting the Common Welfare

THE PRINCIPLE OF THE PUBLIC GOOD

As semipublic governments, public corporations are
more than pieces of property or private contracts.
They have a responsibility to the public good.

*I*n devising changes to our economic system, the real issue is one of choice—of learning to see the invisible choices we don't realize we have. The idea of unseen choice is a lesson my friend Laura taught me, and she did so quite offhandedly one evening, when I saw her confront a toddler who was refusing to go to bed. She rolled her eyes in exasperation and told him—in a routine I could tell was well-rehearsed—"OK, Marcel, the choice is yours. Do you want to wear blue pajamas or red pajamas?" He thought long and hard in his toddler mind and settled on blue, heading off to bed confident he was in control.

Like Marcel, when we purchase shares in corporation A rather than corporation B, we believe we have made a real choice. We don't see the invisible choices denied us: Would we like to buy shares in a bank with a mission of serving the local community, or a bank that extracts the equity from people's homes through predatory lending? We don't have this choice, because in many ways public corporations themselves don't have it. As legal scholar Kent Greenfield of Boston College has commented, "'Corporate social responsibility,' in the eyes of U.S. law, is an oxymoron."[1]

Shore Bank in Chicago is one bank with an overriding commitment to developing deteriorating neighborhoods, but it's privately held. As a representative put it, "If we were publicly traded, we couldn't have as our mission to do community development." After a progressive natural juice company went public, its CEO-founder lamented, "I used to be in the business of making great juice. Now I'm in the business of making money."[2]

The problem is that prevailing legal thought says serving the public good—in a central way, not in a 1-percent-after-taxes kind of way—is not an option for public companies. This is odd in a nation like America, for it contradicts the essential meaning of the very word republic. Although in common usage this term refers to representative government, in its deeper meaning it embraces an overriding concern for the common welfare. Republic stems from the Latin *res publica*, the public affairs, or the public good.

Concern for the public good is the animating force of the democratic order—and it must become the animating force of our emerging democratic economy. We must have a conscious and deliberate concern for the public good built into the system design.

Economic theory may suggest that competing self-interests alone will guide actions to serve the broader good, but democratic theory embraces no such delusion. In the United States, we do not deem it sufficient simply to have broad voting rights, so that vigorous factions might pursue their own interests at the expense of the community at large. We also have a system design called the Constitution, with civil liberties protections, guarantees of due process, and protection of minority rights. Even the highest power in a democracy—government itself—faces institutional restraints on its own power.

Democracies accept self-interest—and harness it—and a democratic economy must do the same, for serving one's own interests is often the engine of prosperity. But self-interest has its limits. In our highest democratic ideals (if not always in practice), democratic cultures seek to protect those who have no power to look after their own interests, like children, the poor, the elderly, or future generations. Government serves public needs not represented by powerful interests—with funding for public parks, public schools, public arts institutions, public maintenance of roads, and public justice systems.

Just as democratic practice does not allow self-interest alone to serve as the force creating and maintaining a just social order, we must no longer allow our economy to embrace this same fallacy. We need a new theory. We need a new economic principle that says public corporations have a responsibility to the public good. As we now ironically preclude public corporations from service to the common welfare, in the future we must require such service. At the very least we must require that the common welfare not be harmed.

AMERICA'S FOUNDING TRADITIONS BETRAYED

While I call this a new principle, it more accurately represents a return to America's oldest economic traditions. At the time of America's founding, corporations were created by state charters *only* to serve the public good. As an 1832 treatise on corporate law put it, "The design of the corporation is to provide for some good that is useful to the public."[3] Or as the Pennsylvania legislature in 1834 declared, "A corporation in law is just what the incorporation act makes it. It is the creature of the law and may be molded to any shape or for any purpose the Legislature may deem most conducive for the common good."[4]

By the midnineteenth century, this original and public purpose of corporations began to be eroded in the courts. As activist Richard Grossman has documented, that erosion was at odds with the intent of America's founders—which we can see in a dissenting opinion in the U.S. Supreme Court's 1855 *Dodge v. Woolsey* case. "Combinations of classes in society . . . united by the bond of a corporate spirit . . . unquestionably desire limitations upon the sovereignty of the people," that opinion said. "But the framers of the Constitution were imbued with no desire to call into existence such combinations."[5]

Again in the late nineteenth century, the Nebraska Supreme Court in the case of *Richardson v. Buhl* warned of the danger of allowing private entities to escape control by the public, writing: "Indeed it is doubtful if free government can long exist in a country where such enormous amounts of money are . . . accumulated in the vaults of corporations, to be used at discretion in controlling the property and business of the country against the interest of the public . . . for the personal gain and aggrandizement of a few individuals."[6]

The phrases here are telling: "the sovereignty of the people," "the interest of the public," "the common good." The corporate form was clearly intended in America's early years to be subject to the sovereign will of the people and to serve the common good. It could not be otherwise, for serving the public good was, as one general put it, the "polar star" of the American Revolution. Serving private groups at the expense of the public was anathema. In a letter to Thomas Jefferson, Horatio Gates wrote that Americans opposed a system holding "that a Part is greater than its Whole; or, in other Words, that some Individuals ought to be considered, even to the Destruction of the Community."[7]

∝

But the waters of wealthy self-interest continued rising in the nineteenth century, and erosion of the democratic tradition could not be held back. As D. Gordon Smith commented in *The Journal of Corporation Law,* by the midnineteenth century a new corporate purpose of serving stockholders emerged in the common law.[8]

This new shareholder primacy norm was augmented by new financial statements dating to the same era. Ralph Estes, former accounting professor, observes that the statements we use today began as a "simple system that stockholders' agents had first set up to report to their principals on how well their investments were doing." This report "was never intended to show the performance of the corporation as a whole, in terms of its chartered purpose." But these reports ultimately became the standard measure of corporate performance.[9]

Still another notion—that a corporation is a private entity—also arose in the nineteenth century. It was embodied in the novel concept that corporations were the result not of public charters but of private contracts. A seminal case here was the Supreme Court's *Dartmouth College* decision in 1819, which said a grant of incorporation was a contract that could not subsequently be altered by the government.[10] The larger meaning of this became clear with the 1905 *Lochner* case, which struck down a law limiting working hours as an infringement on private contracts.[11]

CORPORATIONS AS PRIVATE GOVERNMENTS

The notion that corporations are private is still a legal lynchpin of the stockholder-focused corporation, even though it stretches the word *private* beyond recognition. The original French terms *privé* or *priveté* referred to objects in the family household or to domestic acts not subject to public authority. According to the *Oxford English Dictionary*, the word *private* pertains to the individual body— "private parts"—or to things "peculiar to oneself," as in a "private staircase." It also refers to "a small intimate body or group of persons apart from the general community."

It is valid that our nation protects the genuinely private sphere, allowing individuals religious freedom or the freedom to do largely as they like in their own homes. But imagining that *public* corporations are private— that they are like households or small intimate bodies—is bizarre. The shares of public companies trade hands among a faceless *public* every day. These companies may have more investors than a state has persons, have revenues larger than the gross domestic product of nations, and employ legions of lobbyists intent on bending public legislatures to their will. Their power is so great today and their influence so large that they are in effect private governments, when what they should be is semipublic governments, with all the responsibilities that entails.

The idea that corporations are governments is an observation that has often been made. In a 1970 economics text, for example, Robert Lekachman wrote, "In many ways, giant corporations exercise the power of private government, subject to fewer checks than are applied to legislatures and presidents."[12] Adolf Berle made the same point in different language when he called the corporation "a nonstatist political institution."[13]

Similarly, corporate theorist Earl Latham in *The Corporation in Modern Society* called the corporation "a body politic," with all the characteristics of such bodies, including systems of command, systems of rewards and punishments, and systems for collective decision making. "A system of organized human behavior which contains these elements is a political system," he wrote, "whether one calls it the state or the corporation."[14]

As private governments, major public corporations today represent the private realm swollen so large as to threaten the public realm. Instead of calling these bodies private, we might use the more proper term, which is *feudal.*

℀

"Feudalization represents a privatization of power," Georges Duby wrote in *A History of Private Life.* The classic example of this process occurred in tenth- and eleventh-century Europe, when public power shrank after the fall of the Roman Empire, and private power grew. "Each great household became a private state unto itself," Duby wrote.[15] It was an era when great barons overshadowed kings.

In the nineteenth century's redefinition of the corporation, America underwent a similar process of feudalization. This was, not incidentally, a new aristocratic era, the age of the railroad kings, the lords of capital— men like Rockefeller, Morgan, Carnegie, Vanderbilt, and Gould. Historian Matthew Josephson described their feudal revolution in his 1934 work, *The Robber Barons:*

> The members of this new ruling class were generally, and quite aptly, called "barons," "kings," "empire-builders," or even "emperors." They were aggressive men, as were the first feudal barons. . . . When [they] arrived upon the scene, the United States was a mercantile-agrarian democracy. When they departed . . . it was something else: a unified industrial society, the effective economic control of which was lodged in the hands of a hierarchy . . . the country's natural resources and arteries of trade were preempted, its political institutions conquered, its social philosophy turned into a pecuniary one, by the new barons.[16]

These men exercised power over vast holdings "in a manner which closely paralleled the 'Divine Right' of feudal princes," Josephson wrote. Thus George Baer, the president of the Philadelphia & Reading Company, could declare that industrialists like himself were those "to whom God has given control of the property rights of the country."[17]

As the old aristocracy had looked out and seen peoples fit to be ruled, the industrial barons looked out and saw workers obliged to be obedient. In the 1870s, Carnegie Steel began systematically hiring immigrants because of their docility and their willingness to work long hours without complaint. After breaking the five-month Homestead strike, John D. Rockefeller said that henceforth only "company unions" should be allowed, in the time-honored relationship of "obedient servants and good masters."[18]

If calling the members of this new ruling class "barons" and "kings" was once commonplace, so too was the practice of combating them with the language of democracy—a practice that we might fruitfully revive today. The Great Strike of 1877 was called the "Second American Revolution," and labor leader Samuel Gompers hailed the Clayton Antitrust Act of 1914 as "labor's Magna Carta" (although, sadly, this turned out not to be true). Theodore Roosevelt similarly disparaged the "mighty industrial overlords," writing of the vulgar "tyranny of mere wealth." But industrialists claimed democratic legitimacy for themselves as they attacked what they termed the "tyranny" of labor. In just one example of their victories, in 1888 a federal court put down the Western railway strike as a "conspiracy in restraint of trade."[19]

That case illustrates a second mechanism used to protect the private corporate order: the notion that trade must not be restrained, that the private sector must self-regulate, that barons must not be ruled by anyone but themselves—and that this is for the good of all. Free market theory thus plays a covert political function, and because of that function, the theory has shrugged off even the most blatant real-world tests that disprove it—like the colossal system failure of the Great Depression.

There was a time in the 1930s when the business community at large recognized that business could not in fact self-regulate, that what failed in the Depression "was the doctrine of laissez-faire," as the editors of *Fortune* wrote in a June 1938 editorial. "Every businessman who is not kidding himself knows that, if left to its own devices, Business would sooner or later run headlong into another 1930," the editorial added.[20] Yet because this realization did not serve the powers that be, it in time disappeared.

In the post-Depression years, free market theory rose from the dead, and found its perhaps preeminent expression in Nobelist Milton Friedman's 1962 work *Capitalism and Freedom*, which made the democratic ideal of liberty the cornerstone of the capitalist edifice. Friedman's work is today a standard text in business schools, where memories of the failure of laissez-faire are lost in a kind of collective amnesia.

But what we forget we are doomed to repeat. The industrial barons' first feudal revolution has been renewed in recent decades—with the revived enthusiasm for free markets since the Reagan era, combined with strengthened stockholder control of corporations, and a new frontier in global markets. As a result of this new feudalism, sweatshops are back, environmental damage continues globally, and progressive laws are attacked under the banner of free trade. We have snapped back to the nineteenth century, as though bound to it by a bungee cord.

THE BEQUEST OF THE ROBBER BARONS

Free market theory provides the smoke screen, but the real problem is what that theory conceals, which is structures of power. The problem is that we have never fundamentally altered the corporate structures that the Robber Barons bequeathed to us, which harken back to the aristocratic age. We've yet to reach these core structures effectively with legislation, so in enacting laws we've been like homeowners chopping down nuisance trees that continually spring back because we have failed to eradicate the roots. Our laws have focused on specific symptoms while leaving the underlying illness untouched. That illness is the corruption of the free market known as shareholder primacy, which is made incurable by the legal notion that corporations are private and may not be altered.

In corporate governance theory, this notion takes form in the concept of private contracts: shareholders are said to have contracted for their rights, and since this is considered a private arrangement, the public may not intervene. This one-sided contract is seen as both eternal and unchanging. We shouldn't be surprised to find something familiar in this idea, for it echoes the old notion that the king was above the law, holding power both eternal and divine. Central to both stockholder and monarchical power is the dubious concept of *eternal contract*.

℘

Edmund Burke invoked such a contract in defending the monarchy after the French Revolution. The monarchy, he wrote, was part of "the great primeval *contract* of eternal society," emerging from "a fixed compact sanctioned by . . . *inviolable oath*" (italics added).[21] He may as well have stamped his foot and shouted, "No one can ever change it!"

But he was outshouted by Thomas Paine, who attacked the idea that some past generation had struck a contract we must honor for eternity. The "vanity and presumption of governing beyond the grave is the most ridiculous and insolent of all tyrannies," he wrote.[22] His attack on eternal contracts in *The Rights of Man* is memorable:

> There never did, there never will, and there never can exist a parliament, or any description of men, or any generation of men, in any country, possessed of the right or the power of binding and controlling posterity to the "*end of time*," or of commanding for ever how the world shall be governed, or who shall govern it; and therefore, all such clauses, acts or declarations, by which the makers of them attempt to do what they have neither the right nor the power to do, nor the power to execute, are in themselves null and void. Every age and generation must be as free to act for itself, *in all cases*, as the ages and generations which preceded it. . . . Man has no property in man; neither has any generation a property in the generations which are to follow (italics in original).[23]

Every generation is free to act for itself, Paine reminds us. We are free, as were previous generations before us, who succeeded in overturning some Robber Baron precedents. Even if there is some hypothetical contract that grants stockholders a right to maximum returns, that contract has been shown to be subject to change.

When wage and hour laws were enacted during the New Deal, the *Lochner* decision was effectively overruled. The Supreme Court in the 1930s initially struck down these laws, but ultimately upheld them. The private contracts of the corporation turned out to be subject to legitimate public intervention.

The right of regulating property has of course often been upheld by the Supreme Court—even if in some cases this means "taking" property, supposedly prohibited by the Constitution. The Fifth Amendment stipulates that the federal government shall deprive no individual "of life, liberty, or property, without due process of law," and the Fourteenth Amendment places the same constraint on the states.[24] But the Court has said the demands of due process can be met by the legislative process itself. In other words, legislatures can take property through legislation.[25]

In the 1877 Supreme Court case of *Munn v. Illinois*, where Justice Waite invoked this principle, he wrote that when an individual "devotes his property to a use in which the public has an interest, he, in effect, grants to the public an interest in that use, and must submit to be controlled by the public for the common good."[26] Building a further case for regulation was the 1937 *West Coast Hotel v. Parrish* case, where the Supreme Court upheld the constitutionality of state legislation establishing a minimum wage for women—rejecting a corporate claim that its freedom of contract had been violated. As the Court wrote, the community may use its lawmaking power to "correct the abuse which springs from . . . selfish disregard of the public interest."[27]

After 1937, the Court began regularly to uphold new kinds of regulations on private property. The era of unilaterally protecting property or private corporate contracts—what has been called *substantive economic due process*—was effectively at an end.[28]

Due process protections would in new guises be reborn decades later—a topic to which we'll return in chapter 11. The point I wish to make here is that regulation of property in the public interest is clearly permissible. As William Letwin, professor of political economy at the London School of Economics, wrote in the 1970s, "To regulate property certainly deprives owners of its previous or potential value, but such deprivation the Court regarded as constitutional."[29]

In more simple terms, Supreme Court Justice Owen Roberts wrote in the 1934 case of *Nebbia v. New York*, "Neither property rights nor contract rights are absolute."[30] Nor, we might add, are they eternal.

BROADENING FIDUCIARY DUTY

The idea that corporations are private entities, immune to government control, is today outmoded. Corporations are routinely subject to legal intervention, even in their most internal operations. In a 2000 racial discrimination lawsuit against Coca-Cola, a legal settlement created an independent race task force with the power to change all key human resource policies. A similar task force was earlier put in place at Texaco.[31] In another case involving abusive lending by Delta Funding, a settlement with the Attorney General of New York put in place for three years a neutral monitor with the power to review Delta's loan file, to ensure compliance with the law.[32]

Similar public intervention occurs with antitrust enforcement. The government can require corporations to break up, as it did with AT&T. Or it can make mergers contingent on steps to serve the public interest, as with the recent merger of AOL and Time-Warner, when the federal government required instant messaging and high-speed cables to be opened to rivals.[33]

But now here's the contradictory point. Although government intervention to protect public interests is constitutionally permissible, historically common, and often desirable, state courts continue to act helpless in the face of some imagined immutable legal mandate to maximize returns to shareholders.

This mandate is less firmly grounded than we might think. As legal scholar D. Gordon Smith has written, this concept of fiduciary duty developed in common law, and only in recent years has it been written into state incorporation statutes, where directors are generally required to act "in the best interests of the *corporation*."[34] You'll notice Smith does not say "in the best interests of shareholders." In fact it is judges—reflecting a widespread bias toward wealth—who have narrowly defined corporate interests to mean stockholder interests alone. But new interpretations are possible. And common law can easily be overturned by legislation.

Ultimately, I believe we may want legislation expanding the legal concept of fiduciary duty to include a duty not only to stockholders but to employees and the community, and perhaps to other stakeholders as well. Under traditional interpretations, legal scholar Marleen O'Connor notes, "a fiduciary is a person who undertakes to act in the interest of another or a person who accepts entrusted property of another."[35] But as she and other legal scholars have argued, stockholders are not the only ones deserving such protection. Corporate acts clearly have an impact on the financial well-being of workers and the community, and these interests deserve loyalty from the corporation.

Expanding fiduciary duty in state law may be one step in a process of returning the corporation to its tradition of serving the public good. What is particularly useful about fiduciary duties is that they are open-ended, often depicted as gap-filling devices. Laws need not stipulate every possible means of harm—pollution, relocation, unfair termination, and so forth—but can instead stipulate a broad loyalty to sets of interests. Corporations violating those interests can be subject to lawsuits.

❧

While widened fiduciary duties may be one ultimate aim, it's instructive to note that thirty-two states—including Illinois, Massachusetts, Minnesota, New Jersey, New York, and Oregon—have already enacted stakeholder statutes to move us in that direction.[36] These laws are worth exploring, because they show us that fiduciary duties in many ways have already been altered—though not in really effective ways.

Stakeholder laws began as part of a wave of antitakeover legislation in the 1970s and 1980s. They were designed to empower corporate boards to consider the interests of other stakeholders alongside the interests of stockholders. The stakeholders named in statutes vary, but generally include employees, customers, creditors, suppliers, and communities. Hypothetically, these laws give corporate boards legal cover for resisting takeovers. But in practice they have been little used.[37]

Potentially, these statutes represent a Copernican revolution in corporate purpose. But it is primarily their critics who have recognized their

possibilities. The American Bar Association's Committee on Corporate Laws, for example, warned that stakeholder statutes represent a threat of radical change in corporate law. Others have similarly warned that the laws represent "a revolutionary break from past generations of corporate law."[38]

The case law on these statutes is sparse, but there are hints of small potential. In a 1987 case, for example, the directors at Commonwealth National Financial Corporation decided to merge with Mellon Bank rather than with Meridian Bancorp, in part because employees would have greater opportunity with Mellon. Citing the state's stakeholder statute, the court ruled that considering social issues was consistent with fiduciary duty.[39]

In a 1997 case involving the sale of railway giant Conrail Inc., directors chose to accept an offer from CSX rather than a significantly higher bid from Norfolk Southern Corporation, in part because the CSX deal was better for shippers and employees. Judge Van Artsdalen commented from the bench that the focus on maximum value for shareholders was "myopic," and that Pennsylvania's stakeholder statute allowed the board, in making its decision, to consider the railway's role in the entire economy.[40]

One might see a stirring of revolution in such cases. They represent small chinks in the supposedly impenetrable legal wall protecting shareholder primacy. Perhaps we might use these laws one day to drive a truck (or a Trojan horse) through that wall.

❧

Doing so would probably require strengthening these laws—though even amendments may not succeed in making them effective. As law professor Lawrence Mitchell of George Washington University has written, the effect of these laws is "likely to be minimal," because "stockholders continue to be the sole corporate constituents that have the right to vote for directors, to bring derivative litigation, and to sell control."[41]

Because of these institutional constraints, even genuinely expanded fiduciary duties may not be enough, and we'll look in later chapters at other changes in governance that may also be necessary.

But starting from where we are today, there may be one immediate, if incremental, step we can take, which is a drive to amend one state's law, to give other stakeholders the right to sue when their interests are not considered. The amendment might say boards not only may but must consider stakeholder interests. This is already the case with Connecticut's statute, though it only covers mergers and acquisitions. According to Terry O'Neill in *Connecticut Law Review*, the Connecticut statute "appears to impose upon corporate directors a fiduciary duty of loyalty to constituent corporate groups other than shareholders, at least when a merger is being contemplated."[42] Standing to sue may already be present in this state.

If another state law were amended, it could stipulate standing to sue, and where necessary extend that standing from takeovers to other decisions. Only a few states—among them New York, Iowa, and Missouri—limit stakeholder statutes to acquisition or merger issues. Most draw the statutes broadly, to refer to any board decision.[43]

There may be special potential in Iowa, Indiana, and Pennsylvania, where statutes specifically provide that shareholder interests are not to be considered primary. The Pennsylvania law stipulates that in considering "the effects of any action," the board shall not view the "interests of any particular group . . . as a dominant or controlling interest."[44] Lawyers might attempt to use this wording to establish standing to sue, arguing that a layoff, say, or a merger is only in the interests of stockholders, and thus makes their interests illegally dominant. If standing cannot be established, the argument might be made to state legislators that the laws must be amended to realize legislative intent.

Even without amendments, there may be other ways these laws could be used, and I would recommend that specialists explore how. There is precedent for bringing life to dormant law, as happened with the Community Reinvestment Act, which was largely unused for over a decade after its 1977 passage. Only in the early 1990s, when community groups began forming—coalescing in 1992 into the National Community Reinvestment Coalition—did the act become functional. CRA agreements (commitments to lend to low- and moderate-income communities) from banks totaled less than a billion dollars in the first fifteen years of the law, but had reached a mammoth $353 billion by the end of the next five years, thanks to the NCRC.[45]

Another law long considered dead that has been brought to life is the Alien Tort Claims Act, enacted in 1789, which in recent years has been used to establish U.S. jurisdiction for suing corporations like Unocal and Chevron for human rights abuses abroad.[46]

There may be similarly nascent potential with stakeholder statutes. Certainly they have immediate instrumental use in consciousness-raising. For stakeholder statutes remind us, by their very existence, that *an exclusive duty to shareholders is simply a state law and not only can be changed but has been changed.*

Can courts overturn stakeholder laws as an unconstitutional infringement on private contracts or a taking of private property? It seems unlikely. It's hard to imagine that laws requiring corporations to serve the public good could be unconstitutional, because that was the corporate design when the Constitution was written. Even if courts try to overturn these laws, we should remember that state judges are often elected officials and can be replaced.

Ultimately, the notion of corporations as private property or private contracts, impervious to public control, seems unlikely to prove an enduring hiding place for aristocratic privilege. The real contract is with the American people, who have the sovereign power to require public service from corporations.

⁓

If expanding fiduciary duties could be one key step to serving the public good, there may be other approaches as well. One example is the sweeping amendment to the Pennsylvania corporate code recently drafted by attorney Thomas Linzey at the Community Environmental Legal Defense Fund. His bill stipulates that a corporate director's duty to the corporation is owed equally to stockholders, employees, and the "natural and human communities in which it operates." To enforce public service, the bill would limit corporate charters to thirty years, and require corporations to request renewal by listing activities performed in the public interest. The request would be published in ten newspapers, after which the secretary of state would hold a public hearing. Renewal might be denied if the state found that the corporation's continued existence was not in the public interest.[47]

Linzey's proposed law would not only change the fundamental corporate purpose but would effectively bring civil liberties protections inside corporations. His bill would prohibit corporations from abridging the privileges or immunities of employees guaranteed to them as citizens. And it states that corporations may not "deprive any employee or independent contractor of life, liberty, or property, without due process of law." In yet another provision, it would outlaw corporate welfare by stipulating that neither the state nor any municipality could give money, property, or even loans to any corporation.

It's a lot to take on in one bill, and whether it will be introduced remains to be seen; Linzey was hoping to begin searching for legislative sponsors in 2001. But as a gesture of what might be possible in changing corporate purpose, it's intriguing and inspiring.

A PRINCIPLE WHOSE TIME HAS COME?

What is emerging—or reemerging—in our time is a democratic economic principle: corporations must serve the public good, or at least must not harm it. If this idea runs through stakeholder laws, it also can be seen in anti-tobacco lawsuits, labor laws, environmental laws, and health and safety laws. Corporate responsibility to the public good may well be a principle whose time has come.

That corporations have slipped away from this idea is not inevitable, but neither is it mysterious. We may picture the public corporation as a rational tool of accountants, but it is not. It is the brainchild of brutal men in a brutal age, hell-bent on amassing for themselves untold wealth, and leading a feudal revolt against the notion that corporations must serve the public good. But as Paine might remind us, the presumption that Robber Barons can govern us from beyond the grave is the most insolent of all tyrannies.

We can complete our undoing of the Robber Barons' feudal revolt. We can again harness public corporations for the common welfare. It may seem today that the free market offers us valid choices as we invest in corporation A rather than corporation B. But we're like toddlers choosing between blue pajamas and red pajamas. The real choice is between corporations that serve the public good and those that harm it.

10

New Citizens in Corporate Governance

THE PRINCIPLE OF DEMOCRACY

The corporation is a human community, and like the
larger community of which it is a part, it is
best governed democratically.

We lack real alternatives to the stockholder-focused corporation because virtually all public corporations have that design. There's a word for this style of structural design, one used by my friend Anne, who is an architectural historian. The word is *vernacular*. It describes buildings that aren't so much designed as simply built. Like a barn. Everyone knows what a barn looks like, so that's what they build: the barn in their head. The vernacular barn.

We in America live with the vernacular corporation. We seem to design public corporations in our sleep, following unconscious assumptions we rarely examine. If we can begin to wake up—dare to reconceptualize the public corporation as a semipublic government, designed in part to serve the public good—we can begin focusing on this issue of design: how to structure corporations to be accountable to a broader set of interests.

There are two sets of interests that need to be separately empowered, and those are employees and the community. In the community—that is to say, under the protection of government—I would include other interests, such as the environment or consumers. All such nonfinancial interests are often lumped together as "social" concerns. But there is in fact a key distinction among them: employees are *internal* to the corporation, while most other social interests are *external*.

The notion of internal and external stakeholders is important because corporate governance in its present form recognizes this division. Externally, corporate governance is regulated by state statutes and court interpretations. Internally, corporate governance is controlled by a board and management legally answerable to shareholders.

A COMPASS, NOT A MAP

Along these two dimensions, the direction of democratic change we need can be summarized in a simple way. Externally, corporations must move from being the private domain of shareholders to being responsible to the democratic order, as we saw in the last chapter. Internally, corporations must shift from exclusive governance by shareholders to joint governance by employees and shareholders. This internal shift is the focus of this chapter. Its primary aim is to make the case that employees deserve a legitimate voice as internal citizens of corporate society.

If our ultimate aim is a fully democratized corporate governance system, what this chapter offers is not a map of that territory but a compass pointing toward it. As management theorist D. K. Hurst wrote in *Crisis and Renewal*, "Maps, by definition, can help only in known worlds—worlds that have been charted before." Compasses are helpful when one can gain "only a general sense of direction."[1]

As both quantum theory and chaos theory teach us, the next state of the world is fundamentally not knowable. Our economy is too complex, changes too rapid, the political climate too hostile, and reform efforts too early for anyone to say what the end point of economic democracy can look like. What we can know, with precision, is the direction we need to take. That direction is as crystal clear as the direction America needed when Thomas Paine wrote *Common Sense*—a direction that at that time faced away from monarchy and toward political equality. Today our direction faces away from control by the financial aristocracy and toward control by ordinary people. In broad strokes, that means limiting the power of shareholders by putting *real corporate governance power* in the hands of employees and the community.

VOLUNTARY CHANGE IS NOT ENOUGH

Real power means legal power. In the long run, it won't be enough to rely on voluntary initiatives, toothless codes of conduct, enlightened leadership, or reforms that proceed company by company. We must ultimately change the fundamental governing framework for all corporations in law. Ideas for doing so will be discussed in chapter 11, but a few words are needed here.

The necessity of legal change is too often unappreciated by corporate reformers. I have tracked reform efforts over fourteen years at *Business Ethics*, and have seen almost invariably how they focus on "enlightened management," which is another way of saying "voluntary change." The belief seems to be that if we put managers through ethics courses, write voluntary codes, teach environmental stewardship, and encourage stakeholder management, we can somehow counteract the overwhelming legal and structural power of shareholders. But we can't.

Again and again I've seen the truth of it. Voluntary actions have no staying power. Voluntary codes, for example, are easily trumped by pressure for shareholder profits. As Neil Kearney of the International Textile, Garment and Leather Workers Federation has commented, "The companies say to the contractor, 'Please allow for freedom of association, pay a decent wage,' but then they say, 'we will pay you 87 cents to produce each shirt.'"[2]

Enlightened founders have the most control, but their policies rarely survive into subsequent generations of management, particularly at public companies. Ben Cohen of Ben & Jerry's discovered this in 2000 after he and his board "decided," at the point of a gun, to sell B&J to the highest bidder, Unilever. Cohen and a group of social investors tried to buy the company, and the board might have been protected in selling to them at a lower price had it used Vermont's stakeholder statute. But the board feared lawsuits and declined to test that law. So Cohen instead sought informal assurances about his continued influence at Unilever, but soon found those assurances hollow. At every turn, his enlightened leadership was outmatched by the structural forces arrayed against him.[3]

Similar disappointments have met other progressive company founders. In a study of eleven socially innovative business people in six countries, published in *Beyond the Bottom Line: Socially Innovative Business*, author Jack Quarter found that *in every case* social innovation was followed by a reversion, at least in part, to traditional practices.[4] If the reader will permit an extreme example, our era is akin to the time when a few enlightened slaveholders voluntarily freed their slaves. Such moves were only a prelude to the ultimate step required, which was to eliminate slavery in law.

When a problem is supported by or caused by law, the solution must be in the law. Today, shareholder primacy is in our law. Certainly it's the law as seen by the Delaware courts, which control most major corporations. And in any state—even those with stakeholder laws—directors who fail to maximize shareholder value can be sued. CEOs who fail to do so can be fired. The company itself can be subject to hostile takeover. These are *legal mechanisms* that hold shareholder primacy in place. And legal mechanisms can only be counteracted by other legal mechanisms.

⚬

Reformers are far from agreement on this point, but it's a point that seems vital to me. And it is connected to a second point that I have raised earlier: in making legal changes, we should move beyond laws focusing on specific abuses—like environmental damage, low wages, or unsafe working conditions—and focus on structures for reallocating power. Democracy is fundamentally about structure: structures of voice, structures of decision making, structures of conflict resolution, structures of accountability.

As Abram Chayes remarked in *The Corporation in Modern Society*, it was the judgment of America's constitutional convention "that limitations of structure rather than limitations of substance would best secure our liberties." If the founding generation's work has proved "effective, durable, adaptable," economic reforms have proved less so. It is quite possible, Chayes wrote, "that the difference in approach contributed to the difference in the quality of the result."[5]

We may have a patchwork of laws controlling various behaviors of corporations, but we lack any constitutional framework for these economic governments. The constitutional law of corporations has never been written—even the word *corporation* is absent from the Constitution. Elected representatives of the people have never met to draw up a democratic framework for corporate structures.

"The rise of the modern corporation has brought a concentration of economic power which can compete on equal terms with the modern state," wrote Adolf Berle. Accordingly, he added, "the law of corporations ... might well be considered as a potential constitutional law for the new economic state."[6]

If we take this suggestion to heart, it does not mean we must proceed as America's founders did—writing the entire Constitution at one time. Given the complexity of our economy, it may be more prudent to proceed as Britain did, allowing a constitution to evolve over time. Whichever path we take, the first step is eliciting principles we can agree on. And that work begins by asking simple questions, such as this: Who besides shareholders deserve to have their interests served by the corporation?

THE PROMISE (AND PERIL) OF STAKEHOLDER THEORY

In progressive parlance, there's an emerging formulation that says that instead of serving stockholders alone, corporations should serve all stakeholders: those with a stake in the corporation. This is a concept developed by scholars like R. Edward Freeman and other business ethicists.[7] It has intuitive appeal, perhaps because of the wordplay between "stockholder" and "stakeholder." Theorists commonly draw the list of stakeholders to include customers, stockholders, employees, suppliers, creditors, the community, and the environment.

If this list seems so broad as to include the whole world, scholars are attempting to sort it out. One of the best efforts to do so can be found in a 1997 article by management scholars Ronald Mitchell, Bradley Agle, and Donna Wood, who suggest a typology based on three critical factors: power to influence the firm, legitimate standing, and urgent claim. But although useful conceptually, this typology in the end yielded an essentially shifting categorization, one in which different stakeholders can over time move in and out of legitimacy, or influence, or urgency.[8]

From an ethical perspective such observations are useful, but the more critical perspective is that of the law. And this is the perspective that stakeholder theory too often neglects, says John R. Boatright, professor of business ethics at Loyola University–Chicago. Because of the tendency to ignore existing financial and legal frameworks, stakeholder theory is "widely dismissed as irrelevant" by researchers in financial economics and corporate law, Boatright notes.[9]

This is unfortunate, because the theoretical skills of stakeholder scholars are sorely needed today. We need many good minds working on this issue of reforming corporate governance. And we need ways to rescue stakeholder theory from irrelevancy, because of the intuitive legitimacy it has in the popular mind. It was stakeholder theory, after all, that was imperfectly enacted into law with state stakeholder statutes.

But the weakness of those statutes may have something to do with the weakness of the theory itself. Indeed, its bagginess and shapelessness do seem fatal to its real usefulness. Rather than grappling with the core issue of institutional power—who has it, who should have it—stakeholder theory seems instead to rest on encouragement of management's good intentions. As corporate governance theorist David Ellerman, an economist with the World Bank, has commented, "One sometimes has the suspicion that 'stakeholder' governance ideas are being floated by managers who know that, by being responsible to everyone, they will be accountable to no one."[10]

If I were to suggest future avenues for stakeholder scholarship, I would say we need to give more attention to one basic issue: Who is external to the corporation, and who internal? In other words, whose interests should be protected as part of the larger, external democratic polity? And who deserves an internal voice in governance and a share in profits? All stakeholders do indeed deserve consideration. But that doesn't mean all deserve internal standing.

EMPLOYEES AS MEMBERS OF THE FIRM

One group that does deserve internal standing is employees. Among the theorists who support that view is Ellerman. Stakeholder theorists commonly ask, Who is affected by the corporation? But Ellerman suggests that a more precise query is, Who is governed by the corporation? The answer is employees. "Many are affected, but few are governed," he says, making analogy to the fact that foreigners are affected by U.S. actions, and their rights should be protected, but that doesn't mean they deserve to vote in the United States.[11]

As Ellerman observes, when shareholders elect a CEO to govern the corporation, it is not shareholders who are being governed by that CEO. Employees are the ones whose actions are supervised, who must submit to drug tests or have their phones tapped and their e-mail monitored. They can be governed in the most invasive ways.

Employees are in essence a colonized people. As Ellerman notes, a stockholder board electing someone to govern employees is like the British Parliament electing a ruler to govern America.[12] In corporate governance, he suggests, we need a shift from the master-servant paradigm to a partnership paradigm. Rather than being seen as servants lacking a legal voice, employees should be seen as full members of the enterprise.[13]

Current governance theory takes the opposite view, seeing employees as outsiders who merely sell their labor to the firm. Ellerman argues that this employment contract is illegitimate, for it involves giving up the right to self-control. And in his view, the right to self-control is like the right to self-govern. In a manner akin to the right to vote, it can never legitimately be sold, even voluntarily.[14] He compares the employment contract to the ancient *pactum subjectionis*, the pact of subjection by which a people alienated their right to self-govern and turned it over to a king. If such contracts are no longer considered legitimate politically, they should cease being legitimate economically.[15]

❧

Although Ellerman approaches this along a somewhat radical trajectory, others have arrived at the same point in more conventional ways. Consider Douglas McGregor's famous Theory Y of management, as presented in *The Human Side of Enterprise*. Traditional management operates by Theory X, based on control of employees by authority, he wrote. But Theory Y replaces control with integration. As McGregor put it, "Theory Y assumes that people will exercise self-direction and self-control in the achievement of organizational objectives" when they are genuinely committed to those objectives. The only way to achieve that commitment—and thus to achieve organizational excellence—is to stop seeing employees as serving organizational goals, and instead to integrate them fully in setting goals and benefiting from their achievement.[16]

This is no longer a novel idea in management, for McGregor's book has been a classic since 1960. The problem is that the concept of employee membership in the firm has yet to become more than a management theory; it has not crossed into corporate governance theory, much less into legal reality. Managers speak often of giving employees a sense of ownership. But real employee ownership is in most cases minuscule. So corporate membership, in any legal sense, remains elusive. As Corey Rosen of the National Center for Employee Ownership once said, giving employees a "sense" of ownership is like giving them a "sense" of dinner.

Still, McGregor's theory is persuasive, for it makes the case that the democratically run corporation is in fact the more effective corporation. One can make other instrumental arguments—pointing, for example, to research showing that employee-owned firms generally financially outperform conventional firms. But such arguments seem unnecessary to me. Similar arguments were once used to justify the vote for women—arguments that said this step would improve society. Whether or not that has proved true, the argument today seems superfluous, even insulting. Women deserve a vote because they are full human beings like men. In like manner, employees deserve a role in governance because they are full members of the corporation, just as stockholders are.

☙

Compelling support for this view is offered by democratic theorist Robert Dahl. In his book *A Preface to Economic Democracy*, he notes that the right to self-government is among the most fundamental of all human rights. And because it is an inalienable right—meaning it can never be given up or sold—it necessarily translates fully into the economic realm. As Dahl put it, "If democracy is justified in governing the state, then it must also be justified in governing economic enterprises."[17] In words similar to those used by Ellerman—and in some cases credited to Ellerman—Dahl argues, "Binding collective decisions ought to be made only by persons who are subject to the decisions. . . . For laws cannot rightfully be imposed on others by persons who are not themselves obliged to obey those laws."[18]

Noting the oft-cited conflict between self-governance rights and property rights, Dahl asserts that self-governance is the superior right. He notes, for example, that in Thomas Jefferson's trilogy of rights—"life, liberty, and the pursuit of happiness"—the right to property is conspicuously absent. And Dahl adds that Jefferson viewed property rights as a late development in the growth of democracy. In Jefferson's own words, "Stable ownership is the gift of social law, and is given late in the progress of society." Others might argue that property rights are antecedent to government, but Jefferson saw them as "not so much prior to society as dependent on it."[19]

Those who argued the opposite case—that property rights trump self-governance rights—included Chancellor Kent, whom Dahl also cites. At the New York Convention of 1821, Kent opposed universal (that is, white male) suffrage on the grounds that it would "jeopardize the rights of property." He scoffed at the notion that "every man that works a day on the road, or serves an idle hour in the militia, is entitled as of right to an equal participation in the whole power of government." In his view, this assertion was "most unreasonable" and with "no foundation of justice." Kent, of course, lost that argument.[20]

Ultimately, Dahl argues, there need be no conflict between property rights and self-governance rights. For "if a right to property is understood in its fundamental moral sense as a right to acquire the personal resources necessary to political liberty and a decent existence," he writes, "then self-governing enterprises would surely not, on balance, diminish the capacity of citizens to exercise that right."[21]

❧

It's invigorating stuff, using democratic theory to justify worker self-governance rights. But there are other justifications as well—such as the arguments based on economic risk advanced by corporate governance theorist Margaret Blair.

In dominant corporate governance scholarship, as we have seen, the corporation today is viewed as a nexus of contracts. Stockholders alone are said to have a contract for control because they take residual risk—that is, they receive income that's not fixed but variable, based on firm performance. But Blair argues that employees also bear residual risk when they develop skills that don't easily translate to other firms. Thus when employees are laid off, they often take new jobs at substantially reduced pay and never fully recover their firm-specific investments.[22]

Developing this view in recent scholarship, Blair has joined Lynn Stout to argue in *Virginia Law Review* that corporate boards should be seen as "mediating hierarchies"—not serving shareholders alone, but instead balancing competing interests. The two base this view of board function on the economic theory of "team production." Such a theory is appropriate in cases where productive activity requires the efforts of two or more groups and "output from the enterprise is nonseparable," so it's not clear how economic surpluses should be divided. In such circumstances, the board acts to protect the "enterprise-specific investments of all the members of the corporate 'team,'" overseeing allocation of profits. Its role is to deter "shirking and rent-seeking among the various corporate 'team members'"—which, as we have seen, is rampant today among stockholders.[23]

The team production theory, Blair and Stout argue, is more appropriate to public corporations than the prevailing theory, which views stockholders as principals and managers as their agents. In that view, the core problem of governance is one of controlling agency costs—keeping directors and managers loyal to stockholder interests. That view relies implicitly on the notion that stockholders own corporations, which is irrelevant in modern legal theory, since a nexus of contracts is not something anyone can actually own.[24]

℘

There are many ways to justify an employee role in internal corporate governance. But the fact remains that many progressive thinkers fail to perceive the legitimacy of employee standing, which is disturbing. Among both stakeholder theorists and social investors, for example, the tendency is to cast employee concerns as social concerns, not fundamentally different from community or environmental concerns. In an unconscious way, these groups thus manifest discrimination against employees.

Imagine if we had taken a similar approach with discrimination against women. We might have begun by saying, yes, the patriarchal family is too focused on fathers. But we would then have recommended a new focus on children, grandparents, aunts, uncles, neighbors, and, oh yes, mothers. Discrimination against women would have remained intact. As women had once disappeared into their husbands (losing their property, losing their names, becoming simply Mrs. John Doe), women would later have disappeared into the world. They would have remained invisible, when their invisibility was itself the starting problem. The problem was an inability to see women as human beings equal to men.

Today, we too often fail to see employees as sovereign members of corporate society, equal to stockholders. The point is not that employees are the only stakeholder group that matters, but that they matter in a *different* way—an internal way. They live in the house, so to speak. Other stakeholders are like neighbors or cousins and aunts and uncles, related to the corporation but not part of the nuclear family.

There are instances in which other stakeholders could become internal—as with "captive" suppliers making products for one company alone, or franchisees dependent on the central franchise firm. Such stakeholders may at times deserve a role in internal governance. But employees are one group that *always* deserves such a role.

❧

As for what shape an employee role in governance should take, one vital piece is of course representation. That immediately suggests employees on corporate boards, but it's worth noting that with employee-owned firms this has not proven an enormously effective tool. As Edward Carberry of the National Center for Employee Ownership told me, "It's not that it doesn't do any good, it's that in itself it doesn't dramatically change how the corporation operates. They're not being represented as employees but as shareholders."[25]

A different approach might be to create a separate employee house— a bicameral legislature—modeled on the Works Councils of Germany, which are employee assemblies that must approve all major corporate decisions. As Lord Acton once wrote, democratic systems wisely restrain power by dividing it, and this division "affords the strongest basis for a second chamber, which has been found the essential security for freedom in every genuine democracy."[26]

Whatever shape employee representation takes, ultimately this representation should be mandatory. Today we have optional employee voice through unions, but we must begin to recognize how inadequate this arrangement is. It's like granting Republicans a permanent lock on voting power but permitting Democrats to vote only if they organize city by city. Unions can be conceived of as political parties representing the labor interest, counterbalancing the financial interest, which today runs corporations like one-party states. Unions are vital. But it may be equally vital for employees to have the vote. We must move toward a truly democratic economy, where employees are naturally seen as voting citizens of the corporation. Such a system should augment unions, not replace them.

But representation is only one tool of governance. If we look at stockholder governance of corporations, we find it uses a number of tools. There is hiring and firing the CEO, and setting his or her compensation. There is the right to vote on changes of control, and the right to bring derivative litigation if one's interests are not served, relying on court protection of fiduciary duties. And finally, there is financial reporting focused on stockholder interests.

In any ultimate scheme of democratic governance, employees should have access to all the tools that stockholders now use—based on the principle of equal protection of the laws. This might mean Employee Income Statements, an employee right to impeach CEOs who pay themselves outrageous amounts, and a mandated duty of loyalty to employees.

HINTS, NOT PLANS

But let us not get too far out into utopian musings. We may find that the idea of employee governance never catches on, or that one or two governance tools in employee hands is sufficient to change how corporations operate. The future genuinely is unknowable.

The more practical question is how to craft a workable hook in law to begin pulling ourselves toward a democratic future, starting today. I would suggest a route proposed by Supreme Court Justice Louis D. Brandeis, who said that a single state could serve as a "laboratory" for a novel experiment, "without risk to the rest of the country."[27]

One experiment we could try at the state level is to take a single stockholder tool—like voting on changes of control—and extend it to employees in law. Thus no merger, acquisition, or hostile takeover could be completed without approval by workers. Because such combinations generally lead to layoffs, employees might be roused to fight for the proposed law. Even lobbying for it would allow us to make the case that corporations really aren't pieces of property but rather human communities, and employees are part of those communities. If it were to pass, such a law would spell the beginning of the end for shareholder primacy, because it would immunize corporations against hostile takeovers, a key enforcement tool for maximum shareholder gain.

As Thomas Paine once wrote, "I only presume to offer hints, not plans."[28] What I offer here is a rough draft of ideas for democratizing corporate governance, and if it encourages others to make better drafts, it has served its purpose.

The map is less important than the compass. The particular shape of employee role in governance is less vital than the general direction of employee citizenship. What we need today is not a blueprint, but the fire in the belly to get us moving—and it may be that talk of democratic self-governance rights can stoke that fire. Perhaps the spark is the realization that we need not live forever with the vernacular corporation.

11

Corporations Are Not Persons

THE PRINCIPLE OF JUSTICE

*In keeping with equal treatment of persons before
the law, the wealthy may not claim greater rights than others,
and corporations may not claim the rights of persons.*

*I*magining a new economic order is a first step, but finding a way to bring
that vision into reality will be the final step. Ultimately it will mean working through the judicial and political process, and that means tackling the
system's ingrained prejudice toward wealth. In other words, before we can
use our legal system to control the money-making machines called corporations, we must free the legal machinery itself from the grip of corporations and wealth.

That grip today is lawful because it is supported by the courts. But
the monarchy in its day was also considered lawful. As long as such an
unjust legal order remains in place, it works on society what French
philosopher Jean-Paul Sartre once called "inert violence."[1] It does so not
overtly but covertly, under the guise of justice.

When corporations assert aristocratic privileges like exemption from
taxes, power to control the legislative process, or the right of the private
realm to self-regulate, they do so by co-opting our democratic framework.
They use this framework to claim the constitutional rights of persons for
themselves, even as they deny the same rights to actual persons working
inside corporations.

Untangling the methods by which such conjuring tricks are accomplished is crucial, for it points to places where reformers might intervene.
If our journey through legal reasoning seems convoluted at times, that's

because convolution is its essence. In a system designed to preserve equality of individuals, the rights of wealth and corporations can be asserted only by twisting the law into forms for which it was not designed.

CAMPAIGN FINANCE REFORM: A FIRST STEP

Let's start with a relatively easy topic: campaign finance reform. Today this is the arena where the power of corporate and individual wealth is most clearly seen as unjust—and as a result, public determination for reform is mounting. We have thus met the first requirement for any successful change: the public must understand what is at stake and support reform. As Miles Rapoport, director of *Democracy Works*, has written, support for campaign finance reform is "growing in public consciousness, among candidates, in legislative battles, and even in the courts."[2]

At a deeper level, campaign finance reform invites the question of how wealth gained a right to a disproportionate voice in elections in the first place—if democracy is based on a principle of one person, one vote. The precedent here traces back to the Supreme Court's *Buckley v. Valeo* case of 1976, which declared money is speech, and thus campaign contributions represent the constitutionally protected exercise of free speech rights.[3] And yes, surely we all have the right to contribute a few dollars to our chosen candidates. But taken to the extreme, this is a troubling assertion.

Fortunately, the Court left Congress some room to limit contributions, and it said public financing is legitimate if it's voluntary.[4] So effective legislative remedies are possible, and the best may be the Clean Money reforms passed in Arizona, Maine, Massachusetts, and Vermont. Under these laws, candidates qualify for full public funding if they voluntarily limit spending and forgo private campaign contributions. Rather than directly limiting the amount that individuals can contribute, the Clean Money approach reduces the need for such contributions through public funding.[5]

Not many reforms comply with the money-is-speech dictum, Ellen Miller of Public Campaign has written, but "the Clean Money approach has been approved by the courts on all counts, most recently in February

2000 at the appellate level." Even more promising, additional Clean Money reforms are being pursued by activists in another forty states.[6]

National change of a perhaps more modest sort is also proceeding apace, because campaign finance reform may still stand a chance at the federal level.

❦

But if we can be heartened by this progress, we might also be disquieted. While our public focus is riveted on the issue of campaign finance reform, we may well be like passengers on the *Titanic* watching the tip of an iceberg as it passes by. The real danger is in the great frozen mass that lies submerged and unseen—the ancient right of wealth to control the governing process. Besides campaign finance, other modern manifestations of this archaic privilege are the dominance of corporate lobbying in the legislative process, the appropriation of constitutional protections by corporations, and the seizure of public resources through corporate welfare. All of these have to do with corporate privilege, which in its essence is the same as wealth privilege, because corporations serve the collective interests of wealthy shareholders.

Campaign finance reform is a good beginning step toward reform, but it's only that. Wealth privilege has a way of seeping around the barriers we erect against it. For example, prohibitions against corporate contributions to candidates have been around since the Progressive era in the early twentieth century, but corporations have discovered other ways to control the political process. In one instance, when Massachusetts passed a statute prohibiting corporate spending on an income tax referendum, a consortium of Boston corporations convinced the Supreme Court to strike it down—in the 1978 case of *First National Bank of Boston v. Bellotti.* The Court's finding was that corporate political speech is protected.[7]

That "speech" today is all but deafening. In a tally a few years back, the activist group INFACT counted registered state and federal lobbyists of corporations and found the number staggering. Philip Morris had an astonishing 245. At WMX Technologies, the count was 240, and at

RJR Nabisco and Dow Chemical, around 100 each.[8] All Americans may theoretically have one vote, but unlike the wealthy who own most corporate equity, most of us don't have hundreds of lobbyists representing our interests.

Campaign finance reform doesn't touch the issue of lobbying, and may make it worse. If corporations stop donating to political parties—as some already pledge to do—they may well turn those same budgets over to legislative lobbying. So we may chase the fox out of the henhouse only to find it in the pigpen.

WEALTH PRIVILEGE: THE UNDERLYING PROBLEM

It may be fruitful to turn our attention from the various manifestations of the problem at hand to the underlying problem itself: wealth privilege. At some point we might consider attacking that privilege directly.

But first we need to overcome our unconscious embrace of it. I had a co-worker once who planned to vote for Ross Perot, and when asked why, she laughed and said, "Because he's rich." Too many of us carry the unexamined assumption today that the wealthy are superior. Even if in certain ways we oppose wealth privilege—for example, distrusting large corporations and resenting tax breaks skewed toward the wealthy—in other ways our aim is gaining wealth for ourselves. Rather than fighting the wealthy, we want to join them. So we may be less inclined to become outraged about their perquisites.

Also blocking outrage is the fact that today, wealth privilege—aristocratic privilege—rarely speaks its own name aloud, as it once did. Historian Joyce Appleby, in *Inheriting the Revolution: The First Generation of Americans*, noted that when Jefferson ran for the presidency in 1800, his opponents—the Federalists—"had spoken freely about the need for the steadying hand of the 'rich, the able, and the well-born.'" In many minds it was considered just and proper that the wealthy should rule, and saying so publicly was still acceptable.[9]

It wasn't until the 1800 election campaign that the issue of rule by wealth became a matter of debate. When Federalists were rejected at the polls, Appleby wrote, American politics began to become truly participa-

tory for the first time. It began with Jefferson's victory at the federal level, then moved to the state level when Jeffersonians began agitating to remove property restrictions on the vote. The ancient idea that only the wealthy should rule was fast becoming discredited. As Jefferson's party maintained its hold on the presidency for decades, the Federalists after 1816 never again even nominated a presidential candidate. "The deferential order the Federalists stood for had collapsed," Appleby wrote. One could no longer argue openly that the wealthy were the nation's natural leaders. Wealth privilege henceforth would have to assume new guises.[10]

It took decades for those new guises to develop, but by the late 1800s the nation saw the emergence of one of the most ingenious: the invention of corporate personhood. As the source of wealth shifted from land to corporations in the nineteenth century, these new entities were regulated largely at the level of state government. But the Supreme Court threw a roadblock in the path of such legislation with its 1886 *Santa Clara* decision that declared the corporation a natural person, subject to protection under the Constitution.[11]

Supreme Court Justice William O. Douglas wrote years later, "There was no history, logic, or reason given to support that view."[12] But it shifted the definition of the corporation from an artificial entity created and controlled by states to a natural person with independent existence. And it allowed corporations to seek shelter under the Fourteenth Amendment, which prohibits the states from taking property without due process.

Though this amendment was enacted on behalf of slaves, it was used far more often on behalf of corporations. In 1938, Justice Hugo Black noted that, of all the cases in which the Supreme Court applied the Fourteenth Amendment in the half-century following *Santa Clara*, "less than one-half of 1 percent invoked it in protection of the Negro race, and more than 50 percent asked that its benefits be extended to corporations." Using this constitutional shield, the Court from 1905 to the mid-1930s invalidated some two hundred economic regulations.[13]

As we saw in chapter 9, this was the era of "substantive economic due process," and it came to an end with the New Deal. But the impetus for new protections began after 1960, when new social, environmental, and consumer rights began to take shape in corporate regulation at the federal level. As Hofstra Law School scholar Carl J. Mayer noted, this led corporations in the 1970s to try to block these regulations by claiming rights for themselves under the Bill of Rights.[14]

For example, Mayer cited a 1976 case where "a textile corporation successfully invoked the Fifth Amendment double jeopardy clause to avoid retrial in a criminal antitrust action." In a 1977 example, unannounced inspections by the Occupational Safety and Health Administration (OSHA) were barred when an electrical and plumbing company invoked the Fourth Amendment protection against unreasonable search and seizure.[15]

In 1994, a federal court ruled corporate First Amendment rights had been violated by a Vermont law requiring products with bovine growth hormone to be labeled. And in the late 1990s, a federal court again invoked the First Amendment to invalidate a Burlington, Vermont, law banning advertising by tobacco companies.[16]

◌℞◌

In all these cases, corporations implicitly claimed status as persons—even though the Supreme Court itself had in its own past questioned that view. Consider, for example, the contradictory nature of the Court's 1906 *Hale v. Hinkel* ruling, which declared that Fourth Amendment protection against unreasonable search and seizure did apply to corporations, but Fifth Amendment privilege against self-incrimination did not.[17] (Presumably self-incrimination was disallowed because corporate documents could otherwise never be obtained for prosecution.)

More decisively, in 1950 the Court's *United States v. Morton Salt* ruling said that "corporations can claim no equality with individuals in the enjoyment of a right to privacy." And this, the Court said, is because they have "public attributes" as well as "a collective impact upon society, from which they derive the privilege to act as artificial entities." So in 1950, the Supreme Court apparently did not believe corporations were persons.[18]

But no matter. Mayer wrote that after 1960, "the Court abandoned theorizing about corporate personhood" altogether, instead finding new grounds for conferring Bill of Rights protections on corporations. In the area of free speech, for example, it said the purpose of the First Amendment was to create a marketplace of ideas, and because corporate speech furthered this end, it was protected. If corporate personhood had been explicitly abandoned, it had also somehow been implicitly retained.[19]

(RE)DEFINING THE CORPORATION

Corporations can claim spurious protection under constitutional provisions designed for persons for one reason: our legal system has no coherent theory of the corporation. State statutes treat them as a collection of stakeholders, while many state courts see them as serving stockholders above all others. The public speaks of owning the corporation like a piece of property, but corporate legal scholars speak of the corporation as a nexus of contracts, which is not a thing that can be owned.

With no coherent underlying concept of the corporation, corporate law today remains a patchwork. As legal theorist Bayless Manning wrote in the 1960s, "Since the mid-19th century we have not had any idea what we wanted to accomplish with corporation law." As a result, the body of law built over the years has "slowly perforated and rotted away," he wrote, leaving nothing but "our great empty corporation statutes—towering skyscrapers of rusting girders, internally welded together and containing nothing but wind."[20]

If today we live with a confusing and contradictory system of corporate law and theory, we should remember that at one time the American legal system was clear that corporations were created and controlled by states to serve the public good. But this early clarity was lost, destroyed by the Robber Baron generation—as we saw in chapter 9—because its fundamental principles were never enshrined in the Constitution. We moved away from early principles over time, then in halting steps moved back with piecemeal regulation, but today we remain lost in a conceptual haze.

∽

One solution is to begin a national dialogue on redefining the corporation—perhaps convening stakeholder theorists, legal scholars, state legislators, social investing professionals, employee ownership specialists, and others to develop a coherent new theory. What might come out of such a dialogue is a proposal to amend state constitutions or the federal Constitution, stating what a corporation is. This might be more of a conceptual exercise than a concerted public policy effort, but it might at some point offer concepts that pass into corporate governance and management literature.

As for attempting a real constitutional amendment, this is of course not an easy thing to do, and at the federal level it's highly unlikely that any such amendment would pass. The Equal Rights Amendment never passed into law, though it drew strong majority support. As Northwestern University professor of political science and sociology Jane J. Mansbridge wrote in *Why We Lost the ERA*, "A constitutional amendment needs an overwhelming majority, so once it becomes a partisan issue its chances of passing are minimal." She noted that since the repeal of Prohibition over a half-century ago, no really controversial amendment has been enacted. Among the amendments that have passed—for example, limiting presidential terms to two or giving eighteen-year-olds the vote— "none evoked strong, organized opposition." And to say that opposition to a corporate amendment would be strong and organized is an understatement.[21]

Still, it may be useful to muse about possible amendments—perhaps one day even to launch some noble, doomed drive. Even though the ERA itself failed, equal rights for women have nonetheless been widely embraced in the public consciousness. Agitation for the ERA may have helped. If it's premature today to launch some corporate amendment drive, it's worth beginning to imagine what an amendment might look like—as an exercise in establishing basic principles.

⚓

One possible amendment was proposed by Mayer in a 1990 *Hastings Law Journal* article, where he suggested that we need a "constitutional presumption favoring the individual over the corporation" and declaring that corporations are not persons.[22] The language he suggested was as follows:

This Amendment enshrines the sanctity of the individual and establishes the presumption that individuals are entitled to a greater measure of constitutional protections than corporations.

For purposes of the foregoing amendments, corporations are not considered "persons," nor are they entitled to the same Bill of Rights protections as individuals. Such protections may only be conferred by state legislatures or in popular referenda.[23]

In a similar vein, Ralph Estes, now head of the activist Stakeholder Alliance in Washington, D.C., in 1999 floated a draft constitutional amendment for his alliance possibly to champion, primarily as an educational tool. His suggested language was brief: "A corporation is not a natural person under the U.S. Constitution."[24]

These are useful proposals, and certainly denying corporations constitutional protections would be an enormous step forward. Yet I remain unconvinced that corporate personhood is really the root issue. It seems to me only the latest hiding place for wealth privilege. And as we have seen, the Supreme Court has already found ways to protect that privilege without explicitly resorting to notions of personhood. So it might find ways around even these amendments. In addition, these proposed amendments state what the corporation is *not*, but they say nothing about what it is— so our towering skyscrapers of corporate law would still remain empty.

A more proactive approach has been suggested by Rabbi Michael Lerner, publisher of *Tikkun* magazine, who in 1997 proposed the Social Responsibility Amendment to the U.S. Constitution. It would require every U.S. corporation with annual revenues of $20 million or more to apply for a new corporate charter every twenty years. To receive this charter, the corporation would have to prove it served the common good, which would be demonstrated by producing an Ethical Impact Report every five years.[25]

Although Lerner may take us closer to a definition of what a corporation should be, his proposal seems too detailed for the constitutional level. It has the flavor more of statutory law, and is probably more appropriate for the state than the federal level. But even as a statute, it would leave the public only one tool—charter revocation.

If we added to that an expanded notion of fiduciary duty backed up by lawsuits, accompanied by internal democratic governance, we might go further. What I would say we're groping toward in corporate definition is some combination of public and private ends: corporations should serve the public interest, but they also must make a profit. Finally, we might use an amendment to attack not only corporate privilege but wealth privilege itself.

Drawn in these terms, a constitutional amendment—or at least a definition of the corporation—might look something like this:

> In keeping with equal treatment of persons before the law, the wealthy may not claim greater rights than other persons, and corporations may not claim the rights of persons. The public corporation is a semipublic body, composed of both property and persons, and these persons include employees. The public corporation is to be chartered by states to serve both public and private interests and is to be governed internally by democratic processes.

Such an amendment would eliminate shareholder primacy, while leaving a legitimate place for some property ownership rights in the corporation. Though it wouldn't explicitly mention other stakeholder interests—like the environment—such interests would be subsumed in the public interest. Democratic governance that would include employee participation would be mandated, with details to be worked out by legislatures or companies. And the ability of wealthy persons to dominate the political process would be ended, because they could not claim greater rights than others.

Of course, we might take a far simpler approach and outlaw wealth privilege itself, mimicking the ERA in saying, "Equality of rights under the law shall not be denied or abridged on account of wealth." That would presumably take care of shareholder primacy and campaign finance. It might lead inevitably to democratic internal governance of corporations. Or if we wanted to attract more constituents to lobby for an amendment, we could tackle three forms of ancient discrimination at once: "Equality of rights under the law shall not be denied or abridged on account of race, sex, or wealth." Interesting to think about what discussions that might arouse.

Seeking Restitution Under the Existing Constitution

In the end, we may not even need a constitutional amendment, for essential principles are already there in the Constitution: in the broad principle of one person, one vote; the principle of equality under the law; and explicitly in the Fourteenth Amendment—which says the states may not "abridge the privileges or immunities" of any citizen, nor deny to any person "the equal protection of the laws."[26] It seems that race and sex discrimination—even wealth discrimination—might all be taken care of right there.

When the states create corporations and judges declare they must serve wealth holders alone, the rights of nonwealthy persons under law are abridged. When the legislative process is dominated by wealthy persons, or by corporations representing wealthy persons, the rights of the nonwealthy are abridged.

Such arguments may be at least conceptually worth making, even if they won't fly in today's Supreme Court.

ॐ

But if conceptual arguments are one thing, more tangible legal battles are already being fought against the presumed rights of corporations and wealth. Consider the matter of corporate welfare, particularly state incentives for corporate relocation. In 1995, North Carolina attorney Bill Maready won a case at state trial court level that was bracingly clear: using taxpayer dollars to attract business was an unconstitutional use of public money for private purposes. Unfortunately, the case was overturned by the North Carolina Supreme Court.[27]

Since then, however, the composition of the state high court has changed, and it may be well disposed to a new challenge, says John Hood, president of the John Locke Foundation in Raleigh. He told *Business Ethics* he might work with citizen groups to file a lawsuit, to once again challenge corporate incentives. Possible grounds could be the North Carolina constitutional requirement of just and equitable taxation. "Charging different corporations different tax rates violates that clause," he said. Hood also was considering a federal lawsuit using the commerce clause. "The argument there is that Congress is solely authorized to regulate interstate commerce, and states cannot erect trade barriers," he explained. Thus, giving a tax break solely to an in-state firm constitutes an illegal tariff.[28]

Equal protection under the law is the constitutional angle recommended by attorney Dwight Brannon of Dayton, Ohio. He sued state and local officials and the Hobart Corporation on behalf of former employees who lost their jobs when the company moved twenty miles from Dayton to Piqua, Ohio—because of $2 million in incentives. "It didn't increase employment one job," he said. "No one benefited but the corporation, and it had the highest earnings in its history last year," he said in 1999.[29]

ᘓ

If corporations can use the Constitution in novel ways, so can others. If creative lawyers can use an amendment protecting slaves to protect corporations, surely we can dream up some creative approaches of our own.

Here's one clause I'd like to see dusted off—for consciousness-raising at least, and conceivably for more substantive challenges. It's found in Article I, Section 9 of the Constitution, and it states, "No Title of Nobility shall be granted by the United States."[30]

Now, obviously, throughout this book I have been arguing that the rights of wealth today have created a kind of aristocracy—when the creation of an aristocracy is explicitly outlawed in the U.S. Constitution. The argument goes like this: aristocratic titles, broadly interpreted, constitute a right to a stream of income in perpetuity, detached from productive activity. So when states allow corporations to grant titles of stock in perpetuity, and when they enshrine shareholder rights as superior in law, they have unconstitutionally created aristocratic titles. This might be one angle for attacking the problem of eternal stock ownership.

The nobility clause might also prove useful in a battle to reinstate the estate tax, which is to be phased out by 2010—at least temporarily, perhaps permanently—under legislation recently passed. If aristocratic titles are a right to a stream of income, they're also a right to pass on title to wealth unimpeded from one generation to the next, and thus to create a dynasty. We might use such an argument to say eliminating the estate tax is unconstitutional. Or we might attack varying tax rates on the same ground. Surely it is aristocratic to say that when I labor, my income should be taxed at 33 percent; when I invest, my income should be taxed at 20 percent; and when I inherit, my income should be taxed not at all.

In the matter of inheritance laws, we can find support for an egalitarian approach in Alexis de Tocqueville's writing. In *Democracy in America*, he challenged any scheme of inheritance that "vests property and power in a few hands," saying that it "causes an aristocracy, so to speak, to spring out of the ground."[31]

The whole idea of inheritance itself—in an extreme view—can be considered aristocratic. Instead of simply fighting to reinstate the estate tax, we might one day challenge the very notion of inheritance, or at least try limiting it to some reasonable amount. If we are seriously committed to an economy of equality, how can persons ever be equal when one person is able to start the game already having won it?

&

Despite his own aristocratic standing, Thomas Jefferson might have supported a challenge to inheritance rights. For he once mocked the very idea of a wealth-based aristocracy, writing of the attempt by military officers to create the order of the Cincinnati, which would have endowed a permanent fund "to secure their descendants against want." He wrote scathingly:

> Why afraid to trust them to the same fertile soil, and the same genial climate which will secure from want the descendants of their other fellow citizens? Are they afraid they will be reduced to labor the earth for their sustenance? They will be rendered thereby both

honester and happier. An industrious farmer occupies a more dignified place in the scale of beings, whether moral or political, than a lazy lounger, valuing himself on his family, too proud to work, and drawing out a miserable existence by eating on that surplus of other men's labour.[32]

It is not wealth or property or inheritance Jefferson exalts, but labor—and labor not in a onetime sense, like the labor of the entrepreneur, but labor in an ongoing sense: the labor of generation upon generation. What he exalts is the right to create wealth, not to inherit it.

Principles like these—in the writing of Jefferson and de Tocqueville, and in the Constitution itself—are part of our common democratic heritage, and we can call upon them. By untangling the twisted legal reasoning under which wealth privilege and corporate privilege hide today, we can begin to create public determination for reform.

Since the early 1800s, wealth privilege has not dared to speak its name aloud, but we can speak it—and in so doing discredit it. Our nation may now consider the rights of wealth and corporations in a certain sense lawful, but we need not remain paralyzed in the grip of this inert violence. There are ways—large and small, creative and prosaic—that we can use the law and its principles to agitate for real justice. For until we have justice in the economic realm, we can never become what we profess to be in the political realm: a nation dedicated to equality under the law.

12

A Little Rebellion

THE PRINCIPLE OF (R)EVOLUTION

As it is the right of the people to alter or abolish government,
it is the right of the people to alter or abolish the
corporations that now govern the world.

What remains is the task of marshaling public resolve for change by stirring up a little rebellion. As Thomas Jefferson once wrote, "A little rebellion now and then is a good thing, & as necessary in the political world as storms in the physical."[1]

We need rebellious steps that move us toward revolutionary change—not a French Revolution, but something more akin to the British Glorious Revolution. That is to say, we should aim not for an overthrow of the whole edifice, but for change within an established framework; not for an abolition of stockholder rights, but for extending those rights from stockholders to others, and adding new rights.

We need revolution not so much in terms of revolt but in its original, Copernican sense of return—the revolution that planets make in their orbits as they return to their starting stations. We must return, in some measure, to the traditional liberties that were America's founding ideals: the liberty of states to control corporations, the liberty of casting a vote that has substance, the liberty of enjoying the fruits of our own labor, and the liberty of individuals to enjoy equality under law. These are the liberties that corporations and the wealthy have usurped, and they are liberties we can rightfully reclaim.

It begins with enlightenment. It begins with public acts that raise the public consciousness about the need for change and point to the principles to be embraced. This may be a complex business, but it can best be approached with acts that are simple and immediately compelling.

The American Revolution was itself a complex business, but it began with a prankster's revolt—folks protesting the tea tax by dressing up in native garb and throwing boxes of tea off of ships. The Stamp Act brought further pranks. When Britain began requiring an official stamp on all documents—with an accompanying tax—newspaper editors devised a mocking death's head "stamp," which they printed where the official stamp was to go. Working people, meanwhile, created a secret society called the Sons of Liberty, "solemnly pledged to resist the execution of the obnoxious law." [2]

In other mischief-making, Samuel Adams helped found the ingenious Committees of Correspondence, which organized opposition to the Crown throughout the colonies, and functioned as a kind of government-in-waiting. By the end of their first year, 1772, such committees were in place in more than eighty towns. As historian John Fiske wrote in *The American Revolution*, the Committee of Correspondence was "a new legislative body, springing directly from the people": "It was always virtually in session, and no governor could dissolve . . . it. Though unknown to the law, the creation of it involved no violation of law. . . . The power thus created was omnipresent, but intangible." [3]

Through such acts of resistance, American Revolutionaries gained widespread support for their principles, such as no taxation without representation, while they left wrangling over the details of the Constitution for later. America was born long before the writing of complex laws. It was born in rebellion.

THE RIGHT TO REVOKE CORPORATE CHARTERS

As early Americans fought the centralized power of the Crown, today we fight the centralized power of corporations and wealth. It is time once again to recognize the principle of revolution: *As it is the right of the people to alter or abolish government, it is the right of the people to alter or abolish the corporations that now govern the world.*

That the American people have the right to abolish corporations is no insubstantial, theoretical right—it is a right still present in all state constitutions as the right to revoke corporate charters.[4] Such revocation should not be undertaken, as Jefferson might have reminded us, "for light and transient causes." But when "a long train of abuses" has occurred, it is the people's "right, it is their duty," to put a stop to those abuses.[5] And in the past, this was a power often used. In the mid-1800s, oil, match, sugar, and whiskey trusts found their charters revoked in Ohio, Michigan, and Nebraska. Turnpike corporations in Massachusetts and New York lost their charters for "not keeping their roads in repair."[6]

Writing limitations into charters was a related power. State legislatures once limited corporate existence to a fixed number of years, spelled out permissible lines of business, and held business owners liable for harms. In Maryland, for example, manufacturing charters were granted for forty years, and many others for only thirty years. "Unless a legislature renewed an expiring charter, the corporation was dissolved and its assets were divided among shareholders," Grossman writes.[7]

Today, Grossman writes, "In all states, legislatures continue to have the historic and the legal obligation to grant, to amend, and to revoke corporate charters." In Illinois, the existing law states that a circuit court may dissolve a corporation if it abuses its authority or continues to violate the law. In New York, dissolution is by jury trial and is required when a corporation abuses its power or acts "contrary to the public policy" of the citizenry.[8]

❧

Charter revocation was little used throughout most of the twentieth century, though there have been recent attempts to put it back in use. In 1998, for example, Loyola law professor Robert Benson and a coalition of dozens of public interest organizations petitioned the California attorney general to revoke the charter of Union Oil of California (Unocal), in part because of environmental and human rights abuses.[9] Also in 1998, Alabama Circuit Judge William Wynn sought to revoke the charters of five major cigarette companies.[10]

Though neither effort succeeded, such attempts do remind the public that operating as a corporation is a privilege bestowed by law, and it can be withdrawn from law-breaking companies.

Because charter revocation can be used only against the most egregious corporate lawbreakers, it is a tool of limited use in any enduring scheme of governance. A bludgeon may have its uses, but it's not something to pick up very often. On the other hand, charter revocation is quite useful as a tool of rebellion. Its aim is to raise consciousness about the ultimate power the public retains over corporations.

If this realization is to take root, the editors of *Adbusters* magazine suggest that "the charter revocation movement needs one precedent, one notorious corporate criminal metaphorically sent to the electric chair." In that spirit, the magazine has called for a movement to revoke the charter of Philip Morris, in an attempt to make it the poster child for this emerging movement.[11]

The Right to Alter Corporations

Charter revocation attempts might be viewed as a warning shot across the bow, a wake-up call rather than a tool of governance. The more vital governing power is the right to alter and control corporations.

Here too we retain power in law, and as attorney Thomas Linzey of the Community Environmental Legal Defense Fund has shown, that power can be put to use. He recently helped two townships in Pennsylvania, for example, to pass ordinances prohibiting corporate ownership of farms. At least three other Pennsylvania townships are considering similar ordinances. They are modeled on language used in constitutional amendments adopted in Nebraska and South Dakota, which also prohibit corporate ownership of farms.[12]

Taking a different approach, Wayne Township of Pennsylvania in 1998 passed a three-strikes-and-you're-out ordinance, preventing any corporation from doing business in the township if it has a "history of consistent violations"—defined as three violations over the past fifteen years. This would include any violation of local, state, or federal statutory or regulatory law.[13]

This three-strikes-and-you're-out approach is compelling, for it makes the point—more strongly than charter revocation—that corporate lawbreakers can lose their license to do business. It reflects a concept floated by William Greider in *Who Will Tell the People: The Betrayal of American Democracy*, where he suggested that we must "raise the bottom line cost of lawlessness"—creating "meaningful sanctions" for lawless corporations "in the only language that an 'artificial legal person' understands: profit and loss."[14]

A rare offense is one thing, Greider notes, but repeated offenses should meet with graduated penalties. At the federal level, we might, for example, establish a "felonious status for 'corporate citizens'" that bars them from campaign financing or lobbying—in the same way that we deny political rights to human felons. A recidivist corporation could also be required to divest a subsidiary with a record of fraud, or be ineligible to hold government licenses or contracts.[15]

For at least a short time recently, barring corporate felons from government contracts was the law. Under administrative rules issued by President Bill Clinton on his way out the door in December 2000, contracts were disallowed with companies that had a record of breaking labor or environmental laws. Federal contracting officials were to award contracts only to businesses with "a satisfactory record of integrity and business ethics."[16] Unfortunately, the Bush administration almost immediately set out to overturn this promising though short-lived rule.

But even the attempt to enact this law shows that there are ways, in the existing framework, to make the point that corporate privileges can be lost. When we begin putting laws and regulations like these to full use, it will represent a vital step toward establishing a core principle: corporations must not harm the public good.

Extralegal approaches to raising public consciousness can also be explored, and this might be done by various groups—like employees, business students, investors, citizens, pension fund beneficiaries, activists, unions, and even CEOs. Many of these approaches can be pursued in the prankster's spirit of early American Revolutionaries.

A Manual for Rebellion

Consider the following, then, a manual for a little rebellion.

Ideas for Employees

The point of any effective rebellion is to unsettle settled assumptions—for example, the assumption that only stockholders have a right to vote in corporations. But what about employees?

This issue might be raised by a prank in which some courageous employee runs for the board of directors—in the tradition of Rosa Parks refusing to sit in the back of the bus. He or she could put up campaign posters on cubicle walls. And employees with a few shares of stock could get their hands on proxy ballots and effectively stuff the ballot box with a write-in candidate.

Since this is likely to get a person fired, it should be staged by someone planning to quit anyway. Or anonymous employees could put some fictitious figure (John Q. Employee) on the ballot. Press coverage of the prank might raise interesting issues: Why aren't employees represented in corporate governance?

As feminist rebels once staged a protest at the Miss America Pageant, employees might stage protests at stockholders' meetings, hanging a sign at the entrance saying, "Property restrictions on voting were removed 150 years ago. Why are they still in place in this corporation?" Employees might wear sandwich boards saying, "No Governance Without Representation."

When companies hand out documents to employees, requiring them to understate their hours or pledge never to sue the corporation, some might resurrect the Revolutionary death's head stamp, putting it where their signatures are to go. To maintain anonymity, they could duplicate the documents with names removed, and deluge management with defaced documents, perhaps slipping one to a sympathetic local journalist.

When a buyout is in the offing, employees might protest the notion they are being "sold" along with the firm's other "assets." They could come to work wearing T-shirts saying, "I am 'goodwill' and Company XYZ is buying me. Where's my check?"

If such a move unsettles notions of ownership, there are other notions worth unsettling as well—like the idea that civil liberties are left at the company door. To challenge this, employees might refuse drug tests en masse. After all, the Fourth Amendment to the Constitution says, "The right of the people to be secure in their persons . . . against unreasonable searches and seizures, shall not be violated." It does not say "except by corporations."

Knowledge employees might assert a right to the fruits of their own labors by challenging or refusing to sign noncompete clauses, since it is unjust in a free market to limit competition. Some day, daring employees might even launch a "Dorr's Rebellion," writing their own constitution and electing their own CEO.

&

These kinds of protests may seem all but unthinkable today because of the long tradition of employees as obedient servants. To stir a sense of power, employees might try the feminist tactic of the consciousness-raising group—held off company property and anonymously, so grievances can be aired with no fear of exposure. Some group might even be formed to sponsor such gatherings. Call it the Sons and Daughters of Liberty.

Like the American Revolutionaries before them, employees will be fighting for their own self-interest as well as a just economy. We can unite employee and public interests. That's the kind of force that makes positive and lasting change possible.

Ideas for Business Students

The movement for a democratic economy will ultimately need leaders at the managerial level, and today's business students can become those leaders.

They can start by challenging the hidden bias in what they are taught. An example was set by a rebel group of students at Harvard called Students for Humane and Responsible Economics (SHARE). In Economics 10—taught by Martin Feldstein, former adviser to Ronald

Reagan—students are told they're learning "positive" economics, which describes reality, rather than "normative" economics, which is based on norms or biases. In 1997, students Stephanie Greenwood, Ian Simmons, and others challenged the notion that "objective economic analysis can exist at all." They quoted Nelson Mandela saying that the ideas of economists "operated in the interests of the powerful and not the poorest of the poor." Feldstein finally gave them fifteen minutes in class. After they were written up in *Dollars and Sense,* an alternative economics magazine, they were contacted by people around the nation hoping to support them.[17]

In management courses, students might write papers developing the concept of "stockholder productivity," researching funding of local firms to determine when new equity was sold, in what amounts, and how much return stockholders have since received. They might ask, Is perpetual and increasing return, detached from productive contribution, justifiable in a free market? If they find the data as difficult to gather as I have, they might ask why.

Graduate students might do research to determine how much companies, for example ad agencies, would be worth without their employees. They could develop guidelines for making such judgments, and publish the results in academic journals.

Accounting students could take up the question of defining human capital, asking if it is something that can be owned and if so, who owns it? How could it be represented on the balance sheet?

Outside of classes, students might work with professors to sponsor essay contests or debates. One topic might be, Is the corporation an object that can be owned, a human community, or some combination of both? Given whatever identity one argues for, what then are the appropriate rights and responsibilities for that identity?

More intrepid business students might imitate the feminists who took over the offices of *The Ladies' Home Journal* and refused to leave until allowed to put out a special issue on feminism. Business students could sit in at a business magazine, and insist on a special issue on economic democracy.

Ideas for Investors

Investors can also use their power to challenge the system design. The best way to do so today is to become a social investor, placing funds with socially responsible mutual funds or money management companies. Currently this is the only way for investors to even start being responsible, and supporting this community is critical. By placing funds with these firms, investors are in effect employing sophisticated professionals to make the case for a stakeholder approach to management.

Social investing professionals can begin pushing the envelope—taking their work to a structural level by lobbying the SEC for greater social disclosure. For it may be investors alone who will be heard by the SEC. They might also start an SEC campaign to change the rules for shareholder resolutions, starting with the absurd company practice of reporting only the votes that are *for* a proposal ("just 5 percent approved this proposal"), which leaves the impression that all others voted against it. In truth many proxies may not have been voted at all, and this should be reported. If we permitted such a system in elections, it would be like saying all who cast no ballot had voted for the incumbent.

A still bigger challenge might be to lobby the SEC to make resolutions binding. For if even shareholders can't govern corporations, to whom are managers accountable? The prospect of binding resolutions would change the game dramatically.

Investing professionals can also help colleagues and clients begin openly questioning the system's biases—like the assumption that maximum profit is always the goal. A courageous lead was taken here by Bob Lincoln, senior portfolio manager and chief strategist for United States Trust Company of Boston, which has a social investing division called Walden Asset Management. In a newsletter to clients, Lincoln suggested that modest future growth in the stock market, rather than the maximum growth of recent years, would in fact represent "a healthy change." For by pressing for profits beyond a reasonable point, he said, investors contribute to the widening gap in income distribution. As he put it, "There is little doubt that, in the long run, economic growth that is not shared more equitably will prove to be unsustainable."[18]

Ideas for Citizens and Pension Fund Beneficiaries

It's important to remember that some of the largest pools of investments today are held by public bodies like states and pension funds, and citizens can begin to assert control over these public funds.

Citizens might lobby state treasurers to do as California State Treasurer Philip Angelides did in 1999, when he announced a new policy of "smart investments," which meant supporting sustainable development, livable communities, and environmental responsibility. In just one example, California now directs its $1.4 billion in low-cost infrastructure loans toward projects that help revitalize struggling communities.[19]

Elsewhere in California, the $2.9 billion Contra Costa County employee pension fund voted to divest tobacco holdings, and to begin voting corporate proxies in favor of environmental and social justice issues. Progressive Asset Management cofounder Peter Camejo helped create the impetus for this change, and he says that he hopes other counties will follow. Citizen input can help.[20]

Ideas for CEOs

Even CEOs have a role to play in the revolution, and doing so may well turn them from villains into heroes. Perhaps one day we will see the emergence of a kind of Nelson Mandela of Coca-Cola, or a Thomas Jefferson of Hewlett-Packard—someone willing to make his or her corporation a true model of economic democracy. Such leaders might start by awarding generous stock options, setting up substantial ESOPs, and establishing a place in governance for employees. They may find their companies enlivened in the process, because putting wealth in the hands of those who create it taps the fundamental genius of capitalism.

Though such changes would start as voluntary initiatives, CEOs or chairmen could help the board write democratic structures into corporate bylaws. They might stipulate that bylaws can be changed only by two-thirds vote of both employee and stockholder representatives, helping protect firms from hostile takeovers. Employee-owned firms might be a place to start.

CEOs could also step forward and test stakeholder statutes, rather than simply buckling under the pressure to sell to the highest bidder. Executives are best positioned to make the argument to the courts that a hostile takeover will not serve employees or the local community, and judges might be inclined to listen. If they fail in the courts, CEOs might lead a campaign among legislators to amend state stakeholder statutes.

Ideas for Activists

While we need patricians, we also need the grassroots. To help activists set things in motion, we may need schools for revolutionaries—like the one James Lawson created in the 1960s for his "Nashville kids." He trained students to become leaders in fighting racial segregation, and they in turn led others in lunch-counter sit-ins at Nashville stores.[21]

One existing school for revolutionaries is the Program on Corporations, Law and Democracy (POCLAD), which trains members in resisting corporate rule.[22] Though POCLAD is small, it speaks with a loud voice, for it was the ideas of POCLAD's Richard Grossman that inspired Robert Benson's move to pull Unocal's charter. And it was POCLAD-affiliated folks—like Paul Cienfuegos—who sponsored the innovative Measure F, the Arcata (California) Advisory Initiative on Democracy and Corporations. Passed in 1998, this law required the city to hold town hall meetings to discuss the topic, "Can we have democracy when large corporations wield so much power and wealth under law?"[23]

A kickoff point for activists might be a national day of action, along the lines of the first Earth Day in 1970. *Adbusters* magazine has proposed repackaging the Fourth of July as a Day of Resistance Against Corporate Rule. Such a day, they say, could draw attention to the sovereignty and independence people have lost to corporations, at a time when the nation is celebrating its freedom.[24]

Ideas for Unions

Unions could get in on the act as part of the movement to revive their own democratic legacy. In the early years, labor leaders focused on a broad goal of universal emancipation, and only later focused narrowly on benefiting certain categories of workers, which was one factor in the weakening of unions. But as Bill Fletcher, education director of the AFL-CIO, has said, unions can be "instruments for much more than narrow collective bargaining purposes." They can be agents of "social change and transformation."[25]

To help reestablish unions as a force serving all employees, they might join activists and social investors in a national campaign to make wage data public. Pricing information is a fundamental piece of what makes markets work, yet the price of labor is a closely guarded secret. At one company, employees were told that if they discussed wages, they'd be fired. At another company, Steve Jobs's Pixar, the anonymous e-mail distribution of accurate salaries for all four hundred employees led to a firestorm.[26] Such secrecy is unconscionable—yet it's protected by companies, because it makes expropriation possible.

A lobbying effort could be launched for an Employee Right to Know Act, modeled on the Community Right to Know Act, which mandated corporate disclosure of certain pollutants through a Toxics Release Inventory. Although that act didn't mandate reductions, it did have that result (at least for listed chemicals). In effect, it embarrassed corporations into reducing pollution. A similar law for employees might embarrass corporations into paying higher wages—if they were exposed, for example, in a "poverty census," tallying how many company employees receive wages so low that they qualify for food stamps.

Generating Public Discussion

Through all these rebellious acts, the point is to generate public discussion, to help the public grasp new ideas in simple forms. If the right's agenda has succeeded so magnificently in recent years, it is because its ideas have often been presented in simple terms, like the "death tax." We need similar ideas that will be compelling to journalists, legislators, and the public.

I believe we can find those ideas by returning to the fundamental principles of democracy, for as Alexander Hamilton once said, "the best way of determining disputes" is to ascend to the simplest principles.[27] Today the principles we need are starkly simple, like the principle that corporations must not harm the public good, that employees are part of the corporation, that wealth belongs to those who create it, and that community wealth belongs to all.

We need to inspire broad discussion on such matters—like the discussions in the early years of America, when, as historian Gordon S. Wood observed, even "'peasants and housewives in every part of the land' had begun 'to dispute on politics.'" What they disputed was not complex law but elementary principles, and it was vital that these be broadly understood. For as Josiah Quincy wrote in 1774, if democratic principles were made the "object of universal attention and study," then the rights of humankind could no longer be buried "under systems of civil and priestly hierarchy."[28] If democratic principles of economics were understood today, our rights might no longer be buried under obscure judicial decisions, or lost in the mumbo jumbo of economics and financial analysis.

What can nourish this new understanding is what nourished the American Revolution, which was a combination of three things: an outpouring of political writing, public acts of rebellion, and joint action through organizations like the Committees of Correspondence.

We need more such organizations today. Where, for example, is the ACLU of economic democracy? Where is the NOW to fight discrimination against employees? Where is the Sierra Club of social investors? We need membership organizations like these, as well as think tanks to develop research and disseminate ideas. We need leaders to get things started, and funders to back them. And we need good connections among various groups, via leadership networks and the Internet, so that like the original committees, our working groups can be always "virtually in session" and cannot be dissolved. The power thus created might be intangible but omnipresent. It could make of our separate battles one battle.

A Change of Mind

It all begins with a change of mind. As Joel Barlow suggested in a 1792 work, what separates the free from the unfree of the world is merely a "habit of thinking." Many "astonishing effects," he wrote, "are wrought in the world by the *habit of thinking*" (italics in original). In America, he said, it was the thought "that all men are equal in their rights" that created the Revolution.[29]

Today the time has come for new democratic thoughts: that all persons have equal economic rights, that corporations are subordinate to the people. These are revolutionary concepts, and it is new habits of thinking that bring them into being.

❧

If change begins in the mind, it unfolds into reality through historical moments—through times when the public consciousness cracks open and new ideas can rush in. Financial crisis is one way such an opening can develop, as we saw in the 1930s. But there is another way to open a space for system change, and that is through crisis at the level of legitimacy, crisis at the level of ideas, as happened with feminism in the 1970s.

What will create the opening, we cannot know. But that an opening will come seems probable, for history has shown democracy to be an unstoppable historical force. If it has not stopped at the doors of kings, it is not likely to stop at the door of the financial aristocracy.

The right to rebel against such powers is a right people have retained since the time of the Magna Carta. It was a right John Locke recognized when he stated that the purpose of his *Two Treatises of Government* was to provide the philosophical foundation for revolution.[30] It was a right Thomas Jefferson recognized when he wrote the words that today, more than two centuries later, still retain the power to stir the blood:

> We hold these truths to be self-evident: that all men are created
> equal; that they are endowed by their creator with certain inalienable
> rights; that among these are life, liberty, and the pursuit of happiness;

that to secure these rights, governments are instituted among men, deriving their just powers from the consent of the governed; that whenever any form of government becomes destructive of these ends, it is the right of the people to alter or abolish it, and to institute new government, laying its foundation on such principles, and organizing its powers in such form, as to them shall seem most likely to effect their safety and happiness.[31]

Corporations today are governments of the propertied class, exercising power over Americans that is greater than the power once exercised by kings. They are governments that have become destructive of our inalienable rights as a people. We can end their illegitimate reign and institute a new economic government, laying its foundation on such principles as seem most likely to effect our safety and happiness. We can one day complete the design in the economic realm that the framers began in the political realm, the design of *novus ordo seclorum*—a new order of the ages.

Notes

PREFACE

1. In 1998, "about 90 percent of the total value of stocks, bonds, trusts, and business equity were held by the top 10 percent of households," according to Edward N. Wolff, professor of economics, New York University, in "What Has Happened to Stock Ownership in the United States?" unpublished paper, September 2000. Citing data Wolff compiled, Economic Policy Institute researchers note that the share of household wealth held by the richest 1 percent of individuals in 1976 was about 20 percent; in 1997, that 1 percent held an estimated 39.1 percent. Wealth was defined as net worth (household assets minus debt). See Lawrence Mishel, Jared Bernstein, and John Schmitt, *The State of Working America: 1998–99* (Ithaca, N.Y.: Cornell University Press, 1999), 261–262, table nos. 5B, 5.5.
2. My father, James Kelly, founded Graphic Engraving Inc. in Columbia, Missouri, after World War II. My maternal grandfather, C. M. Anderson, founded Anderson Tool and Die from his basement in Chicago during the Depression. I am cofounder, with Miriam Kniaz, of Mavis Publications, Inc. in Minneapolis, publisher of *Business Ethics* [www.business-ethics.com].

INTRODUCTION

1. In 1999, sales of new common stock were $105.7 billion, according to *Federal Reserve Bulletin* figures compiled in *Statistical Abstract of the United States, 2000* (Washington, D.C.: U.S. Census Bureau, 2000), 523. Also in 1999, the total value of all shares traded was $20.4 trillion; sales of new common stock represent less than 1 percent of all stock trading. This was typical of the 1990s.

2. Eldon S. Hendriksen, *Capital Expenditures in the Steel Industry, 1900 to 1953*, The Development of Contemporary Accounting Thought Series (New York: Arno Press, 1978), 143–177.

3. Karl R. Popper, *The Open Society and Its Enemies, Vol. 1: The Spell of Plato* (Princeton, N.J.: Princeton University Press, 1966 [originally published 1943]), 70.

4. Wolff, "Stock Ownership."

5. Paul Hawken, interview with Sarah van Gelder, "The Next Reformation," *In Context*, Summer 1995, 41, 17–22; cited by David C. Korten, *The Post-Corporate World: Life After Capitalism* (West Hartford, Conn.: Kumarian Press, and San Francisco: Berrett-Koehler, 1999), 65.

6. The value of all stocks listed on exchanges in 1948 was $81.9 billion; in 1998 it was $10.5 trillion, a 128-fold increase, according to the 1996 and 1999 annual reports of the Securities and Exchange Commission, p. 211 (1996 report), p. 195 (1999 report). The description of environmental decline is paraphrased from *The State of the World 1998* report from the Worldwatch Institute, cited by Korten, *Post-Corporate World*, 67.

7. This fact was noted by David C. Korten in *When Corporations Rule the World* (San Francisco: Berrett-Koehler, and West Hartford, Conn.: Kumarian Press, 1995), 220. Korten cited 1991 GNP data versus corporate sales data, and found fifty of the one hundred largest economies were corporations; the number has since been updated to fifty-one.

8. Franklin D. Roosevelt, acceptance speech, Democratic National Convention, June 27, 1936; quoted by Ralph Estes, *Tyranny of the Bottom Line: Why Corporations Make Good People Do Bad Things* (San Francisco: Berrett-Koehler, 1996), 88.

9. Francis Fukuyama, *The End of History and the Last Man* (New York: Free Press, 1992), 15. In a chapter titled "The Weakness of Strong States," RAND Corporation consultant Fukuyama observed, "The critical weakness that eventually toppled these strong states was in the last analysis a failure of legitimacy—that is, a crisis on the level of ideas."

10. Michel Foucault, *Discipline and Punish: The Birth of the Prison* (New York: Vintage Books, 1975), 102–103. Foucault wrote, "A stupid despot may constrain his slaves with iron chains; but a true politician binds them even more strongly by the chain of their own ideas . . . this link is all the stronger in that we do not know of what it is made and we believe it to be our own work. . . . on the soft fibers of the brain is founded the unshakable base of the soundest of Empires."

CHAPTER 1

1. Theo Aronson, *Crowns in Conflict: The Triumph and Tragedy of European Monarchy 1910–1918* (Manchester, N.H.: Salem House, 1986), 187.

2. David Cannadine, *The Decline and Fall of the British Aristocracy* (New York: Anchor Books/Doubleday, 1990), 8.

3. Cannadine, *Decline and Fall*, 2, 15.

4. Arthur O. Lovejoy, *The Great Chain of Being: A Study of the History of an Idea*, The William James Lectures Delivered at Harvard University, 1933 (Cambridge, Mass.: Harvard University Press, 1936), 7.

5. Edward W. Said, *Culture and Imperialism* (New York: Vintage Books, 1994 [originally published 1993]), 225.

6. Those making poverty-level wage or below were 30 percent of the workforce in 1995, up from 24 percent in 1979. Poverty-level wage is the "hourly wage a full-time, year-round worker must earn to sustain a family of four at the poverty threshold, which was $7.28 in 1995 (in 1994 dollars)." Lawrence Mishel, Jared Bernstein, and John Schmitt, *The State of Working America: 1996–97* (Washington, D.C.: Economic Policy Institute, 1996), 147–148.

7. Center on Budget and Policy Priorities, Washington, D.C., cited in "Rising Tide, Falling Boats," *The Economist*, Dec. 20, 1997, 28.

8. Robert F. Kennedy Jr., "Petrofied Forest: How American and Ecuadorian Oil Firms Slimed the Oriente Forest," *The Village Voice*, Feb. 12, 1991, 17. Other oil companies are involved in Amazon drilling, although Texaco has been a leader. According to Kennedy, "Production pits dump an astounding 4.3 million gallons of toxic production wastes and treatment chemicals each day into the Amazon rivers, streams, and groundwater." The practice of burying toxic drilling muds is industrywide.

9. Kennedy, "Petrofied Forest," 18.

CHAPTER 2

1. A long discussion of the difference between gentlemen and commoners in early America is found in Gordon S. Wood, *The Radicalism of the American Revolution* (New York: Vintage Books, 1991), 24–42. The pretense that economic work is for pleasure is noted on p. 36; "the only Gentlemanlike Way of growing rich . . . ," p. 38. The John Adams quote, from his *Defence of the Constitution of the United States*, written 1787–88, is cited by Wood in footnote 1, p. 374.

2. Wood, *American Revolution*, 33.

3. *Whitaker's Peerage, Baronetage, Knightage, and Companionage for the Year 1914* (London: Whitaker's, 1913), 11.

4. C.B.A. Behrens, *The Ancien Régime* (London: Thames and Hudson, 1967), 107–108.

5. Reinhard Bendix, *Kings or People: Power and the Mandate to Rule* (Berkeley and Los Angeles: University of California Press, 1978), 336.

6. George Rudé, *The French Revolution: Its Causes, Its History, and Its Legacy After 200 Years* (New York: Grove Press, 1988), 2.

7. Bendix, *Kings or People*, 376.

8. Alexis de Tocqueville, *The Old Regime and the French Revolution* (New York: Anchor Books/Doubleday, 1983), 31.

9. de Tocqueville, *Old Regime*, 30.

10. A commemorative medal celebrating France's revolutionary National Assembly of Aug. 4, 1789, shows the delegates assembled under the slogan, *"Abandon de tous les privileges"*—Abandon all privileges. Cited by Bendix, *Kings or People*, 376.

11. Staff, Social Sciences I (eds.), *The People Shall Judge: Readings in the Formation of American Policy*, Vol. 1, Part 1 (Chicago: University of Chicago Press, 1949), 235. John Adams was complaining about the new aristocracy arising from "banks and land-jobbing," in a letter to Thomas Jefferson, December 19, 1813.

12. *Clean Yield Newsletter* (Greensboro, Vt.: Clean Yield Asset Management), Feb. 5, 1998, 3.

13. Private-sector real (inflation-adjusted) hourly wages from 1987 to 1997 dropped from $15.87 to $14.72, a decline of 7.2 percent, according to Bureau of Labor statistics, analyzed by Mishel, Bernstein, and Schmitt, *Working America: 1998–99*, 126.

14. The number for 1999 sales of new common stock is from Federal Reserve data in *Statistical Abstract of the United States, 2000* (Washington, D.C.: U.S. Census Bureau, 2000), 523. The value of all public shares traded in 1999 is from figures supplied by the Securities Industry Association in Washington, D.C.

15. The value of all exchange-listed stock in 1998 ($10.5 trillion) is from *1999 Annual Report of the Securities and Exchange Commission*, 195; 1999 value ($11.6 billion) is from SEC phone interview. The value of common stock issued by U.S. corporations ($83 billion in 1998) is from Federal Reserve data in *Statistical Abstract 2000*, 523. This second figure does not include private placements or preferred stock. A footnote explains that it represents gross proceeds and excludes secondary offerings and employee stock plans.

16. Federal Reserve Flow of Funds Accounts of the United States [www.federalreserve.gov].

17. The dividend figure is from the table "Corporate Profits and Their Distribution," based on data from U.S. Department of Commerce, *Survey of Current Business;* cited in the *Federal Reserve Bulletin,* May 2001, A32.

18. Federal Reserve Flow of Funds Accounts of the United States, Annual Flows, Web site shows net new equity issues since 1946. The first year this figure was negative was 1963; the next negative years were 1965 and 1968. Since 1978, negative years have been more common than positive years. The last positive year was 1993. The negative $540 billion figure is obtained by adding up net new equity issues from 1981 to 2000.

19. Floyd Norris, "With Bull Market Under Siege, Some Worry About Its Legacy," *New York Times,* Mar. 18, 2001, A1. A chart on that page notes that the stock market bottomed in 1982, when the Dow Jones industrial average hit 777. It climbed from there—through the crash of Oct. 19, 1987, when it retreated to about 2,000—and was above 10,000 in 2000.

20. Norris, "Bull Market Under Siege," A1, A16.

21. Adolf A. Berle and Gardiner C. Means, *The Modern Corporation and Private Property* (New Brunswick, N.J., and London: Transaction Publishers, 1991 [originally published 1932]), jacket quote.

22. Berle and Means, *Modern Corporation,* xxxiv–xxxv.

23. The 1964 AT&T issuance of new stock was noted by Berle and Means in *Modern Corporation,* xxxiii. GM's $2.2 billion stock offering in 1992 was at the time the largest in history. Then in January 1997 it bought back $2.5 billion of stock, as noted in *Hoover's Handbook of American Business 1998* (Austin, Tex.: Hoover's Business Press), 654. Another $4 billion buyback was announced Feb. 9, 1998, as noted in Standard & Poor's periodical *Standard Corporation Descriptions,* 8786. See also Agis Salpukas, "Conoco Raises $4.4 Billion in a Record Initial Offering," *The New York Times,* Oct. 22, 1998, C1.

24. Berle, *Modern Corporation,* xxxiii, xxxv.

25. "Over the past decade, productivity has risen by at least 1.5% annually, a figure three times the 0.5% average annual gain in workers' real compensation per hour." Stephen S. Roach, "The Hollow Ring of the Productivity Revival," *Harvard Business Review,* Nov.-Dec. 1996, 86. To see if this had changed in 1998, I phoned Roach on June 25, 1998, and in a personal interview got the quote used here: "But we still have fifteen years. . . ."

26. From 1977 to 1997, the number of workers working fifty or more hours a week jumped from 24 percent to 37 percent, according to James T. Bond, vice president of the Families and Work Institute. Cited in James Lardner, "World-Class Workaholics," *U.S. News & World Report,* Dec. 20, 1999, 42.

27. In 1989, the real (inflation-adjusted) hourly wage for median workers was $11.30; in the first half of 1998, it was $11.13, according to statistics from the Economic Policy Institute. Cited in *LRA Economic Notes* (Labor Research Association, 145 West 28 St., New York, N.Y. 10001; 212/714-1677), Sept. 1998, 5.

28. Mishel, Bernstein, and Schmitt, *Working America: 1998–99*, 5.

29. Andrew Bary, "The Unsinkable Dow Hits 7,000, But What Comes Next?", The Trader column, *Barron's*, Feb. 17, 1997, MW5.

CHAPTER 3

1. Teresa Michals, "'That Sole and Despotic Dominion': Slaves, Wives, and Game in Blackstone's *Commentaries*," *Eighteenth Century Studies*, Winter 1993–94, 27(2), 209, 201.

2. Michals, "'Sole and Despotic Dominion,'" 202.

3. Michals, "'Sole and Despotic Dominion,'" 199–201.

4. Wood, *American Revolution*, 50.

5. John Locke, *Two Treatises of Government* [originally published in London, 1698], in *Cambridge Texts in the History of Political Thought* (Cambridge: Cambridge University Press, 1988), 271.

6. Richard B. Morris, *Studies in the History of American Law: With Special Reference to the Seventeenth and Eighteenth Centuries* (New York: Columbia University Press, 1930), 170.

7. Michals, "'Sole and Despotic Dominion,'" 202.

8. This varies. Some utilities pay 100 percent of after-tax income as dividends; other companies pay no dividends at all. In 1995, S&P 500 companies on average paid out 37.5 percent of after-tax profits to shareholders, which was historically low. In 1994 the ratio was 43 percent. Shirley Lazo, "Companies Hold Tight to Cash," *Barron's*, Jan. 8, 1996, 25.

9. In mid-March 2001 the price-earnings ratio of the Standard & Poor's 500 was 24. By contrast, the Nasdaq p-e ratio was then at 154, down from 400 a year earlier. At the end of the S&P's last bear market in 1987, the p-e ratio was 12. Stock prices were just seven times earnings in Dec. 1974, at the end of a two-year bear market. Bridget O'Brian and Susan Pulliam, "The Really Bad News About the Market: Stocks Are Still Pricey," *Wall Street Journal*, Mar. 13, 2001.

10. The market value of the S&P 500 at year-end 1995 was $4.6 trillion; the combined book value of the companies totaled $1.2 trillion. "Intangibles" were worth $3.4 trillion. From *CFO* magazine, cited in "Musings," *Business Ethics*, July-Aug. 1997, 5.

11. Bernard Wysocki, Jr., "Why an Acquisition? Often, It's the People," *Wall Street Journal*, Oct. 6, 1997, 1.

12. Wysocki, "Why an Acquisition?," 1.

13. John S. Pratt and Peter Dosik, "Whose Idea Is It? Company Sues Ex-Employee," *National Law Journal*, Oct. 20, 1997. The lawsuit *DSC v. Evan Brown* was still languishing in court on Aug. 28, 1998, when I had e-mail correspondence with Evan Brown, who said he was waiting for a response to a motion and noted that DSC was in the process of being bought out by Alcatel, France.

14. Morton J. Horwitz, *The Transformation of American Law, 1780–1860* (New York and Oxford: Oxford University Press, 1992 [originally published 1977]), 55–58.

15. Stevan Alburty, "The Ad Agency to End All Ad Agencies," *Fast Company*, Dec.-Jan. 1997, 6, 117–124. Also see "2000 Millennium-End Business Ethics Awards," *Business Ethics*, Nov.-Dec. 1999, 8–9; and Andy Law, *Creative Company: How St. Luke's Became "the Ad Agency to End All Ad Agencies"* (New York: Wiley, 1999). It's interesting to note that Law and his rebels could have walked off with all the clients, without paying Omnicon anything. One suspects Omnicon realized this. That realization—plus Law's determination to resolve things ethically—led to the eventual "earnout" arrangement. Law allowed the acquisition to go through with the entire company intact (the London branch represented 5 percent of Chiat/Day revenues). He then struck the deal with Omnicon to purchase the company for $1, plus a percentage of profits for seven years, with an option to buy it outright for $2 million (representing roughly one times London-branch revenue at the time). His rebellion pointed up the absurdity that outsiders could own a company composed of nothing but human relationships. Yet in agreeing to "buy" the company, the final legal arrangement kept that fiction intact. However, Omnicon got only a portion of profits for seven years. Without Law's rebellion, they would have gotten all the profits forever.

CHAPTER 4

1. Brett D. Fromson, "Nice Work If You Can Get It," *Washington Post National Weekly Edition*, Feb. 16, 1998, 31. The boards Jordan sat on included American Express, Bankers Trust of New York, Dow Jones & Co., J.C. Penney, Revlon, Union Carbide, and Xerox. The ten companies had a total market value of about $100 billion. For his services, Jordan earned $1.1 million in 1998.

2. Frederick Rose, "Goofing Off?", Work Week column, *Wall Street Journal*, Nov. 25, 1997, 1.

3. Lawrence E. Mitchell, "A Theoretical and Practical Framework for Enforcing Corporate Constituency Statutes," *Texas Law Review*, Feb. 1992, 601.

4. Phone interview with Richard Saliterman, July 7, 2000.

5. Berle and Means, *Modern Corporation*, xxxviii, li. The authors noted that by the end of 1929 two-thirds of the nation's industrial wealth had been transferred from individual ownership to ownership by publicly held corporations, run by managers rather than founders. Thus, they maintained, ownership had for the first time been separated from control, which worked a revolution in the private property tradition. "The American corporation had ceased to be a private business device and had become an institution," even a kind of "adjunct of the state itself."

6. Mishel, Bernstein, and Schmitt, *Working America: 1998–99*, Figure 5D, 268. According to their analysis, using an index set to 100 at 1960, the U.S. stock market was around 80 in 1983.

7. For an excellent discussion of the governance revolution, see Marina Whitman (former vice president of public affairs, General Motors, and former member of the President's Council of Economic Advisers), *New World, New Rules: The Changing Role of the American Corporation* (Cambridge, Mass.: Harvard Business School Press, 1999). The figure of about one-third of the Fortune 500 targeted for hostile takeovers in 1990 is from p. 9.

8. Laura Holson, "A Slightly Kinder and Gentler Era for Hostile Takeovers," *The New York Times*, Nov. 12, 1999, C1.

9. Joann S. Lublin, "Corporate Chiefs Polish Their Relations with Directors," *Wall Street Journal*, Oct. 15, 1993, B1.

10. The practice of ousting CEOs is still going on. In a few short months in late 1999 and early 2000, for example, CEOs were forced out at BankOne Corp., Coca-Cola, Aetna, and Mattel. Directors are so powerful today that they need not even resort to firing. At Coca-Cola, directors Warren Buffett and Herb Allen (who controlled about 8 percent of shares) were "nonconfrontational—even sympathetic" when they met privately in Dec. 1999 with CEO Doug Ivestor. They simply said they'd lost confidence in him. Within a week he had resigned. See Betsy Morris and Patricia Sellers, "What Really Happened at Coke," *Fortune*, Jan. 10, 2000.

11. Michael Useem, *Investor Capitalism: How Money Managers Are Changing the Face of Corporate America* (New York: Basic Books, 1996), 10.

12. Whitman, *New World*, 9.

13. In 1997, 28.7 percent of American workers were employed in nonstandard (or contingent) jobs, a slight decline from 1995, when the share was 29.4 percent. "No Shortage of 'Nonstandard' Jobs," Economic Policy Institute Briefing Paper, Dec. 2, 1999 [www.epinet.org]. Temporary work increased 75 percent from 1992 to 1997; see Andrew Hermann, "Temporary Insanity," *Boston Phoenix*, 1999 [www.Alternet.org].

14. GE anecdote from Thomas F. O'Boyle, "Profit at Any Cost: A Look at How Ethics Suffered in GE's Relentless Drive to 'Get the Numbers,'" *Business Ethics*, Mar.-Apr. 1999, 15; excerpt from Thomas F. O'Boyle, *At Any Cost: Jack Welch, General Electric, and the Pursuit of Profit* (New York: Knopf, 1998), 73–75.

15. From 1960 to 1997, corporate income taxes as a percentage of government revenue dropped from 23 percent to 12 percent; this figure was cited in Frederick Strobel and Wallace Peterson, *The Coming Class War and How to Avoid It* (Armonk, N.Y.: M.E. Sharpe, 1999), 56.

16. In 1994, Minnesota spent $143 million on Aid to Families with Dependent Children and work-readiness programs but $1 billion on corporate welfare, according to the *Report on Corporate Welfare*, Feb. 1995 (Minnesota Alliance for Progressive Action, 1821 University Ave., Suite S-307, St. Paul, Minn. 55104, 651/641-4050).

17. Adolf A. Berle, *The 20th Century Capitalist Revolution* (New York: Harcourt Brace, 1954), 64–65.

18. The Revolution in its widest sense extended from 1640 to 1689, and encompassed an earlier unseating of a different king, as well as the Restoration of 1660. This extended Revolution "reasserted the authority of the 'natural rulers' of the country, the gentry and merchant oligarchies, both against . . . monarchical absolutism . . . and against a radical republic." Christopher Hill, *Some Intellectual Consequences of the English Revolution* (Madison: University of Wisconsin Press, 1980), 3.

19. John Emerich Edward Dalberg-Acton, First Baron Acton, "Selected Writings of Lord Acton," in J. Rufus Fears (ed.), *Essays in the History of Liberty*, Vol. 1 (Indianapolis: Liberty Fund, 1985), 48.

20. Financial Markets Center, *Employee Stock Options Background Report*, Apr. 2000 (Financial Markets Center, P.O. Box 334, Philmont, Va. 20131, www.fmcenter.org); David Binns, *Employee Ownership in the New Economy* (Foundation for Enterprise Development, 7911 Herschel Ave., Suite 402, La Jolla, Calif. 92037, www.fed.org).

21. Financial Markets Center, *Employee Stock Options*.

22. Mishel, Bernstein, and Schmitt, *Working America: 1996–97*, 278–279.

23. Mishel, Bernstein, and Schmitt, *Working America: 1996–97*, 278.

24. Employers cannot literally take away benefits already earned, but they can cut the rate at which future benefits are earned or take away those future benefits entirely, wrote Ellen E. Schultz in "Companies Find Host of Subtle Ways to Pare Retirement Payouts," *Wall Street Journal*, July 27, 2000, A1. "At General Electric Co., almost 9 percent of 1999's operating income can be traced to its $4 billion pension credit," wrote Nanette Byrnes, "The Perils of Fat Pension Plans," *Business Week*, Apr. 24, 2000, 91–92. Other companies where pensions contributed 7 to 8 percent of

1999 operating profit included SBC Communications, IBM, BellSouth, and Weyerhaeuser.

25. Bendix, *Kings or People*, 6–7.

26. Popper, *The Open Society*, 57.

27. Popper, *The Open Society*, 57–61.

28. Popper, *The Open Society*, 53, 47, 12, 295.

29. Popper, *The Open Society*, 86–87, 107.

30. Phone conversation on Oct. 9, 1997 with Ellen Braune, National Labor Committee (275 7th Ave., New York, N.Y. 10001, 212/242-0986). This group, led by Charles Kernaghan, has done a great deal to put overseas sweatshops on the national agenda.

31. Kent Greenfield, "The Place of Workers in Corporate Law," *Boston College Law Review*, Mar. 1998, 1 (39 B.C.L. Rev. 283).

32. Report based on union elections from 1993 to 1995, by Cornell University researchers, in a study commissioned under NAFTA for the U.S. Labor Department. Aaron Bernstein, "NAFTA: A New Union-Busting Weapon," *Business Week*, Jan. 27, 1997, 4.

33. Bendix, *Kings or People*, 7–8.

34. Dalberg-Acton, "Selected Writings of Lord Acton," 12.

35. Don Herzog, *Poisoning the Minds of the Lower Orders* (Princeton, N.J.: Princeton University Press, 1998). Herzog writes, "We have long associated conservatism with the reaction against the French Revolution. The association isn't arbitrary or mistaken" (p. x). For conservatism at its very beginning "was locked in combat with democracy" (p. ix). It sought to marshal arguments against the rising debate favoring democracy, for as the aristocracy saw it, "that debate was poisoning the minds of the lower orders." (p. xi). In countering democratic theory, Edmund Burke, in *Reflections on the Revolution in France*, pointed to the great chain of being as the legitimate base of society, praising "the great primeval contract of eternal society, linking the lower with the higher natures, connecting the visible and invisible world, according to a fixed compact sanctioned by the inviolable oath which holds all physical and all moral natures each in their appointed place" (p. 34). These "lower orders" to be held in their place, Herzog wrote, included "women, blacks, Jews, and workers" (p. 245).

36. Whereas changes in voting rights for women and blacks were made at the federal level, changes in voting rights concerning property were made by the states. This may be one reason we know little of this struggle, for it was not one struggle but many. They occurred over a period of years, and were completed nationwide by the 1850s.

37. See entries for Dorr Rebellion and Thomas Dorr at www.Britannica.com. An excellent discussion of changes in suffrage

requirements is also found in Joyce Appleby, *Inheriting the Revolution: The First Generation of Americans* (Cambridge, Mass., and London: Belknap Press of Harvard University Press, 2000), 28–30.

CHAPTER 5

1. "In fact, sophisticated lawyers these days don't use the 'ownership' term," said Margaret Blair in a phone interview on Oct. 31, 1996. "The corporation is a nexus of contracts. It's not a thing that can be owned."
2. R. H. Coase, "The Nature of the Firm," *Economica*, 1937, 4, 386, reprinted in Coase, *The Firm, the Market, and the Law*, (Chicago: University of Chicago Press, 1988), 33–55; Coase's insights were elaborated on by Frank H. Easterbrook and Daniel R. Fischel, *The Economic Structure of Corporate Law* (Cambridge, Mass., and London: Harvard University Press, 1991).
3. Berle and Means, *Modern Corporation*, ix, xx, li, xxxviii.
4. In recent years the nexus-of-contracts formulation has become "accepted wisdom, if not outright dogma," wrote Margaret Blair in "Rethinking Assumptions Behind Corporate Governance," *Challenge*, Nov.-Dec. 1995, 12.
5. Blair, "Rethinking Assumptions," 13.
6. Margaret Blair, e-mail correspondence, July 13, 1999.
7. Easterbrook and Fischel, *Economic Structure of Corporate Law*, 15, quoted by Kent Greenfield, "From Rights to Regulation in Corporate Law" in Fiona Patfield (ed.), *Perspectives on Company Law* (London: Kluwer Law International, 1997), 15. Greenfield's insightful critique of the contractarian view of the corporation is that it is based on the "historically misguided belief in the private nature of corporate law," and he argues for a view of corporate governance based on theories of public regulation. He offers a valuable overview of an enduring issue in corporate governance theory: Is the corporate form created by the state (thus subject to regulation by the state)? Or is it a matter of private contracts among individuals (hence government should keep out)? He notes that contract language is used to oppose social responsibility requirements, because the public is not party to the contract, but calls this "unhelpful," since explicit contracts are not involved (p. 15).
8. Fukuyama, *End of History*, 1992, 15.
9. Robert Anchor, *The Enlightenment Tradition* (Berkeley, Los Angeles, London: University of California Press, 1967), 11.
10. Voltaire, *Candide* (New York: Quality Paperback Book Club, 1991 [first published 1759]), 171.
11. Voltaire, *Candide*, 16.

12. Karl Polanyi, *The Great Transformation: The Political and Economic Origins of Our Time* (Boston: Beacon Press, 1960 [originally published 1944]), 93.

13. Quoted in Polanyi, *Great Transformation*, 129.

14. Eric Hobsbawm, *The Age of Extremes: A History of the World, 1914–1991* (New York: Pantheon, 1994), 269–273.

15. Mishel, Bernstein, and Schmitt, *Working America: 1996–97*, 147. Those making poverty-level wage or below were 30 percent of the workforce in 1995. See again chapter 1, note 6.

16. According to a 2000 American Management Association survey, "nearly three-quarters of major U.S. firms now record and review some form of their employees' communications—either telephone calls, e-mail, Internet connections, or computer files. That's more than double the number of just two years ago." Sarah Boehle, "They're Watching You," *Training*, Aug. 2000, 51.

17. David F. Linowes, "A Research Survey of Privacy in the Workplace," 1996, unpublished paper based on survey (see www.oc.uiuc.edu/NB). Linowes, a professor at University of Illinois at Urbana-Champaign who chaired the U.S. Privacy Protection Commission during the 1970s, surveyed eighty-four Fortune 500 companies representing more than 3.2 million employees. He also found that 35 percent use medical records in making employment-related decisions.

18. "Ending Nabisco's Bathroom Brawl," *Business Week*, April 29, 1996, 50.

19. John Kenneth Galbraith, "Free Market Fraud," *The Progressive*, Jan. 1999, 63(1).

20. As Ray Stringham wrote in *Magna Carta: Fountainhead of Freedom* (Rochester, N.Y.: Aqueduct Books, 1966), the rights secured in the Magna Carta were "obtained by and for barons" (p. 6). Of the charter's sixty-three clauses, twenty-one concerned property rights (p. 29).

21. G.W.F. Hegel, *Introduction to the Philosophy of History*. Leo Rauch, trans. (Indianapolis and Cambridge: Hackett, 1988), 22, 56. Hegel died in 1831; this work was published posthumously from lecture notes and is far more accessible than his other writings.

CHAPTER 6

1. An excellent reference is Eric W. Orts, "Beyond Shareholders: Interpreting Corporate Constituency Statutes," *George Washington Law Review*, Nov. 1992, 61(1), 14–135. "Most legal commentators greet them with a loud hiss," Orts wrote (p. 48). "The ABA [American Bar Association]'s Committee on Corporate Laws, in the best-known and most trenchant attack, warns not only of 'opportunities for misunderstanding' and

'potential for mischief,' but of a threat of 'radical' change in corporate law" (p. 17).

2. Bendix, *Kings or People*, 7.

3. As Robert Lacey wrote in *Aristocrats* (London: Hutchinson & Co., 1983): "The king allowed his mightiest subjects to hold their lands in return for their support in times of war; they, in turn, sublet sections of their territories to lesser lords, and the lesser lords sublet further to create links of personal allegiance which stretched from the monarch to the humblest peasant tilling the soil" (p. 43).

4. *Concise Dictionary of American History* (New York: Scribner's, 1962), 593–594, 987.

5. *Concise Dictionary*, 987.

6. James Morris, *Heaven's Command: An Imperial Progress* (London: Folio Society, 1992 [originally published 1973]), 87. The East India Company was dechartered by the Crown before Gandhi began his campaign for independence, so Gandhi did not fight the old Company, but rather the Crown.

7. Fernand Braudel, *The Wheels of Commerce: Civilization and Capitalism 15th–18th Century, Vol. 2* (Berkeley: University of California Press, 1992 [originally published 1979 under the title *Les Jeux de l'échange*]), 439–440.

8. Household-owned equity, including mutual funds, represents close to two-thirds of all stock (see www.conference-board.org). According to Greg Ip, "Are Fears of 'Wealth Effect' Exaggerated?," *Wall Street Journal*, Mar. 23, 2001, A2, household holdings of stock and mutual funds in March 2000 were $12.2 trillion. Total equity at year-end 1999 was $18.9 trillion, according to Donovan Hervig, research analyst with the Conference Board Global Corporate Government Research Center in New York, in a Mar. 14, 2001 telephone interview. Edward Wolff reported that in 1998, the richest 10 percent accounted for 78 percent of the total value of stock held by households, directly or indirectly ("What Has Happened to Stock Ownership"). If the 10 percent wealthiest held an estimated 78 percent of $12.2 trillion, that's a total stock ownership of $9.5 trillion—or just over 50 percent of all stock.

9. Richard Waters, "10,0001: A Stock Odyssey," *Financial Times* (London), Mar. 17, 1999, 12.

10. For the twelve months ended September 30, 1998, average return on common equity for the nine hundred companies in *Business Week*'s "corporate scorecard" was 15.5 percent (*Business Week*, Nov. 23, 1998, 175).

11. In 1999, stock market capitalization reached a peak of nearly 160 percent of nominal GDP. The pre-1990s high was August 1929, at 81 percent;

the low was around 1941, when capitalization was under 20 percent of GDP. In the 1970s and 1980s it was in the 40 to 80 percent range. Alan Abelson, "Thanks, Yanks," *Barron's*, Nov. 1, 1999, 5 (chart based on data from Bianco Research).

12. "Getting Companies Off the Dole," *Business Ethics*, Mar.-Apr. 1999, 4.

13. "Why Is Theft of Public Resources Legal?" *Business Ethics*, Sept.-Oct. 1998, 5. This article on the 1872 mining law drew much of its research from the Mineral Policy Center (1612 K St. NW, Suite 808, Washington, D.C. 20006, 202/887-1872).

14. Reuven S. Avi-Yonah, "World-Class Tax Evasion," *The American Prospect*, May 22, 2000, 28–29.

15. Lon L. Fuller, *Legal Fictions* (Stanford, Calif: Stanford University Press, 1967), cited by Richard Saliterman, "Some Perceptions Bearing on the Public Policy Dynamics of Corporation Law," appendix to four-volume set *Advising Minnesota Corporations and Other Business Organizations* (Charlottesville, Va.: Lexis Law Publishing, 1995), 340.

16. Saliterman, "Some Perceptions," 319. This appendix (see previous note) was also published in revised form as "Perceptions Bearing on the Public Policy Dynamics of Corporation Law," *Hamline Law Review*, Winter 1996, 20(2) (quote used here is on p. 261).

17. Ernst H. Kantorowicz, *The King's Two Bodies: A Study in Medieval Political Theology* (Princeton, N.J.: Princeton University Press, 1981 [originally published 1957]), 4–5, 131, 331.

18. Kantorowicz is quoting from Edmund Plowden, *Commentaries or Reports* (1816), concerning a legal case that provided the "first clear elaboration of that mystical talk with which English Crown jurists enveloped and trimmed their definitions of kingship and royal capacities." The case, around the year 1550, concerned the validity of the lease of certain lands in the Duchy of Lancaster, which the Lancastrian kings owned not as property of the Crown, but as private property. Edward VI, predecessor to Queen Elizabeth, in whose reign the case was tried, had made the lease while not yet of age. Kantorowicz writes: "The judges, after thus having gained a foothold on, so to speak, firm celestial ground . . . pointed out that, if lands which the King has purchased before he was King, namely, 'in the capacity of his Body natural,' later were given away by him, such gift . . . had to be recognized as the King's act" (*King's Two Bodies*, 7).

19. Kantorowicz, *King's Two Bodies*, 13.

20. Kantorowicz, *King's Two Bodies*, 5.

21. D. Gordon, "The Role of the History of Economic Thought in Understanding Modern Economic Theory," *American Economic Review: Papers*

and Proceedings, 1965, 55, 123, 124. Cited by David E. Schrader in *The Corporation as Anomaly* (Cambridge: Cambridge University Press, 1993), 10. Shrader writes: "Most discussions of the U.S. economic system . . . appear to be premised on the view that corporations are simply artificial persons and that their behavior in the market is substantially the same as that of other persons. Given the dominant economic view that individuals invariably act as maximizers of their utility, this translates into a view of the business corporation as an individual acting in the market to maximize its utility" (p. 2). Schrader's thesis is that the corporation represents an anomaly in economic theory that has yet to be fully recognized. He quotes Alfred Chandler as noting that the advent of "managerial capitalism" was a "phenomenon" that was "revolutionary." But, he writes, "the mainstream of contemporary economic theory has carried on its theoretical endeavors as if this 'economic phenomenon' didn't really constitute anything fundamentally new in the economic world" (p. 4).

22. Daniel Yergin and Joseph Stanislaw, *The Commanding Heights: The Battle Between Government and the Marketplace That Is Remaking the Modern World* (New York: Touchstone, Simon & Schuster, 1999 [originally published 1998]), 11.

23. In *Managers vs. Owners: The Struggle for Corporate Control in American Democracy* (New York, Oxford: Oxford University Press, 1995), authors Allen Kaufman, Lawrence Zacharias, and Marvin Karson wrote: "When the Court took up the constitutional validity of a tax on railroads in this case, it decided that corporate properties were subject to the equal protection provisions of the Fourteenth Amendment and that the states must therefore treat them just as they would the private property of ordinary 'persons,' including the associated owners of a business corporation. This decision . . . thus simply extended the logic of the corporate fiction or 'artificial entity' that had long prevailed. Moreover, by identifying the corporation with private property instead of with public grants and state interests, *Santa Clara* also came close to extinguishing whatever prior claims the public may have made on corporate charters and properties" (p. 19). In *Santa Clara County v. Southern Pacific Railroad Co.* 118 U.S. 394 (1886), the court extended to the corporation the due process and equal protection that the Constitution had originally intended for individual persons. The case is considered a judicial endorsement of the laissez-faire philosophy—viewing the corporation as a "natural entity" with natural rights, rather than as a creation of the state subject to control by the state, which was a view that prevailed earlier.

24. Fukuyama, *End of History*, xv.

CHAPTER 7

1. Edward S. Mason (ed.), *The Corporation in Modern Society* (New York: Atheneum, 1966), 10.
2. Thomas Paine, *Common Sense: Addressed to the Inhabitants of America,* Feb. 14, 1776, in Thomas Paine, *Collected Writings* (New York: Library of America, Literary Classics of the United States, 1995), 28.
3. Paine, *Common Sense,* 28.
4. "The Old Regime was dedicated to defending the institution of absolute monarchy and the privileges of a hereditary nobility. It depended upon tradition, custom, and convention for its sanctions," wrote Anchor in *The Enlightenment Tradition* (p. xi). The Enlightenment, by contrast, was devoted to reason, and "hostile to tradition" (p. ix).
5. Immanuel Kant, *Groundwork of the Metaphysics of Morals.* H. J. Paton, trans. (New York: Harper & Row, 1956 [originally published at end of eighteenth century]), 95, 96.
6. On a ten-year annualized basis through third quarter 2000, the socially screened Domini Index beat the S&P 500, with 21.3 percent returns compared to 19.4 percent for the S&P. Kevin O'Keefe, "When the Going Gets Tough: How SRI Mutual Funds Fared in a Tough 2000 Market," *Business Ethics,* Jan.-Feb. 2001, 22.
7. Bernard Bailyn, *The Ideological Origins of the American Revolution* (Cambridge, Mass., and London: Belknap Press of Harvard University Press, 1967), 55, 56.
8. Bailyn, *Ideological Origins,* 56
9. "Patricia Ireland: The Progressive Interview," *The Progressive,* Aug. 1999, 36.
10. Geoffrey Brewer, "A Supportive Environment," interview with Royal Farros, CEO of iPrint.com, an online printing service, *The New York Times,* Sept. 13, 2000, C1, C8.
11. Marleen O'Connor observes: "Employees themselves should not be viewed as assets; rather, it is necessary to rethink firms' investment disclosure of human capital practices. The most important reason for not talking about employees as assets does not involve accounting, but morality. Specifically, the firm does not own its workers. Rather, employees should be thought of and used as a resource." She points to the European firm Skandia, for example, which sees human capital more as debt than asset; it sees itself as borrowing human capital from employees to leverage it into financial returns. In a related vein, Tom DeMarco, in *The New York Times* ("Human Capital Unmasked," Apr. 14, 1996), wrote, "If corporations booked their investments in workers as capital

assets, as I believe they should, AT&T would not have been able to eliminate [forty thousand knowledge workers' jobs] without writing down $4 billion to $8 billion of assets. Then the market response would be different. Instead of applauding the company's executives, we'd be looking to give them the boot." Cited by O'Connor in "Rethinking Corporate Financial Disclosure of Human Resource Value for the Knowledge-Based Economy," University of Pennsylvania *Journal of Labor and Employment Law*, Fall 1998, V, 530, 527 (footnote 13).

12. O'Connor, "Rethinking Corporate Financial Disclosure," 541.
13. David C. Korten, "A New Focus: Corporate Cost Internalization," *Business Ethics*, July-Aug. 1997, 16.
14. "The Sunshine Standards for Corporate Reporting," special report from *Business Ethics*, Dec. 1996.
15. Hazel Henderson, "Overview of the Calvert-Henderson Quality of Life Indicators," paper presented to the National Conference on Sustainable Development Indicators, Mar. 27, 2001, Ottawa, Canada [www.hazelhenderson.com].
16. Henderson, "Overview of Calvert-Henderson," 6–13. See also Clifford Cobb, Ted Halstead, and Jonathan Rowe, "If the GDP Is Up, Why Is America Down?" *Atlantic Monthly*, Oct. 1995, 59–76. For more on the work of economist Herman Daly and professor of philosophy and theology John Cobb Jr., see their work *For the Common Good: Redirecting the Economy Toward Community, the Environment, and a Sustainable Future* (Boston: Beacon Press, 1989).
17. Henderson, "Overview of Calvert-Henderson," 4–6.
18. O'Connor, "Rethinking Corporate Disclosure," 528–529.
19. Cited by Ralph Estes in "Sunshine Standards."
20. "Leading Investors Urge CEOs to Adopt New Reporting Guidelines," press release, Nov. 13, 2000, Fenton Communications, for the Global Reporting Initiative [www.globalreporting.org].
21. "Launching a Worldwide Revolution ... in Accounting (?!)," *Business Ethics*, millennium-end double issue (Sept.-Oct., Nov.-Dec.) 1999, 18. See also the GRI Web site (address in previous note).
22. "Launching a Worldwide Revolution," 18.
23. "Making Social Disclosure as Routine as Financial Disclosure," *Business Ethics*, Sept.-Oct. and Nov.-Dec. 1999, 6. Cynthia Williams's quotes are drawn from remarks at the October 1999 SRI in the Rockies conference and from her Apr. 1999 *Harvard Law Review* article, "The SEC and Corporate Social Transparency."
24. "Making Social Disclosure Routine," 6. For a complete list of data that Williams suggests be disclosed, see "The SEC and Corporate Social Transparency" (see previous note).

25. Amy Domini's remarks were made at the October 1999 SRI in the Rockies conference, quoted in "Making Social Disclosure Routine," 6.

26. Ralph Estes, "The Corporate Social Accounting Movement of the 1970s: Enormous Success—and Tragic Failure," Dec. 1999 (Stakeholder Alliance, c/o Center for Advancement of Public Policy, 1735 S St. NW, Washington, D.C. 2009). Ernst & Ernst (later Ernst & Young) tabulated social disclosure by large companies. In 1978, it reported that 89 percent of the Fortune 500, 94 percent of Fortune 50 commercial banks, and 88 percent of life insurance companies were reporting on social performance. By the early 1980s those numbers had dropped "to virtually zero," Estes wrote. When social accountability drew back, "there was no voice of the people to disagree, to present the case for continued reporting, to confirm the need, to engage these leaders in dialogue— to bring constructive pressure to bear."

27. John Adams in a letter to Thomas Jefferson, 1815, quoted in Bailyn, *Ideological Origins*, 1.

CHAPTER 8

1. These are the opening lines from Paine, *Common Sense*, 5.

2. Paine, *Common Sense*, 20.

3. Thomas Jefferson, in a letter to John Adams, Oct. 28, 1813, wrote: "For I agree with you that there is a natural aristocracy among men. The grounds of this are virtue and talents. . . . There is also an artificial aristocracy founded on wealth and birth, without either virtue or talents." Thomas Jefferson, *Writings* (New York: Library of America, Literary Classics of the United States, 1984), 1305–1306.

4. Locke, *Two Treatises*, 170.

5. Cited by Richard Ashcraft, *Revolutionary Politics and Locke's Two Treatises of Government* (Princeton, N.J.: Princeton University Press, 1986), 266.

6. Adam Smith, *The Wealth of Nations*, Vol. 1 (New York: The Modern Library, 2000), 140.

7. Cited by Eric Hobsbawm in *Uncommon People: Resistance, Rebellion, and Jazz* (New York: The New Press, 1998), 4.

8. Jefferson, *Writings*, 494.

9. Abraham Lincoln, "Annual Message to Congress," Dec. 3, 1861, in Roy P. Basler (ed.), *The Collected Works of Abraham Lincoln: 1861–1862*, Vol. 5 (New Brunswick, N.J.: Rutgers University Press, 1953); cited by Marleen O'Connor, "Organized Labor as Shareholder Activist: Building Coalitions to Promote Worker Capitalism," *University of Richmond Law Review*, Dec. 1997, 1345.

10. Speaking of natural rights, Paine wrote that every man is a natural part of society. "Society *grants* him nothing. Every man is a proprietor in society, and draws on the capital as a matter of right." Thomas Paine, *The Rights of Man*, in Paine, *Collected Writings* (New York: Library of America, Literary Classics of the United States, 1995), 465.

11. Paine, *The Rights of Man*, 465.

12. Living wage laws require companies receiving government contracts to pay decent wages and reasonable benefits. The first living wage campaign was won in Baltimore in 1994; other living wage laws have been adopted in Boston, Los Angeles, Milwaukee, New York, and Portland, Oregon. Robert Pollin and Stephanie Luce, *The Living Wage: Building a Fair Economy* (New York: The New Press, 1998).

13. Ashcraft, *Revolutionary Politics*, 268, 264, 273.

14. Cited by Ashcraft, *Revolutionary Politics*, 280.

15. Locke, *Two Treatises*, 329.

16. Ashcraft, *Revolutionary Politics*, 9, 281.

17. Smith, *Wealth of Nations*, 48.

18. Paul A. Samuelson, *Economics: An Introductory Analysis*, 3rd ed. (New York: McGraw-Hill, 1955), 602.

19. Cited in David E. Schrader, *The Corporation as Anomaly* (Cambridge, England, and New York: Cambridge University Press, 1993), 61.

20. John Bates Clark, *Essentials of Economic Theory* (New York: Macmillan, 1924 [originally published 1907]), 376–377; cited by Schrader in *Corporation as Anomaly*, 12.

21. From keynote address by Roberto Eisanman, Business for Social Responsibility conference, Nov. 11, 1998.

22. Jacquelyn Yates and Marjorie Kelly, "The Employee Ownership 100: The 100 Largest Majority-Employee-Owned Companies (and What Makes Them Great)," *Business Ethics*, Sept.-Oct. 2000, 10–13.

23. Yates and Kelly, "The Employee Ownership 100," 10.

24. Yates and Kelly, "The Employee Ownership 100," 10.

25. Yates and Kelly, "The Employee Ownership 100," 10.

26. I am indebted to Leslie Christian, president of Progressive Investment Management in Portland, Oregon, for questioning the notion that if the "right" people own shares, it's OK to have shareholders be top dogs. She raised this point in private correspondence March 14, 2001, in her review of a draft manuscript of this book.

27. Yates and Kelly, "The Employee Ownership 100," 13.

28. John Logue and Marjorie Kelly, "It's Time to Renew Our National Enthusiasm for Employee Ownership," *Business Ethics*, Sept.-Oct. 2000, 16–17.

29. The concept of sliding-scale tax benefits for employee ownership was suggested by Deborah Groban Olson, attorney with Jackier, Gould, Bean, Upfal & Eizelman, P.C., Grosse Pointe Park, Michigan [www.esoplaw.com].

30. Logue and Kelly, "It's Time to Renew," 17.

31. Deborah Groban Olson, e-mail correspondence, April 4, 2001.

32. Deborah Groban Olson and Alan F. Zundel, "A Half-Dozen Bold New Ideas for Spreading Capital Ownership," *Business Ethics*, Sept.-Oct. 2000, 18–19. The Capital Ownership Group is a nonprofit network of professionals, activists, academics, and leaders of business, labor, and government who are working to broaden ownership [http://cog.kent.edu]. See also Shann Turnbull, "Should Ownership Last Forever?" *Journal of Socio-Economics*, 1998, 27(3), 341–363 [http://papers.ssrn.com/paper.taf?abstract_id=137382].

33. Olson and Zundel, "A Half-Dozen Bold New Ideas," 18–19.

34. Olson and Zundel, "A Half-Dozen Bold New Ideas," 18–19.

35. L. Ling-Chi Wang, "For This Ex-Hong Kong Resident, a Story of Humiliation Ends Today," *Minneapolis Star-Tribune*, June 30, 1997, A9. The British possession of Hong Kong was ended peaceably—and without payment—after 158 years.

36. Locke, *Two Treatises*, 409–411.

37. Locke, *Two Treatises*, 411.

38. *The People of the State of California v. American Trading Transportation Co. Inc.* 64 6339 (Super. Ct., Orange Co., Calif.), a 1997 lawsuit, concerned a 1990 oil spill near Huntington Beach, Calif., by the tanker *American Trader*, owned by Attransco Inc. It was brought by the state of California, the cities of Huntington Beach and Newport Beach, and Orange County. The plaintiffs were able to calculate a specific value for the lost recreational use by looking at attendance data and correlating it with weather patterns on the dates the beaches were closed. The Clark Ford River basin case was *Montana v. ARCO*. "Causes of Action: 10 New Bases for Suits," *National Law Journal*, July 20, 1998, A13–A17.

39. Olson and Zundel, "A Half-Dozen Bold New Ideas," 18–19. For the figure on 2000 income from the Permanent Fund, see Sam Howe Verhovek, "Alaskans Know Which Side Bread Is Oiled On," *The New York Times*, Mar. 18, 2001, A1; each man, woman, and child in Alaska in fall 2000 received a check for $1,963.86.

40. Peter Barnes, "The Pollution Dividend," *The American Prospect*, May-June 1999.

41. Olson and Zundel, "A Half-Dozen Bold New Ideas," 18–19.

42. Olson, e-mail correspondence, April 4, 2001.
43. Verhovek, "Alaskans Know," A1.

CHAPTER 9

1. "'Corporate social responsibility,' in the eyes of U.S. law, is an oxymoron. A corporation has fiduciary responsibilities only to shareholders," according to Greenfield, "From Rights to Regulation," 2.

2. The comment about Shore Bank was made by a bank representative at the Making a Profit While Making a Difference conference in New York, June 14, 1999. The juice maker quoted was the founder of Odwalla.

3. D. Gordon Smith, "The Shareholder Primacy Norm," *Journal of Corporation Law*, Winter 1998, 285, 295.

4. Cited by Richard L. Grossman, "Claiming Our Sovereignty: Establishing Control Over the Corporation" (n.d.), 1; unpublished paper distributed by Program on Corporations, Law and Democracy (www.poclad.org).

5. Richard L. Grossman and Frank T. Adams, *Taking Care of Business: Citizenship and the Charter of Incorporation* [pamphlet] (South Yarmouth, Mass.: Charter Ink./Program on Corporations, Law and Democracy, 1993), 13.

6. Grossman, "Claiming Our Sovereignty," 2.

7. Horatio Gates to Thomas Jefferson, Feb. 2, 1781; cited by Gordon S. Wood, *The Creation of the American Republic 1776–1787* (New York and London: W.W. Norton, 1969), 55.

8. Smith, "Shareholder Primacy Norm," 285, 295.

9. Estes, *Tyranny of the Bottom Line*, 28.

10. *The Trustees of Dartmouth College v. Woodward* 4 Wheaton 518 (1819), in Henry Steele Commager (ed.), *Documents of American History* (New York: Appleton-Century-Crofts, 1958), 220. See also the discussion in Ralph Nader and Mark Green (eds.), *Corporate Power in America* (New York: Grossman Publishers, 1973), 69.

11. *Lochner v. New York* 198 U.S. 45 (1905), cited in Greenfield, "From Rights to Regulation," 11. This article offers a valuable and readable overview of the history of two opposing legal views of the corporation, as subject to public regulation, or as private and thus beyond the reach of regulation.

12. Robert Lekachman (State University of New York–Stony Brook), introduction to Paul A. Samuelson, *Economics: An Introductory Course*, 8th ed. (New York: McGraw-Hill, 1970), xi.

13. Berle, *20th Century Capitalist Revolution*, 60.

14. Earl Latham, "The Body Politic of the Corporation," in Edward S.
    Mason (ed.), *The Corporation in Modern Society* (New York: Atheneum,
    1966), 220.

15. Georges Duby (ed.), *A History of Private Life, Vol. II, Revelations of the
    Medieval World* (Cambridge, Mass., and London: The Belknap Press of
    Harvard University Press, 1988), 9.

16. Matthew Josephson, *The Robber Barons: The Great American Capitalists,
    1861–1901* (New York: Harcourt Brace, 1934), vii–viii.

17. Josephson, *The Robber Barons*, 372, 374.

18. Josephson, *The Robber Barons*, 362, 372.

19. Josephson, *The Robber Barons*, 448, 367.

20. "Business and Government: Business, Faced with an Overwhelming
    Political Fact, Should Favor a More Socialized State," unsigned editorial,
    Fortune, June 1938, 52.

21. Cited by Herzog, *Poisoning the Minds*, 34.

22. Paine, *The Rights of Man*, 438.

23. Paine, *The Rights of Man*, 438.

24. The Constitution of the United States, in Commager, *Documents of
    American History*, 146–147.

25. In *Munn v. Illinois* 94 U.S. 124 (1877)—cited by William Letwin,
    "Economic Due Process in the American Constitution and the Rule
    of Law," in Robert L. Cunningham (ed.), *Liberty and the Rule of Law*
    (College Station and London: Texas A&M University Press, 1979), 3—
    Justice Waite spoke to the matter of "due process," writing that "the very
    essence of government" is its power to make laws "requiring each citizen
    to so conduct himself, and so use his own property as not unnecessarily
    to injure another."

26. *Munn v. Illinois*, cited by Letwin, "Economic Due Process," 39.

27. *West Coast Hotel v. Parrish* 300 U.S. 379 (1937), cited by Letwin,
    "Economic Due Process," 64–65.

28. Carl J. Mayer, "Personalizing the Impersonal: Corporations and the Bill
    of Rights," *The Hastings Law Journal*, Mar. 1990, 41(3), 589. Mayer wrote
    that with *West Coast Hotel v. Parrish*, "the doctrine of substantive due
    process was abandoned by the New Deal Supreme Court." Letwin
    ("Economic Due Process," 67) made the same observation: "Many have
    said that the Supreme Court in 1937 did away with substantive due
    process."

29. Letwin, "Economic Due Process," 30, 49.

30. Supreme Court Justice Owen Roberts, in the five-to-four decision on
    Nebbia v. New York 291 U.S. 523 (1934), sustained a New York law that
    created a board to set minimum and maximum retail prices for milk.

William E. Leuchtenberg, *Franklin Roosevelt and the New Deal, 1932–1940* (New York: Harper & Row, 1963), 144.

31. "When the CEO Ignored Racial Issues, the Lawyers Came Calling at Coke," *Business Ethics*, Jan.-Feb. 2001, 7.

32. "(Un)Fair Lending," *Business Ethics*, July-Aug. 1999, 8.

33. Paul Krugman, "Mergers Most Foul," *The New York Times*, Jan. 14, 2001, WK-17.

34. Smith, "Shareholder Primacy Norm," 289.

35. Marleen O'Connor, "Restructuring the Corporation's Nexus of Contracts: Recognizing a Fiduciary Duty to Protect Displaced Workers," *North Carolina Law Review*, June 1991, 69, 1247.

36. The count of thirty-two was made by Terry O'Neill, "Employees' Duty of Loyalty and the Corporate Constituency Debate," *Connecticut Law Review*, Spring 1993, 682.

37. Orts, "Beyond Shareholders," 16. Also see Larry E. Ribstein, "Takeover Defenses and the Corporate Contract," *Georgetown Law Journal*, Oct. 1989, 78.

38. James J. Hanks, Jr., "Non-Stockholder Constituency Statutes: An Idea Whose Time Should Never Have Come," *Insights*, Dec. 1989, 20, 22. James J. Hanks, Jr., "Playing with Fire: Nonshareholder Constituency Statutes in the 1990s," *Stetson Law Review*, 1991, 21, 97. Cited by Orts, "Beyond Shareholders," 17.

39. Orts, "Beyond Shareholders," 33.

40. Karen Donovan, "Titans Clash in Takeover Battle in Pa.: Judge Approves First Use of Toughest Anti-Takeover Law," *National Law Journal*, Jan. 20, 1997, A1.

41. Lawrence Mitchell, "Cooperation and Constraint in the Modern Corporation: An Inquiry into the Causes of Corporate Immorality," *Texas Law Review*, Feb. 1995, 73(3), 533.

42. O'Neill, "Employees' Duty of Loyalty," 681.

43. Orts, "Beyond Shareholders," 26–31.

44. Orts, "Beyond Shareholders," 73–74. The codrafter of the Pennsylvania statute, SEC commissioner Steven Wallman, argues that the law leaves directors' duties where they have always been—to the corporation as a whole rather than to any particular group. He maintains that the focus on shareholder interests, increasingly defined as short-term stock price, is a recent misguided tendency in the law. See Mark G. Robilotti, "Codetermination, Stakeholder Rights, and Hostile Takeovers: A Reevaluation of the Evidence from Abroad," *Harvard International Law Journal*, Spring 1997, 543.

45. Report on the twentieth anniversary of the Community Reinvestment Act, published March 18, 1998, by the National Community Reinvestment Coalition (733 15th St. NW, Suite 540, Washington, D.C., 202/628-8866, ncrc@essential.org). "Responsible Banking's 20th Anniversary," *Business Ethics*, Mar.-Apr. 1998, 8.

46. The first time an Alien Tort Claims Act suit was allowed to proceed in the United States was in 1998, when then–U.S. District Judge Richard Paez ruled Unocal could be tried in the United States for alleged human rights abuses—including slavery and rape—committed by authorities in Myanmar (formerly Burma) acting on Unocal's behalf. The case was *Doe v. Unocal*. Paez said foreign plaintiffs can be heard in U.S. courts if a company "knew or should have known" that its business partner was violating the law of nations on behalf of a joint venture. A second case allowed to proceed in U.S. courts was *Bowoto. v. Chevron*, which concerned Chevron's role in the May 1998 killing of two people on an offshore oil rig by Nigerian troops flown there in Chevron helicopters. *National Law Journal*, Apr. 24, 2000; cited in "BizEthics Buzz," May 2000, an online newsletter produced by *Business Ethics*.

47. "Who Says Corporations Have Eternal Life?" *Business Ethics*, Nov.-Dec. 2000, 5. A copy of the proposed bill was provided by Thomas Linzey (Community Environmental Legal Defense Fund, 2859 Scotland Rd., Chambersburg, Pa. 17201, 717/709-0457).

CHAPTER 10

1. D. K. Hurst, *Crisis and Renewal* (Boston: Harvard Business School Press, 1995), 168. Cited by Karl E. Weick, "Leadership as the Legitimation of Doubt," in Warren Bennis, Gretchen Spreitzer, Thomas Cummings (eds.), *The Future of Leadership* (San Francisco: Jossey-Bass, 2001), 92–93.

2. Keri Hayes, "Made in the USA (Sort of . . .), *Business Ethics*, Mar.-Apr. 1998, 6.

3. Jim Steiker and Michael Golden, "Hot Fudge Partners: An Insider's Story on How Social Investors Failed in Their Attempt to Buy Ben & Jerry's," *Business Ethics*, May-June 2000, 5.

4. Jack Quarter, "The Innovator's Dilemma," *Business Ethics*, Jan.-Feb. 2001, 4. Adapted from Jack Quarter, *Beyond the Bottom Line: Socially Innovative Business Owners* (Westport, Conn.: Quorum/Greenwood, 2000).

5. Abram Chayes, "The Modern Corporation and the Rule of Law," in Edward S. Mason (ed.), *The Corporation in Modern Society* (New York: Atheneum, 1966), 38.

6. Berle and Means, *Modern Corporation*, 313.

7. R. Edward Freeman, *Strategic Management: A Stakeholder Approach* (Boston: Pitman, 1984); cited by Orts, "Beyond Shareholders," 20.

8. Ronald K. Mitchell, Bradley R. Agle, Donna J. Wood, "Toward a Theory of Identification and Salience: Defining the Principle of Who and What Really Counts," *Academy of Management Review*, Oct. 1997, 23(4), 853, 866, 879. This article offers a valuable overview of various stakeholder definitions in other management literature.

9. John R. Boatright, "Business Ethics and the Theory of the Firm," *American Business Law Journal*, Dec. 1996, 34(2), 217–219. Also see Steven N. Brenner and Philip Cochran, "The Stakeholder Theory of the Firm: Implications for Business and Society Theory and Research," paper presented at International Society for Business and Society conference, Sundance, Utah, March 22–24, 1991.

10. Comment by David Ellerman in "From Employee Ownership to Workplace Democracy via 'Residual Claimancy,'" presentation given at the meeting of International Institute for Corporate Governance and Accountability, George Washington University Law School, Washington, D.C., June 2, 2001 (see www.Ellerman.org).

11. Ellerman, "From Employee Ownership to Workplace Democracy."

12. This argument was made by Ellerman, "From Employee Ownership to Workplace Democracy," and in his book *Property and Contract in Economics: The Case for Economic Democracy* (Oxford and Cambridge, Mass.: Blackwell, 1992). The book is out of print but available at www.Ellerman.org.

13. Ellerman, "From Employee Ownership to Workplace Democracy."

14. Ellerman, *Property and Contract*, 1–2.

15. David Ellerman, "The Libertarian Case for Slavery," in *Intellectual Trespassing as a Way of Life: Essays in Philosophy, Economics, and Mathematics* (Lanham, Md.: Rowman & Littlefield, 1995), 81. If we allow sale of labor by the hour, why not allow sale of labor for life—as in slavery? If we disallow one, shouldn't we logically disallow the other? In this article, Ellerman makes this point, arguing, tongue-in-cheek, that voluntary slavery should be permitted. As he wrote, "Any thoroughgoing and decisive critique of voluntary slavery . . . would carry over to the employment contract."

16. Douglas McGregor, *The Human Side of Enterprise* (New York: McGraw-Hill, 1960), 47–56.

17. Robert A. Dahl, *A Preface to Economic Democracy* (Berkeley and Los Angeles: University of California Press, 1985), 57, 162, 111.

18. In a footnote on p. 91 of *A Preface*, Dahl writes that he has "profited greatly from a number of unpublished papers by David Ellerman." The Dahl quote cited here is from p. 57.

19. Dahl, *A Preface*, 67.
20. Dahl, *A Preface*, 67.
21. Dahl, *A Preface*, 112–113.
22. Blair, "Rethinking Assumptions," 12–17. Also, Margaret M. Blair, "Corporate 'Ownership,'" *The Brookings Review*, Winter 1995, 16–19.
23. Margaret M. Blair and Lynn A. Stout, "A Team Production Theory of Corporate Law," *Virginia Law Review*, Mar. 1999, 85(2), 249, 250, 253.
24. Blair and Stout, "A Team Production Theory," 249, 250, 253.
25. Research on having employees on the board is inconclusive. "It doesn't show companies do amazingly well or do poorly," Edward Carberry said in a phone interview, Jan. 13, 1997. "Companies that do it think it's a good idea. But a lot of times employee owners don't care about board representation; they want to be involved at the job level." He does not know of any companies that have a "bicameral legislature."
26. Dalberg-Acton, "Selected Writings of Lord Acton," 84.
27. Quoted by John D. Donahue, "The Disunited States," *The Atlantic*, May 1997, 18.
28. Paine, *Common Sense*, 43.

CHAPTER 11

1. Braudel, *Wheels of Commerce*, 21.
2. Miles Rapoport, "How Money Reform Connects to Issues Reform," *The American Prospect*, Sept. 25–Oct. 9, 2000, 24.
3. *Buckley v. Valeo* 424 U.S. 1 (1976; see http://laws.findlaw.com/us/424/1.html). For commentary see Cass Sunstein, "Chipping Away at Buckley," *The American Prospect*, Sept. 25–Oct. 9, 2000, 23–24.
4. Cass Sunstein, "Rescuing Politics From Money: Round Two," *The American Prospect*, Sept. 25–Oct. 9, 2000, 25. "Buckley v. Valeo is poorly understood. The Court did not strike down campaign finance reform as a whole. Instead, the Court suggested three different points. First, Congress could not limit direct expenditures on campaigns, by candidates for themselves (consider the case of Ross Perot). . . . Second, the Court said that Congress could limit contributions to campaigns, to reduce the risk and reality of corruption. Third, the Court indicated that public financing is entirely legitimate so long as it is voluntary and does not forbid private expenditures."
5. Ellen S. Miller, "The Clean Money Solution," *The American Prospect*, Sept. 25–Oct. 9, 2000, 22. The article was part of a collection of pieces, "Rescuing Politics from Money: A Symposium," which offers a valuable overview of campaign finance reform.

6. Miller, "Clean Money Solution," 22.

7. *First National Bank of Boston v. Bellotti*, cited by Mayer, "Personalizing the Impersonal," 615–616. Mayer wrote, "Prohibitions against corporate expenditures on election of candidates . . . date back to the Progressive era." In a footnote, he says that the Tillman Act, repealed in 1909, provided that corporations could not directly fund candidates for federal office. "Since then, Congress and the state legislatures have repeatedly limited or prohibited corporate contributions or expenditures." But in striking down *Bellotti*, the Court in effect declared that spending money was "an important property right to be guarded."

8. INFACT, *1997 People's Annual Report*, reported in "Company Watch: Says Who?" *Business Ethics*, Jan.-Feb. 1998, 8.

9. Appleby, *Inheriting the Revolution*, 27–28.

10. Appleby, *Inheriting the Revolution*, 32–33.

11. *Santa Clara County v. Southern Pacific Railroad*, cited in Joseph B. James, *The Framing of the Fourteenth Amendment* (Urbana: University of Illinois Press, 1965), 194.

12. Grossman and Adams, *Taking Care of Business*, 20.

13. Mayer, "Personalizing the Impersonal," 589.

14. Mayer, "Personalizing the Impersonal," 578. Writing in 1990, Mayer noted various corporate uses of the Bill of Rights, adding, "Twenty years ago, the corporation had not deployed any of these Bill of Rights provisions successfully."

15. Mayer, "Personalizing the Impersonal," 578.

16. Richard L. Grossman, "Corporate Omnipresence—Even in Vermont," *Annals of Earth*, 1999, 17(1), 1.

17. Mayer, "Personalizing the Impersonal," 592.

18. Mayer, "Personalizing the Impersonal," 626.

19. Mayer, "Personalizing the Impersonal," 620, 633, 650.

20. Bayless Manning, *Economic Policy and the Regulation of Corporate Securities*, 1969; also "The Stockholders' Appraisal Remedy: An Essay for Frank Coker," *Yale Law Journal*, 1962, 72, 223, 245. Cited in Donald E. Schwartz (ed.), *Commentaries on Corporate Structure and Governance: The ALI-ABA Symposiums, 1977–1978* (1979), which was in turn cited by Richard Saliterman, "Some Perceptions," 342. (See earlier notes for full information on Saliterman work.)

21. Jane J. Mansbridge, *Why We Lost the ERA* (Chicago and London: University of Chicago Press, 1986), 19, 29.

22. Mayer, "Personalizing the Impersonal," 660.

23. Mayer, "Personalizing the Impersonal," 661.

24. Ralph Estes, correspondence with author, Dec. 10, 1999.

25. Michael Lerner, "The Social Responsibility Amendment to the U.S. Constitution," *Tikkun: A Bimonthly Jewish Critique of Politics, Culture & Society*, July-Aug. 1997, 12(4), 33–42, 79. This cover section includes an outline of the amendment, an article on "The Content of Ethical Impact Reports," and a collection of "SRA Responses" from people like Hazel Henderson, Richard Grossman, and Ward Morehouse.

26. Fourteenth Amendment to the Constitution of the United States, in Commager, *Documents of American History*, 147.

27. "Getting Companies Off the Dole," 4.

28. "Getting Companies Off the Dole," 4.

29. "Getting Companies Off the Dole," 4.

30. The Constitution of the United States, Article I, Section 9, in Commager, *Documents of American History*, 142. The paragraph reads in full: "No Title of Nobility shall be granted by the United States: And no Person holding any Office of Profit or Trust under them, shall, without the Consent of the Congress, accept of any present, Emolument, Office, or Title, of any kind whatever, from any King, Prince or foreign State."

31. Alexis de Tocqueville, *Democracy in America*, Vol. 1 (New York: Vintage Books, 1990 [originally published 1835]), 48.

32. Jefferson, "Observations on Démeunier's Manuscript" [June 22, 1786], in Jefferson, *Writings*, 588.

CHAPTER 12

1. Letter from Jefferson to James Madison, Paris, Jan. 30, 1787, in Jefferson, *Writings*, 882.

2. John Fiske, *The American Revolution*, Vol. 1 (Boston and New York: Houghton Mifflin, 1891), 24, 23.

3. Fiske, *American Revolution*, 79.

4. Thomas Linzey has researched all fifty states and found that the power of charter revocation is legally present in all.

5. "Declaration of Independence," in Jefferson, *Writings*, 19.

6. Edwin Merrick Dodd, *American Business Corporations Until 1860* (Cambridge: Harvard University Press, 1934); Lawrence M. Friedman, *A History of American Law* (New York: Simon & Schuster, 1973); cited by Grossman and Adams, *Taking Care of Business*, 17.

7. Morton J. Horwitz, *The Transformation of American Law, 1780–1860* (Cambridge, Mass.: Harvard University Press, 1977); cited by Grossman and Adams, *Taking Care of Business*, 8.

8. Illinois Business Corporation Act, Revised Statutes, chapter 32, part 1.01 et. seq.; New York Business Corporation Law 101 et. seq.; cited by Grossman and Adams, *Taking Care of Business*, 22–23.

9. The 127-page petition against Unocal is available at www.heed.net. Russell Mokhiber, "Death Penalty for Corporations Comes of Age," *Business Ethics*, Nov.-Dec. 1998, 7.

10. Mokhiber, "Death Penalty," 8.

11. In *Adbusters*, Aug.-Sept. 2000, the editors said they hope to launch a three-pronged strategy: a radio-TV campaign about Philip Morris's long criminal history, a boycott of the company's popular food brands like Kraft and Maxwell House, and the collection of cyberpetition signatures to be sent to New York Attorney General Eliot Spitzer demanding that he revoke the company's charter. Reported in "Activist Notes," *Business Ethics*, Nov.-Dec. 2000, 5.

12. "Who Says Corporations Have Eternal Life?" (interview with Thomas Linzey), *Business Ethics*, Nov.-Dec. 2000, 5.

13. "Who Says Corporations Have Eternal Life?" 5.

14. William Greider, *Who Will Tell the People: The Betrayal of American Democracy* (New York: Simon & Schuster, 1992), 354–355.

15. Greider, *Who Will Tell the People*, 354–355.

16. "When Brilliant Ideas Become Law: Punishing the Corporate Felon," *Business Ethics*, Jan.-Feb. 2001, 6.

17. Paul Precht, "Robed Rebels," *Dollars and Sense*, July-Aug. 1998, 6. Other information was from e-mail correspondence with Stephanie Greenwood, Sept. 28, 1998, and from a flyer put out by the Students for Humane and Responsible Economics entitled "Economics: What Do You See?" Greenwood said they received assistance from faculty adviser Phinneas Baxindall, who sits on the editorial board of *Dollars and Sense*, and from faculty member Juliet Schor. Other core members of the group in 1998 were Jane Martin, Mitch McEwen, and Adam Storeygard.

18. Bob Lincoln, "Return to Judgment III," *Walden Asset Management Newsletter*, Spring 2001, 3. My thanks to Leslie Christian of Progressive Investment Management in Portland, Oregon, for pointing out this article.

19. "New Inroads in Public Finance: SRI Is Popping Up Everywhere in California," *Business Ethics*, Mar.-Apr. 2000.

20. "New Inroads."

21. David M. Oshinsky, "Freedom Riders," *The New York Times Book Review*, Mar. 15, 1998, 9, a review of David Halberstam, *The Children* (New York: Random House, 1998).

22. Program on Corporations, Law and Democracy. *Short Reading List* (South Yarmouth, Mass.: Program on Corporations, Law and Democracy, 1998).

23. "Vote Yes on Measure F" brochure, Citizens Concerned About Corporations, P.O. Box 27, Arcata, Calif. 95518. See also Paul Cienfuegos, "Sprouting Wings: A New Movement Takes Flight," *Business Ethics,* July-Aug. 2000. The article details more than a dozen initiatives to reign in corporate power. Cienfuegos leads workshops on "First Steps in Dismantling Corporate Rule," and runs a bookstore with over two hundred titles on democracy and corporations [www.100fires.com].

24. "Activist Notes," *Business Ethics,* Nov.-Dec. 2000, 5.

25. "A Dialogue About Capitalism: The AFL-CIO's Bill Fletcher Speaks His Mind," *Dollars and Sense,* Sept.-Oct. 1998, 26–27. See also Paul Buhle, *Taking Care of Business: Samuel Gompers, George Meany, Lane Kirkland, and the Tragedy of American Labor* (New York: Monthly Review Press, 1999), reviewed by Jane Slaughter, "Big Labor's Little Problem," *The Nation,* Oct. 25, 1999, 36–39.

26. E-mail correspondence with Terry South, Feb. 1998.

27. Wood, *Creation of the American Republic,* 5.

28. Wood, *Creation of the American Republic,* 4–6.

29. Wood, *Creation of the American Republic,* vii.

30. Will Durant and Ariel Durant, *Rousseau and Revolution* (New York: Simon & Schuster, 1965), 579.

31. "The Declaration of Independence," in Jefferson, *Writings,* 19.

Index

About the Author

MARJORIE KELLY is the cofounder and editor of Minneapolis-based *Business Ethics*, a national publication on corporate social responsibility launched in 1987. For fourteen years, *Business Ethics* has been the core publication of the movement to bring greater ethics into business. It offers news and analysis of ethical scandals, corporate best practices, social investing, and social activism.

Kelly's writing has appeared in publications such as *The Utne Reader*, *The Progressive Populist*, *Earth Island Journal*, *Hope* magazine, and the *Minneapolis Star-Tribune*. Her work has been anthologized in a half-dozen books, including *The New Entrepreneurs* and *The New Paradigm in Business*.

Kelly is a regular speaker and commentator on business ethics and corporate social responsibility—featured in *The Wall Street Journal*, quoted in the *New York Times*, and interviewed frequently on NPR and other radio programs. She has been profiled on the cover of *Minnesota Corporate Report*, in the book *Women's Venture, Women's Visions*, and in other books and articles.

She is a board member of the Capital Ownership Group, which is working to spread capital ownership, and of the International Institute for Corporate Governance and Accountability at George Washington University Law School.

Contact Kelly at Business Ethics, P.O. Box 8439, Minneapolis, MN 55408; phone: 612/879-0695; Web site: www.DivineRightofCapital.com.

Berrett-Koehler Publishers

BERRETT-KOEHLER is an independent publisher of books, periodicals, and other publications at the leading edge of new thinking and innovative practice on work, business, management, leadership, stewardship, career development, human resources, entrepreneurship, and global sustainability.

Since the company's founding in 1992, we have been committed to supporting the movement toward a more enlightened world of work by publishing books, periodicals, and other publications that help us to integrate our values with our work and work lives, and to create more humane and effective organizations.

We have chosen to focus on the areas of work, business, and organizations, because these are central elements in many people's lives today. Furthermore, the work world is going through tumultuous changes, from the decline of job security to the rise of new structures for organizing people and work. We believe that change is needed at all levels—individual, organizational, community, and global—and our publications address each of these levels.

We seek to create new lenses for understanding organizations, to legitimize topics that people care deeply about but that current business orthodoxy censors or considers secondary to bottom-line concerns, and to uncover new meaning, means, and ends for our work and work lives.

See next pages for other publications from Berrett-Koehler Publishers

Macroshift
Navigating the Transformation to a Sustainable World

Ervin Laszlo

Preeminent futurist Ervin Laszlo confronts the global crisis and shows how we can shape our future. *Macroshift* informs readers about the dangers, opportunities, and choices we face—in business, in politics, and in our private lives—and motivates them to make informed and responsible lifestyle, civic, and professional choices. Laszlo expertly combines insights into the science of rapid and irreversible change with practical guidelines for managing that change.

Hardcover, 200 pages • ISBN 1-57675-163-5 • Item #51635-383 $24.95

When Corporations Rule the World
Second Edition

David C. Korten

David Korten offers an alarming exposé of the devastating consequences of economic globalization and a passionate message of hope in this well reasoned, extensively researched analysis. He documents the human and environmental consequences of economic globalization, and explain why human survival depends on a community-based, people-centered alternative.

Paperback, 400 pages • ISBN 1-887208-04-6 • Item #08046-383 $15.95

The Post-Corporate World
Life After Capitalism

David C. Korten

The Post-Corporate World presents readers with both a profound challenge and an empowering sense of hope. It is an extensively researched, powerfully argued, eye-opening critique of how today's corporate captialism is destroying the things of real value in the world—like cancer destroys life—including practical alternatives that will help restore health to markets, democracy, and every day life.

Paperback, 300 pages • ISBN 1-887208-03-8 • Item #08038-383 $19.95

Berrett-Koehler Publishers
PO Box 565, Williston, VT 05495-9900
Call toll-free! **800-929-2929** 7 am-12 midnight
Or fax your order to 802-864-7627
For fastest service order online: **www.bkconnection.com**

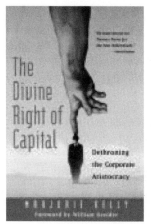